Religion and the Life of the Nation

RELIGION
and the
LIFE OF THE NATION

AMERICAN RECOVERIES

EDITED BY

Rowland A. Sherrill

UNIVERSITY OF ILLINOIS PRESS
Urbana and Chicago

This book is printed on acid-free paper.

Library of Congress Cataloging-in-Publication Data

Religion and the life of the nation : American recoveries / edited by
Rowland A. Sherrill.
    p. cm.
   ISBN 0-252-01693-9 (cloth : alk. paper).—ISBN 0-252-06111-X
(paper : alk. paper)
    1. United States—Religion. 2. United States—Religion—1960–
I. Sherrill, Rowland A.
BL2525.R461   1990
291'.0973—dc20   89-35983
                                         CIP

for Joy
"every blessed day"

Contents

Preface and Acknowledgments

Except for the introductory chapter, each of the essays appearing in this volume was first presented as a "working paper" in one or another of several conferences held between 1982 and 1985 in a project entitled "Re-Visioning America: Religion and the Life of the Nation." This project, funded by the Lilly Endowment, Inc., was cosponsored by the Department of Religious Studies and the Center for American Studies of Indiana University, Indianapolis. The editor here gratefully acknowledges the support of the Lilly Endowment, especially the wisdom and learning supplied by Robert Wood Lynn, then its senior vice-president for religion, and expresses thanks as well to colleagues and support staff in Religious Studies and American Studies in my home university, who made the "going" smoother as I labored at the editorial tasks. Among these, Karl Illg, Jan Shipps, James F. Smurl, E. Theodore Mullen, Jr., Anne T. Fraker, and Conrad Cherry deserve high praise. Those three dozen or more colleagues from other institutions who participated in the project have been an intellectual boon in thinking through our subject and have no doubt contributed decisively to the learning of those who wrote the following chapters.

But each of these essayists whose work appears here also has my deep appreciation. While occasionally chafing under a rough editorial hand, each has been wonderfully congenial about staying at the work necessary to move his or her original paper into the final excellent piece which now appears. And, although such things cannot be guaranteed, I hope that their efforts will be as significant now for a broader community of inquiry as they have been for my own understanding of religion in American culture.

Many, many thanks are due Elizabeth G. Dulany of the University of Illinois Press for her interest in the project, her patience, her help. I would also like to thank the manuscript editor, Patricia Hollahan, and the many others at the Press who have helped in the production of this book.

The colleagues who wrote the following chapters will, I know, both understand and approve of the dedication of this volume to my wife, Joy, who has, they know, persisted.

Finally, for the use of the poem by Emily Dickinson at the end of

John Roth's essay, grateful acknowledgment is made. Reprinted by permission of the publishers and the Trustees of Amherst College from *The Poems of Emily Dickinson*, Thomas H. Johnson, ed., Cambridge: The Belknap Press of Harvard University Press, Copyright 1951, © 1955, 1979, 1983 by the President and Fellows of Harvard College. Reprinted by permission of Little, Brown, and Company from *The Complete Poems of Emily Dickinson*, edited by Thomas H. Johnson. Copyright 1929 by Martha Dickinson Bianchi; copyright © renewed 1957 by Mary L. Hampton.

Rowland A. Sherrill

Recovering
American Religious Sensibility:
An Introduction

True to the title of this volume, each of the essays presented here picks up an instance of American life at a highly disclosive intersection of religious meanings and energies with other systems, patterns, or issues of cultural existence. Each author's attention is trained not only on the singular character of his or her focal case but also on the terms in which this intersection is "telling" with respect to broader patterns and meanings of the national life. In variety and in cumulative thrust, then, the collection attempts to suggest how religious thought and action in America have insisted on and continue to persist in ramifying throughout other realms of American culture and have frequently done so in forms quite beyond what is generally considered their predictable "places"—institutional histories, theological systems, and doctrinal frames. The stuff of religion in America, these essays contend, is not only a matter of a separate, private sphere of understanding and commitment (with its ornamented, distinctive, and constitutionally protected house in the American republican village); and religion, as a structural category in the wider American polity, is not only the functional servant of democratic institutions, as Alexis de Tocqueville observed in 1835 in *Democracy in America*. Religion permeates the character, lives and works in the guts, of the village itself; it propels the people in matters of *res publica;* and it can loom up, asserting itself, in deeply camouflaged as well as highly visible ways.

Working with such a perspective, the essays thus aim as well at the matter of the subtitle—*American Recoveries*—for each is bent on discerning how its exploration of this or that topos of religious life illumines some more general aspect of American existence. Whether the author works on a religious movement intent on helping America "recover" (recuperate) from some ill time or action, concentrates on "recovering" (going over again) an old issue with new perspectives, or attempts to "recover" (to retrieve) some lost or neglected dimension of potential significance, each understands his or her work as a labor of interpretive recovery. Each, too, takes seriously the idea that religious sensibility always assumes its character and expresses itself distinctively in reciprocity with its cultural modifiers—in the case of these explorations, the modifiers supplied by various American contexts and conditions. To study formations and expressions of religious life as elements of culture, shaped by other cultural energies and shaping them in turn, is therefore to enlist the study of American religion in the broader effort of general cultural studies. Likewise, as the containing circumferences and the substantial media for whatever importance religious life in America might be thought to have, the specificities of the culture itself pose other contextualizing questions, apart from which the matter of accounting for American religion can never be settled. None of this diminishes the significance of religion, much less delivers over to the sly and facile determinisms of bad social science something called "religion," viewed as an isolated feature or trait of American life. Such an approach is animated, rather, by the notion that religious life, for good or ill, has its fullest efficacy and influence and most completely discloses itself for interpretation, not as a "floating" concept in its own separate sphere but as a species of cultural action. This is to see the manifold ways of "being religious" as engaged, performative matters of living in the gnarled stuff of circumstance and of meeting that requirement with a certain kind of understanding, a distinctive and encompassing acumen, from which flows a dynamic, continuous form of self-explanation.

At first glance, working toward such ends, seeking to understand elements of American culture by delineating its religious entanglements, would seem likely to encounter no special problems beyond those always faced by labors of scholarship—as if, indeed, the enormous complexities of "religion" and "culture" were not enough. In fact, however, contemporary critical inquiry of this order runs headlong not only into a host of issues in the various fields of cultural studies but also into some of the most cherished conventions of the scholarship on American religion itself. This introductory chapter, then, has the task of exploring in broad terms some of the difficulties to be met—with possible solutions to be gained—in dealing, in this time and place, with the character of American culture and with the various shapes, parts, and implications that make up American religion. Such explorations propose no means of "containing" the essays which follow, much less of enclosing the subject of religion and American culture. But, along with the much more refined work of the essayists, perhaps they will have served a particular purpose if some of the calculations ventured prove challenging to others dauntless enough to undertake the intellectual recovery of American religious sensibilities.

I. *Cultural "Loss" and Cultural "Recovery"*

Allowing briefly for the conceit of a "corporate personality," at least one element of the irony of American history has been that the nation periodically undergoes intense periods of self-consciousness and self-scrutiny about its own nature and meaning, despite observations by foreign visitors from de Tocqueville to the present about the unreflective, even unthinking, character of the American folk. Perhaps the old Puritan disposition to the jeremiad, ingrained later in national habits even as a "ritual of assent"[1] in various political and social rhetorics, has continued over the decades to reassert itself. But, for whatever reason, the American populace has intermittently gone in for intense and renewed inspections of its cumulative character and destiny— inspired, at different moments, by wars, by other national crises, by social discontents, by religious groups in reformative moods, by great and singular prophetic figures, by small grass-roots movements which trigger broader cultural convulsions, or simply by a pervasive sense of decline, misdirection, or anxiety.

By the middle of the 1980s, America yet again had become a fully public and serious question to itself, at least for those who cared to ask. Taught since the Vietnam era about its capacities for self-deceit and about the duplicities and corruptions of authority, introduced sometimes violently to the fragility of the social order in a wildly pluralistic framework, and tutored in the huge complexities of new geo-political formations and vast, almost unimaginably intricate, environmental systems, the nation, now schooled decisively on the limitations of its vaunted self-sufficiency and faced with the problematic of its special destiny, apparently had also to pose the question of its own core meanings, its nature, part, and place in a world "newly complicated."

Such questions are fundamentally cultural questions or, better, are questions about those persisting and containing traditions, values, traits, notions, and behaviors which figure into the commanding and distinguishing "logic" of American thought and experience. They are the kinds of questions raised most often in fully public terms in periods of crisis—when there are serious and widespread reasons to think that the traditions might suffer atrophy, that the traits might betray, that the cultural logic might cease to obtain.

An indication of the extent to which these and related questions pressed on American society by mid-decade appears in the pages of two large-circulation magazines. In the March 1984 issue of *Harper's Magazine,* the "Forum" section was entitled "Does America Still Exist?"—a question to which a number of thinkers/writers (among them Robert Nisbet, Richard Rodriguez, Eric Hoffer, Philip Berrigan, and Michael Harrington) were invited to respond in brief essays. The central problems posed by America were seen as the diffusions created by individualism and compounded by the dilemmas of American pluralism, both felt at a level of pain "on the pulses" as a great loss of any common core of values, meanings, loyalties, and purposes. The section is introduced, in part, as follows:

> The multiplication of so many purposes has led to a good deal of confusion as to what, if anything, the dreamers of so many American dreams hold in common. Americans are forever asking the questions in variant forms—"Where is the lost consensus?" "What is the national interest?" Even a federation of sardonic democrats requires a store of common value and a lexicon of public myth, but among a people dedicated to the ruthless pursuit of individual liberty, how is it possible to sustain belief in a political entity greater than the sum of its collective desire? (p. 43)

Again and again, the writers—in celebration or lament—answer from their various senses of the situation that if America *exists,* in all of its great and real diversity, it no longer possesses any sustaining continuity of values, any persisting fund of common meanings. It appears, rather, only as a huge, kaleidoscopic collection of meanings stemming from all those individualistic versions of America and pluriform enclaves in America. Whatever the writers find to applaud, however much richness they discover in diversity, regardless of the abundance they locate in variegated forms, the collectivity apparently remains just, and only, that. Any shared national culture seems improbable, the reader senses, prevented by a rampage of self-denominations and the arrival of the myriad new tribalisms. The question of the "lost consensus" goes unanswered.[2]

The "news" from *Esquire* seemed only slightly more sanguine, perhaps because of the editorial format selected for its Golden Collector's Issue of June 1985, entitled *The Soul of America,* with a cover which announces that "Two years ago, Esquire went looking for the real America. We found it." Instead of sending their writers into assigned isolation for "thought-pieces," the editors of *Esquire* pushed their writers—Ken Kesey, David Halberstam, Tom Wolfe, Sally Quinn, Bob Greene, George Plimpton, and another dozen others—out into the daily stuff of American life, from Westwood, California, to New York City, from Pendleton, Oregon, to Lafayette, Louisiana, to see what they could see of the "soul" of America in the human forms to be found in rodeos, oyster bars, and oil fields, Vietnamese fishing villages, Indiana basketball, Pennsylvania mill towns, and Houston opulence. With this cumulative quest, of course, the editors and writers thus hoped for something of a presiding spirit, at least a kind of metaphorical "soul," within or attached to their own presumption of the American "corporate personality." One need be neither cynical nor mischievous to suggest that the editors found that for which they had ostensibly craved. While each writer's piece fixes on and seeks to evoke the singular feature of this or that character, the telling quality of specific detail, the sense of the unique action, the feeling of the immediate scene, in his or her assigned "place," the editorial staff, clearly bent on searching out rubrics of organization with which to control all of that "difference," finds the "soul" of America much less in the particularities of persons and places, sensibilities and actions (as the writers drive these home) than in their own vapid and sometimes contradictory labels: the Albany oyster-shucker, the Philadelphia debutante circle, the Wall Street process, all species of the *genera* "Tenacity and Lasting Tradition"; a hotel staff in Salt Lake City, a military school in South Carolina, a laid-off steel family in Pittsburgh, all commonly denominated under "Loyalty and Common Purpose"; the "Blues" in Chicago, Jewish humor in the Catskills, "sanctuary" activists in Tucson, all *exempla* of "Individuality and Reckless Imagination." Even with such a typology of the American "soul"—found in the counterdrives of longevity and currency, teamwork and individuality, loyalty and autonomy—the country remains a question for itself, to be answered only with an encyclopedic sprint across an intractable and incommensurable landscape.

But the point is not so much to size up the failures of these magazines as they took up their queries into the possibility of common American meanings as it is to suggest both the pervasive character of the questioning and the odds against satisfactory answers. The country had become too enormously variable, too complex and contradictory, it appeared, to sustain some set of core meanings inclusive for, shared by, the citizenry, and inquiries into the defining nature of the culture seemed bound to meet a paradox.

Such general perplexity about a containing set of American cultural traditions and meanings in the mid–1980s was matched in the academy among those whose fields or disciplines in any way attached to the subject of American culture, and, at least in some cases, there has been an equivalent concern among these university people that a vital American legacy of common understanding and values is by way of being lost. Again, two sources—both essays in the *American Scholar*—serve to suggest the character of the quandary: Clifford

Geertz explored the confusions appearing in "cultural studies" generally,[3] and E. D. Hirsch, Jr., "worried" the nature and maintenance of American "core" culture particularly.[4]

Geertz's essay points to a situation in current styles of interpretive discourse which itself suggests a vast upheaval in cultural studies and portends the complexities implied in his subtitle, "The Refiguration of Social Thought." With efforts to account for social and cultural forms and meanings more or less up for grabs in a rushing reorganization of knowledge generally, he notes, there have appeared many instances of blurred genres, in which some contemporary texts mingle, interpenetrate, and *con*-fuse forms of description and modes of exposition traditionally thought remote from each other or not ordinarily thought appropriate for the cases under scrutiny. One finds "scientific discussions looking like belles lettres *morceaux* (Lewis Thomas, Loren Eisley), baroque fantasies presented as deadpan empirical observations (Borges, Barthelme), . . . documentaries that read like true confessions (Mailer), parables posing as ethnographies (Castenada), theoretical treatises set out as travelogues (Lévi-Strauss)" (p. 20), and so on. Such instances of what Geertz calls "genre dispersion" (p. 21) arrive neither as simple intellectual curiosities nor as arcane resorts to artifice: they both stem from and signal the dilemmas of interpretive life in the face of enormous and intricate social and cultural realities which pose incredible odds against interpreting anything—"cultural studies" caught in throes similar to chaos-science. For Geertz, of course, this "jumbling of the varieties of discourse" requires not "just another redrawing of the cultural map" but rather "an alteration of the principles of mapping" (p. 20), and, committed to the charges of the new interpretive ethnography, he is also prepared to think that cultural studies possess more profound possibilities at just such a moment, when the secure cartography of the arts and sciences begins to discover it might well have missed a continent. "The woods," he suggests, "are full of eager interpreters" (p. 21).

For his part, E. D. Hirsch, Jr., found the challenges of the cultural scene much less bracing as he undertook a different kind of "cultural studies" in his essay "Cultural Literacy" in 1983, followed in 1987 by his book bearing the same title. His own studies of culture having led him to the virtues of the ancient Greek concept of *paideia,* Hirsch wants to propose that culture consists in a kind of "shared knowledge" in a populace which supplies the "background" of all of its discourse and social interaction, that cultural literacy requires the ability to trade in this currency, and that the vitality and efficacy of cultural

identity and tradition therefore ride on the intergenerational continuity of such knowledge. Hirsch's vested concern in the maintenance
of the American tradition is something about which he makes no pre-
tense as he sets out to expose the "scandalous" decline of such shared
knowledge, of culture, in contemporary America.

Even without entering into the momentous issues of "cultural literacy," it can be noted that Hirsch's questions and purposes, especially
in the book-length study, touch on many of the same issues of common values, incumbent knowledge, and the like which tugged at the
editors of *Harper's* and *Esquire*. Since 1983, he and a number of others
have participated in intensive and extensive quarrels about the items
of indispensable information for Americans, questions of the existence or construction of "shared" learning, the identification of the
"classics" of American culture, the selection and character of an authoritative American cultural "canon," with which and into which
"aura" the American generations ought to be educated. What is at
stake is nothing less than the national "language," the possibility of
public discourse in the midst of American diversity, the very life and
health of national culture. And, despite Hirsch's own assured tone
about how the culture can right itself, his work, viewed in the context
of wider discussions of American cultural literacy, not only reflects the
problems of defining what are or ought to be the central meanings,
the centripetal pulls, of American cultural existence but also signals
some of the ambiguities into which "American cultural studies" at
large have fallen.

Such predicaments for cultural self-understanding—conundrums
of an order and depth which force America to question its own nature
and meaning—are difficult enough without adding religion to the
mix. But each of the "samples" in the preceding brief but studied
"survey" also suggests that something called "religion" plays an important role: the *Harper's* "Forum" sees it as instrumental in the rich
diversity of American forms; the *Esquire* editors hint at the presence
of an American "soul"; Geertz, in other essays, understands religion
as a commanding systemic formation in cultural life;[5] and Hirsch's
book, which borrows the concept of "canon" from biblical studies,
traces the efficacy of Horace Kallen's notion of an American "Bible"
in his call for a "civil religion" for American culture.[6] Indeed, even as
one meets such assertions regarding the powerful influence of religion in American culture, the sheer variety of working definitions of
religion utilized by various practitioners of cultural studies compli-
cates the question of America further still. And when one turns to

those who work specifically to account for the nature, roles, and effects of religion in American life, the problems in some respects only increase.

II. *Finding American Religion: Normal Forms and Formal Norms*

As William Scott Green has recently reminded the community of higher education, the emergence of religion as a subject of study is the upshot of some curious twists of seventeenth- and eighteenth-century intellect in the West, and the appearance of this subject in the curriculum of the modern American "secular" university is an even later phenomenon.[7] Green also notes, however, that the new academic rectitude on which scholars of religion have preened themselves over recent decades has been fraught with problems. The academicians have demarcated themselves from those religionists whose perspectives and practices represent the primary data for such academic study and, thus, the modern scholars have seen their subject take its full and rightful place among the humanities and social sciences as fitting and proper in the university array of critical inquiry. But, according to Green, those who carry on the study have too often done so in ways which "finesse" the matter of any defensible theory by "trying to account for religion while [at once] claiming that it is *sui generis* and irreducible" (p. 24), thus insisting on a privileged status for "religion" enjoyed by none of the other human activities taken as subjects of intellectual inquiry.

Such an impasse of logic, Green suggests, is all the more vexing still in America wherein "religion is a native category"—that is, a "given" as a paradigm for construing life which "carries a claim to concretion, self-evidence, and inherent significance" (p. 23). On a bad day, the scholarship grapples with intractable "public" comprehensions of religion, present categorically, as something significant and "evocative but inarticulate" which is to be "taken for granted as a . . . conventional trait of human being" (p. 23). This, along with the widespread and cherished assumption of religion's "private" nature, tends to make it not only an improbable but a virtually unassailable subject of study. On a worse day, the scholarship succumbs and aims its discourse at interpreting *other* peoples' religious lives in terms of this American native comprehension, with the alien religion divorced, in its utterly pristine status, from all other aspects of cultural existence and with American religion itself beyond the limits even of circumspect inquiry. On a worse day yet, of course, American scholars of religion vigorously reify this American foundational category, become themselves religionists in the actions of their inquiry, and persist in several species of gnostic self-evidencing—provoked perhaps to glance at others' beliefs and practices for the sake of evaluation but not inclined to exercise any thoroughgoing critical inspection of their own standpoints and assumptions.

Beyond these kinds of false starts in the study of religion generally, three characteristic modes of scholarship on American religion have further circumscribed the critical understanding of religion as they have attached their inquiries only to the most visible and predictable phenomena. Perhaps because of the peculiar status "religion" has had and the most obvious forms it has taken in the United States, this kind of scholarship has constructed, or at least tended to abide with, assumptions about religion which are largely auxiliary for the apparently prepossessing religious forms found in institutions, formal theology, and "civil religion" and has, in doing so, neglected some singularly important features of the subject which would permit a firmer grasp on the implications of religious life in other spheres of American cultural existence.

One form of this tendency shows itself very quickly in the kinds of truncated definitions of "religion" which appear in simplistic or even more complex equations of religion with some of its "accustomed" public appearances—in the various social groupings associated with Temple, Church, Mosque, or in the defining doctrinal systems thought to typify persons or groups, or in the traditions through which doctrines and institutions have persisted. These are, of course, important and powerful elements of religious life, signally significant in accounting for religion in its cumulative or social or "collective" formations. Frequently, however, such predictable, even patent, topoi of the dimensions of religion become, even in the academy, the whole of the matter. Regarded as the essentially definitive formations of religious life in America, they become paradigmatic and controlling, iconic and static, for a kind of scholarship which confuses one form of American religious manifestation with what it takes to be the whole of American religion. *Homo religiosus Americanus* is seen as nothing other than a function of the particular creedal framework inherited, group identified with, or institution belonged to, as these exist in some immaterial manner—as something like the taxonomic native category Green points out—apart from the remainder of American cultural-historical existence. With American religion viewed as no more than the sum of its individual "organized" parts, the story of American religion, for this form of scholarship, amounts to a collection of those exhaustive historical accounts of every group, institution, and doctrinal system—from the Anabaptists to the Zen Buddhists—in the visible pantheon of American religious associations.

A second, perhaps ancillary—but in any event broadly practiced and equally attenuating—disposition in the scholarship appears more subtly in treatments of great theological figures and religious sensibilities when these are proposed as "representatives" of the entirety of American theological expression and religious sensibility in their eras and when, thus, the full range of American religious thought and life is nothing other than these figures "writ small." To the extent that this approach rightfully insists on viewing, say, a Jonathan Edwards or a Horace Bushnell or an Abraham Heschel not only as delivering the most highly articulate and deeply nuanced kinds of theological reflection but as "giants" in this regard who were conditioned by and responsive to their respective times, such scholarly work is undeniably valuable. Even if this form of inquiry and exposition often tends to posit theology as a kind of activity stringently and exclusively in the keeping of "official" theologians and to discern the actions of religious expression only in these most overt forms, it can at its best serve the useful functions both of presenting refined accounts of one important dimension of American religious life and of providing a special kind of access to the cultural-historical ages of the American religious tradition. Quite beyond what is frequently an abridged, partial, or partisan definition of "theology," however, such an approach hits its limits, falls to error, when it assumes, tacitly or more aggressively, that it accounts for American religion in large part or in total, that its great looming figures completely represent their religious communities, much less the religious *demos* of their ages. It errs as well, indeed, when it fails to see that these big, hovering personages have their status in the American tradition only as, and perhaps just because of, the outsized idiosyncrats they actually were, however much they might have later been incorporated into the so-called mainstream and however much they might, then, cumulatively comprise *one* powerful feature of American religion, "the Great Tradition in Theology." The remainder, omitted from that particular record, of course, is what and how all those other, *un*represented, less intellectually commanding, less socially powerful Americans understood and believed, felt and practiced, suffered and imagined, religiously.

Although those who want to work on "civil" or "public" religion suggest that their foci and objectives can lead to critical understanding of a broader, more populous "American faith" which vivifies cultural life, their inquiries into the terms and nature of American religion likewise reveal another, frequently employed, albeit quite different, kind of problematical assumption appearing in a third convention in the scholarship. Such an assumption is revealed frequently when the scholars propose a "civil religion" which draws on, yet both underlies and supersedes, the huge varieties of specific religious identification in America, or when they argue for a "public religion" which confounds discrete features of Judeo-Christian, but mainly Protestant, viewpoints in a discernible but largely indistinct presentation of itself, or when they posit some species of nationalist faith—belief in, loyalty toward, trust in, orientation by[8] the American polity and "way of life." This manner of approaching American religion aims to locate the inclusive, a cultural "universal." It looks for, among other things, the key texts and doctrines of that religio-political "canon" which animates Kallen's, and Hirsch's, desire for an "American Bible," the conflations of political and pulpit rhetorics which express an "orthodox" form of American identity, the public ceremonies which arrive with adumbrations of "the sacred," the cultural values, symbols, and myths which are dyed in religious coloration, and the habits and customs of public life which are "consecrated" in spiritual allusion. And, to the degree that such studies calculate repeated, significant patterns of expression and behavior, constellations of images and meanings, and connections among the disparate realms of American experience, they serve religious and cultural studies well.

All too often, however, these scholarly quests for a "civil religion" are accompanied by assumptions about "religion" which apparently tempt them to overreach. The working conviction, defended or not, seems to be that, in some fully pervading way, this American "religion" swings through the night like a nearby moon, radiating uniformly over the variegated and complex fields of the republic, washing over or washing out not only religious and general cultural but larger human "difference," and, thus, compelling equally—like gravity—all who live under its lunar (lunatic) influence. If the simile surely leads to semantic excess, perhaps it serves nonetheless to suggest a deep faultiness in this way of thinking about religion—that is, the inclination, when this style of scholarship is pushed to its limits, to think of a religion, once in place in some distinguishable form, as an immutable object, a *thing* "out there" which, if experienced as effectual and absorbed into the human lives under its light, is always and everywhere internalized in precisely the same ways, always and everywhere soaked through the skin and into the veins with a constancy of content, always and everywhere a univocal form of possession.

Several crucial rudiments are missed when such assumptions about

American religion run to extremes. First, the approach is unable to account for the varieties of sects, denominations, and so on, which must be thought instrumentally important in the makeup of American life as a whole, not only religious life.[9] And, indeed, the varieties of "civil religion" itself cannot be accommodated. Further, such approaches fail to take seriously the singular character and presence of those major eccentrics—Edwards, Emerson, Orestes Brownson, and the like—who are significant in religious and cultural traditions at least in part just because they internalized the more collective and uniform stuff of their American religious "worlds" through the unique subjectivities of their genius and, thus, veered away from any immutable commanding thing which might have possessed them. But this is only to observe that the scholars of "civil religion" inhabit a different ground than the other two conventional approaches. What is more important is that their modes of grasping after the containing "American religion" prevent their attending to the ways people, who are not only possessed by ways of being religious, take possession of the various dimensions and possibilities that religious legacy and contemporary life present to them and do so in terms pertinent to, meaningful for, and significant within their particular contexts of cultural existence—their backgrounds, families, and groups; their times, places, and situations; their self-understanding; their "America."[10]

Now, the purpose of such a critique of some prevailing scholarly conventions—in portrayals which are admittedly stunted, even caricatures—is not to tar all equally with the same broad brush. Few, if any, practice so erroneously or fail so egregiously as this presentation suggests. Indeed, the main point of issuing such extreme depictions is only to remark how each approach is hampered: with its specific focus on and approach to one dimension, or activity, or visible expression of religion in America, each adopts at least a working definition of religion which is constrained by its focus, and which thus severely limits what can properly be regarded as "religious" or delivers an obscured view of religion in America. By concentrating on what seem to them to be the "normal forms" of religion as found in America—in systems and histories of social groupings, in powerful or regnant "theological" interpretations, in the efforts of pulpit-patriotic rhetorics to capture public fields—these conventional modes have largely succeeded in accounting for American religion under the self-fulfilling aegis of an apparently standard American definition of "religion." With this, the objects of inquiry supply the more or less exclusive definitions of the subject of inquiry, the structures become dictatorial for the strategies of inquiry, and the "normal forms" in which religion in America has been seen become "formal norms" for thinking about what American religion is or can be. The problem, again, is that the most obvious objects of scrutiny—certainly not the only appropriate objects—have been inordinately influential in constricting the definitions of "religion" utilized by the scholarship to explore the issues of religion and American culture.[11]

The exertions of these conventions and the exercise of their "formal norms" respecting what significantly belongs to the study of American religion have caused the scholarship largely to ignore some several rudiments which not only belong within its subject but figure as important dimensions of it. What these ways of proceeding miss, in general and from the outset, is the mood to take seriously the importance of the "religious sensibilities" of people in the ordinary actions of their general cultural lives, and thus they make no provisions to account for how their own "normal forms" of religion—doctrine, social group, "theology," rhetoric, and the like—might "translate" for, and into, the complex, heterogeneous subjectivities which make up the American religious populace.[12]

Apparently lacking interest in the messy and maculate ways the big paradigmatic forms are taken up in the interpretations of individual sensibility, personal desire, particular enclave, or local circumstance, such approaches might well avoid the singular, eccentric, or even aberrant expressions of religious life to be found among ordinary people in favor of the commanding paradigm, personage, or pattern, but they foreclose as well on any surer understanding of the dynamics between the "canonical" stuff of religion and the performative stuff of religious lives, as lived in the midst of daily actions and accidents of cultural existence. It is one thing to account for the sources of official theological musing which underlay a decade of Presbyterian life in New England; it is another to generate an adequate means of accounting for how that Presbyterian*ism* assumed a distinctively American form and how it obtained and had its broad, nearly uniform "affect" for Presbyterians not only among the elite in Princeton but in the common parishioner elsewhere. It is another thing yet to be able to see, and to take seriously as religious performance, the actions of that corrupt or misguided Presbyterian civic leader whose "honest" but aberrant hold on and "internalization" of the authoritative religious world leads him to error. Finally it is quite another thing altogether to possess an effectual definition of religion which permits one to approach all of these cases with an equal eye, prepared to find the actions of the civic leader as significantly disclosive, in one way, with respect to the question of the nature and terms of American religion as are the meditations of the great theologians in their particular ways. All of these "instances" belong to American religion and no fuller understanding of the implication of religion in American culture can be achieved without an approach which can treat them each and all.

In order to deal more successfully with the matter of American religion, then, there seems required a reconception which can accommodate both the storied traditions—the general formations, the large paradigms, the canonical data—and the specific twists and turns of more particular and individual religious subjectivities and responses along a continuous spectrum of religious thought, expression, and action and which understands the complex reciprocities occurring on this kind of continuum. Nothing less will allow some crucial entanglements of religious sensibilty with other spheres of American culture to come foward for fuller critical inspection, and, in this sense, nothing else will permit that deeper understanding of the parts and places of religious sensibility which might be fundamental in and for American cultural studies. But such a reconception necessarily begins with, and finally depends on, an attending recognition that categories like "tradition," "canon," and "theology" also need to come in for reexamination as forms and actions within a cultural table of operations.

III. *Locating American Religious Sensibility*

As Green and a number of others know full well, there are in fact movements, however nascent, in the currents of the contemporary reorganization of knowledge—some in part signaled by the kinds of "blurred genres" Geertz identifies—which drive to interpret religious forms, utterances, and actions as they move and function and make meaning in and as cultural terms and dynamics. Some of this work, especially as it seeks to detach the study of religion from formal theological proclivities and to move it toward some of the new insights in anthropological learning and other fields of cultural studies, has deep pertinence for any efforts to locate the terms of that American religious sensibility which has too frequently fallen outside the purview of the conventional scholarship. And, even without any full survey of such work, itself interested more often in its particular *praxis* than in what would seem its sustaining *theoria,* it is nonetheless possible to see in some of its thrusts a vital new endowment for studies of American religion.[13]

Concerned not only for the subject of religion but for theoretical ways and means adequate to it, the work of Jonathan Z. Smith points up one kind of a possible course. Smith has been keen to see that "the map is not the territory," that not only new maps but, as Geertz notes, "new principles of mapping" are necessary, and that these new principles will emerge only through the full intellectual project of thinking again through the stuff and matter of religion in cultural terms, without the theological privileging and ethnocentric cant. His essays in *Imagining Religion* are provocative cases in point. Although focusing only occasionally on American instances, Smith wants in part to occupy a "position to offer a redescription of certain categories of religious experience and expression which we associate primarily with the West"[14] and, in the present context, his reflections on the nature, function, and implication of "canon" supply rich resources for conceiving crucial elements in the character and continuity of religious sensibility.

Threading his way between observations by Cicero and Freud, Smith aims toward "a conception of religion as human [hence cultural] labor" (p. 43) which, among other things, involves the work of ingenuity in meeting limitation, a continuous reciprocity of canon and exegesis. If a "canon, broadly understood . . . [is] the arbitrary fixing of a limited number of 'texts' [also broadly understood[15]] as immutable and authoritative," then, Smith insists, it "is far from unusual" (p. 44): it is one, albeit a highly significant one, among other cultural operations or processes, the religious one through which, by which, a community posits vital, constituent elements of its self-definition in decisions about what are for it, out of the wide world of possibilities in thought and experience, the central inscriptions of "the sacred," the delimitation of what can obsessively bear significance. The specific terms of such a "reduction of the plenum" (p. 43) of possibilities, of course, provide nurture for but are also conditioned by the historical and cultural unit in question, within which the canon reaches a *kind* of closure. While a canon figures as a central formation in a religious community which proposes explanations of and to itself, however, it is not "religion." For Smith, it is only a central element in a continuing tradition of the community as its members "labor" religiously in the process of keeping the authoritative ascriptions of sacrality decisive and meaningful in their interpretations of experience.

In this view, if a canon is in a sense "closed" by definition, as it posits self-imposed limitations for a community in its regard for "the sacred," it is far from being a static or autotelic thing. Stemming from processive religious labor and "fixing" or closing itself only by dint of cultural agreements, it thus presents itself to the ongoing life of the community for its own perpetuation.[16] Thus a canon, once closed, is

also "open" in the one sense at least that its sustained, effectual life—
and the "persistence of the sacred" for the community—depends on
the ingenuity of the exegetes it invites to take up the work of interpretation, application, and extension. In terms of the taxonomy,
Smith observes:

> The only formal element that is lacking to transform a catalogue into
> a *canon* is the element of closure: that the list is held to be complete.
> This formal requirement generates a corollary. Where there is a canon,
> it is possible to predict the *necessary* occurrence of a hermeneute, of an
> interpreter whose task it is continually to extend the domain of the
> closed canon over everything that is known or everything that exists
> *without* altering the canon in the process. It is with the canon and its
> hermeneute that we encounter the necessary obsession with [that effort
> of] exegetical totalization [which is the only thing, if anything, Smith
> believes, that is "distinctive about religion as a human activity" (p. 44)].
> (p. 48)

Without the hermeneute, the exegete, the stuff of the canon will eventually become anachronistic, its reach truncated, its bearing on life
either unintelligible for those who feel no connection with the past or
omniapplicable in paralyzing literalist ways for those who cannot
break into the present. Supplying the community with limitations, the
canon itself in turn requires the ingenuity of interpretive life not only
for the sake of that "sacred persistence" definitive for the continued
life of the community but also for that obsessive effort of "exegetical
totalization" religious life seeks under the rule and sway of its canonical center.[17] For Smith, such a process of work in a religious community—"the radical and arbitrary reduction represented by the notion
of canon and the ingenuity represented by the rule-governed exegetical enterprise of applying the canon to every dimension of human
life . . . [which is its] most characteristic, persistent, and obsessive religious activity" (p. 43)—is essentially theological labor.

With this, of course, the category of "theology" has also come in
for real redescription, now understood as the indigenous exertions of
individuals in a community "who may be termed tribal theologians
. . . [as they attempt to] raise the endeavors of exegetical ingenuity to
the level of a comprehensive system" (p. 52). This means on its face
that theology is not the exclusive possession of "official" theologians,
that it is to be found whenever, wherever, people work theologically
or, that is, when they enlist themselves in the labor of sustaining and
extending "their sacred" in those canonically ruled exegetical attempts which aim to interpret every dimension of the experience they
meet. While the tribes might necessarily have their working theologi-

ans, however, the work of those theologians—the struggles of contained interpretation and fettered ingenuity—is "profoundly cultural," thus calling for an "essentially anthropological viewpoint" (p. 43) on the part of that critical scholarship which would study such decisive shapes and actions of religious life.

As Smith carries out his redescriptions of the Western category of "canon," he works in part to enable further critical reflection on the religious *Sitz im Leben* of Yoruba and Ndembu divination-practices and other instances of religious activity which might analogically be illuminated, and, in this way, he participates in the anthropological project of "translation," as Clifford Geertz understands it: "the reshaping of categories (ours and other people's—think of 'taboo') so that they can reach beyond the contexts in which they originally arose . . . [in order] to locate affinities and mark differences is a great part of what 'translation' comes to in anthropology" (p. 12). And, while Geertz does not make note of the fact, it ought to go without saying that any such "reshaped category" might well also release for inspection important new dimensions of the very source and context of origination. In other words, it surely follows that the category of canon in the West, once reshaped, might not only illumine Ndembu divination, might not only open new ways to think about the Chinese *I Ching*, but might lead to unexpected objects and altered approaches to profound processes of canon-exegesis, limitation, and ingenuity, in American instances as well. One might be prepared to find various unanticipated "canons" presented to various traditions and various examples of the cultural processes of exegesis at work and, thus, various stripes of American "tribal theologians" involved in the characteristic, persistent, obsessive labor of intrepreting life under the rules of their canons and energized by their prospects for interpretive comprehensiveness.

Geertz's own version of "interpretive anthropology" provides warrants for being so prepared, in fact for *expecting* such variety in the canonical-exegetical processes instanced in American religious labors. Indeed, as one measures the utility of Smith's "anthropological viewpoint" in grappling with this signal dimension of American religious sensibility, Geertz provides a crucial corollary in his own descriptions of the nature and conditions of contemporary ethnographical work— most specifically, on the loci of such religious activity. In dealing with the acts and expressions of "alien" cultures, the ethnographer, even in his or her most "generalizing" mood, must finally own that the specific stuff under scrutiny—the forms and actions disclosive of cultural knowledge, the expressions revelatory of ways of cultural self-understanding—are always rooted in, participatory in, "local frames of awareness" (p. 6) or, to use one of Geertz's own favored locutions, are always "texts" to be read in *context.* What he remarks about remote cultures is clearly applicable to, and important for, any efforts to "read" the acts of American religious sensibility: "To an ethnographer, sorting through the machinery of distant ideas, the shapes of knowledge are always ineluctably local, indivisible from their instruments and their encasements. One may veil this fact with ecumenical rhetoric or blur it with strenuous theory, but one cannot really make it go away" (p. 4).

In terms of present purposes, the moral seems clear. All actions in the American canonical-exegetical process, all "texts" of American religious sensibility, whether appearing in what Geertz terms "the small imaginings of local knowledge [or] the large ones of cosmopolitan intent" (pp. 15–16), appear first in the sharp immediacies of the cultural life in which they occur and apart from which shaping *ecos* they cannot be understood. Canons are forged and continue to propose their authoritative limitations in encasements which belong to local frames of cultural awareness. Exegesis performs its ingenuities with the cultural instruments and through the cultural machinery which stems from local knowledge. Those "tribal theologians" (official and otherwise, eccentric or otherwise) understand their lives, extend their sacred, seek interpretive "wholes," in cultural actions which are predicates of local senses of circumstance and possibilty, fear and hope, need and desire. Instances and cases of religious sensibility in America reveal themselves in a huge variety of "acts" of local cultural knowledge, in myriad local expressions of "knowing" cultural action.[18] In this view, Amish withdrawal presents itself as cultural "expression" every bit as much as the Southern Christian Leadership Conference's more vocal reformative urges, various American religious "quietisms" as much forms of cultural "action" as the new Religious Right's political purges, the new pursuit of Zen in America as much a kind of limitation-ingenuity operation as the old revivalism in its impassioned surges. In this view, James Agee's vivid, "obsessive" struggle of "canonical-exegetical totalization" in locating the sacrality of Alabama tenant farmers[19] is an instance of American religious sensibility which is equal in kind in the process of religious labor, if not as "official theology," to Reinhold Niebuhr's effort of comprehensiveness in *The Nature and Destiny of Man:* both operate under the charge and both have status as American "tribal theologians."

But the point is not simply to create a new lexicon which might enable interpretation of the meaning of this or that formation of

American religious sensibility in some autotelic or self-containing set of terms, one among many such possible meanings in cultural life. The objective is also to discern how local instances of religious sensibility operate to make meaning—drawing on their various canonical ascriptions of "the sacred," proposing their special ingenious exegetical "logics," thus presenting their defining, sustaining knowledges and gaining their distinctive characters—just as American cultural actions in their great varieties of American locale.

This view might encourage students of American religion to recover instances of religious life from heretofore hidden or unaccustomed "places," and it might admit of a fuller and more textured critical recovery of the complex shapes and forms of American religious sensibility in its processive cultural labors. Indeed, it might rescue or aid in recovering discussions of an "American canon," for people like Hirsch, with a far more nuanced sense of the dynamics of authoritative knowledge in a cultural tradition. But it will not, cannot, issue up *the* soul of America, will not and cannot reinvent some American "consensus" feared lost if ever it existed. With an enlarged notion of the parts and places of religious sensibility, it is no doubt possible to discern in more complicated ways how religion in America has insisted on "mattering" beyond its conventionally confined quarters, has persisted in extending itself in cultural terms, but its ways and means, ineluctably rooted in the cultural and tied to the corrigible and tangible stuff of the historical, admit of no univocal "American religion." The drive of intellect under the insight of the honest ethnographer is, rather, toward an apprehension of and respect for the irreducibly various cultural forms and shapes of American religious sensibilities even as one carries out the attempt to conceive the more or less constant cultural process, labor, of religious sensibility in America.

Such a condition of inquiry does not lead back into any stylized form of "cultural relativism": it *does* invite acts of intellectual decency—respectful efforts of full interpretation, reconstructions of exclusivist categories, analogical arts of "translation"—which will allow us both to preserve the sacred "differences" in all of those past and present American religious "worlds" and yet to travel among them confident of finding Americans religiously at the labor of making meaning, according to their "lights," according to their "canons." As Geertz suggests, "in the last analysis, then, as in the first, the interpretive study of culture represents an attempt to come to terms with the diversity of the ways human beings construct their lives in the act of leading them" (p. 16). Without necessarily trading in the anthropological "vocabulary" of this chapter, the following essays participate in such an attempt by following out their own forms of cultural labor, the best metaphor for which, perhaps, is archaeological excavation— as they dig, first to last, through the temporal layers of American life, from the imaginations of "outer space" in the national present to the operations of "inner space" in Puritan New England.

NOTES

1. See the chapter entitled "Ritual of Consensus" in Sacvan Bercovitch, *The American Jeremiad* (Madison: University of Wisconsin Press), pp. 132–75.

2. This once-present, now-lost national "consensus," of course, is perhaps more a conjuration, stemming from hope or dream, than an empirical social reality, as much a matter of American myth as of American history. The very existence of what Bercovitch describes as "rituals of consensus" suggests a frequent cultural sensation in American historical experience that no such consensus is present. Even so, it is nonetheless a powerful object for creative nostalgia in a community which feels itself "uncentered." At another level, of course, it can be argued that the public expression of "crisis" is a function of a "crisis" felt by those "consensus theorists" whose politics require the continuity of the values which belong to the status quo. To stand as defender of the symbolic values of a culture, of course, can be a political act of empowerment and possession.

3. Clifford Geertz, "Blurred Genres," *American Scholar* 29 (1980). Reprinted in Clifford Geertz, *Local Knowledge: Further Essays in Interpetive Anthropolgy* (New York: Basic Books, 1983). Hereafter, all parenthetical page numbers in the text following quotations from Geertz refer to *Local Knowledge*.

4. E. D. Hirsch, Jr., "Cultural Literacy," *American Scholar* 32 (1983). This essay was followed by Hirsch's book on the subject, *Cultural Literacy: What Every American Needs to Know* (Boston: Houghton Mifflin Company, 1987).

5. See especially "Religion as a Cultural System," in Clifford Geertz, *The Interpretation of Cultures: Selected Essays* (New York: Basic Books, 1973), pp. 87–125.

6. Hirsch, *Cultural Literacy*, pp. 98–104.

7. William Scott Green, "Something Strange, Yet Nothing New: Religion in the Secular Curriculum," *Liberal Education* 75, no. 5 (1987): 21–25. Subsequent parenthetical page numbers following quotations from Green refer to this article.

8. For a "starter set" on this matter, see Robert Bellah, "Civil Religion in America," which appeared first in *Daedalus* 1 (1967): 1–21, and is widely reprinted; Robert Bellah and Phillip E. Hammond, *Varieties of Civil Religion* (New York: Seabury Press, 1975); John F. Wilson, *Public Religion in American Culture* (Philadelphia: Temple University Press, 1979); Will Herberg, *Protestant, Catholic, Jew: An Essay in American Religious Sociology* (Garden City: Doubleday and Company, 1960). On various forms of "social faiths," see H.

Richard Niebuhr, *Radical Monotheism and Western Culture* (New York: Harper & Row, 1960).

9. Hirsch, for instance, places heavy importance on the necessity for a "civil religion" in America to sustain the common values and meanings of cultural identity and tradition, but, in this, he radically underestimates the reliance of any such civil religion on the various traditions of Judaism and Christianity so instrumental in the making of American life. A quick indication of Hirsch's failure to understand not only the decisively shaping influence of these religious traditions in America but the derivative character of any effectual "civil religion" appears perhaps in the fact that his book on American identity, culture, and tradition manages three separate listings for civil religion in its index (as well as entries for C. P. Snow, Cicero, and Daniel Defoe) but makes no mention there of Protestantism, Catholicism, or Judaism, much less Methodists, Baptists, Episcopalians, and so on. An index is not necessarily axiomatic of an author's scale of importance, but such omissions seem quite telling when regarded in relation to the text.

10. It is important to observe in passing that the "civil religion" proponents who might well seek forms of entitlement in the *construction* of such a "religion" are not altogether different from the "consensus theorists" of American social life (see n. 2) and that both groups might be thought to exist in a strange triad with those who would insist on certain forms of "cultural literacy" (see n. 9). One cannot ignore the possible political motivations of such efforts at cultural possession.

11. Much of this problem of "definitions" is no doubt attributable to the rise of academic specializations not only within the study of religion but within the study of American religion, as each specialty adopts a definition, or at least a set of assumptions, regarding "religion" which is congenial to the particular objects under scrutiny.

12. I am *not* advocating the end of those studies of religious institutions, theological figures, or civil-religious patterns, nor indeed do I want to disregard their undeniable value. I am only recommending the development of a much more inclusive view of the phenomena of religious life than any of these three forms of scholarship is able singly or cumulatively to afford. Nonetheless, I recognize that no such broader approach is at all possible which forfeits on the gains made by such studies.

13. Despite the tack taken in the remainder of this introduction, I am *not* proposing that the entire study of religion in America be given away to the anthropologists or even to those in the field called "History of Religions" as they try on the anthropological "wardrobe." The point, rather, is simply to size up potential resources for the study of religion in America which are adequate when the subject has been pulled, without privileged status, into the broader ambit of "cultural studies." Such resources might arrive from any of the humanities and social sciences which are bent on seeing religion as cultural activity with cultural implications and significance. Besides, as Geertz recognizes (see "Blurred Genres" above), anthropology itself is by way of be-

coming not just anthropology but linguistics, literary criticism, psychology, and so on.

14. Jonathan Z. Smith, *Imagining Religion: From Babylon to Jonestown* (Chicago: University of Chicago Press, 1982), p. 36. Hereafter, all parenthetical page numbers following quotations from Smith refer to this book.

15. The term *texts*, for Smith as for Geertz, refers not only to written documents but to anything which can be thought to inscribe and propose human meanings and which, therefore, can be "read" as a bearer of cultural content.

16. Again, the political dimensions of canon-construction cannot be overlooked, even if here I have adopted Smith's more "neutral" taxonomic tones. *People* work at the business of the formation of a canon, and that work is always filled with potential interpenetrations of other cultural actions with the discernible efforts of religious life.

17. In understanding this processive work for what it is, it is important for Smith, and it is important in the present context, to resist what Adolf Jensen called the "iron law of semantic depletion" (*Myth and Cult among Primitive Peoples* [Chicago: University of Chicago Press, 1963])—that is, the notion that the first utterances, first acts, and so on, represent the only pure formulations of religious "expression" and that all subsequent "applications," interpretations, and so on, are degenerations from these *primordia*. Smith is surely correct in asserting the reciprocity, and processive equality, of canonical formulations and exegetical activities, for it is in that reciprocating process of work that religious sensibility is to be discerned and, if efficacious, not in any depleted form. See Smith's discussion of this, p. 42.

18. If "texts" refers to more than written documents (see n. 13), then "canonical texts"—the sources of religious knowledge in a community—alludes to all of those cultural inscriptions of "the sacred" which give religious limits in a community, which are authoritative for its self-identity, and which "rule" the exegetical struggles of religious sensibility: thus, canonical "texts" might include, among other things, mythic expressions, ritual configurations and performances, doctrinal articulations, artworks, and moral codes, which define the community's sense of itself and, while falling within the necessary "closure," invite the exegesis which will extend the sway of the canon.

19. James Agee, *Let Us Now Praise Famous Men* (Boston: Houghton Mifflin Company, 1941).

EDWARD TABOR LINENTHAL

Restoring America:
Political Revivalism in the Nuclear Age

Americans, wrote Nathan Scott, have from their beginnings imagined historical experience in melodramatic terms, "an affair," he said, "of clashing contraries."[1] Since the formative years of the nuclear age, Americans have clashed over the nature of the supreme danger that threatened the nation: the Soviet Union or nuclear war. Fear of one could not rear its head without engendering fear of the other. These "clashing contraries" were evident in the activities of two groups who profoundly shaped the nation's hopes and fears during the late 1970s and early 1980s, a time of renewed cultural attention to the threat from the Soviet Union and the danger of nuclear war. The Committee on the Present Danger (CPD) and Physicians for Social Responsibility (PSR) asked that Americans become attentive to different risks, risks selected because of allegiance paid to the lessons of different historical paradigms. These historical events are often perceived as revelatory—"shared crucial examples."[2] It is clear that the ideological civil war that has continued with such virulence in the United States since the end of World War II has been largely about the nature of what "shared crucial examples" should help citizens of the nation correctly perceive the internal and external dangers that presumably threatened the nation's existence.

The nature of this ideological civil war became clear when America emerged as the preeminent world power after World War II. The war shaped a series of contending perceptions about the role of America in the postwar world. Many hoped that it would bring about the creative transformations necessary to end war. Douglas MacArthur expressed this during the ceremonies concluding hostilities in September 1945: "It is my earnest hope and indeed the hope of all mankind that from this solemn occasion a better world shall emerge out of the blood and carnage of the past."[3] What emerged from the blood and carnage of the war, however, was the transmutation of a perennial evil from the guise of National Socialism into the guise of Communism. For others, the advent of the nuclear age forever changed the way human beings must think about the nature and function of warfare. The power of these clashing perceptions about the nature of the world, and, by extension, America's role in that world, were expressed shortly after the conclusion of World War II. Speaking before Congress on March 12, 1947, President Truman portrayed the bipolar world that still confronted the United States:

> At the present moment in world history nearly every nation must choose between alternative ways of life. The choice is too often not a free one.
>
> One way of life is based upon the will of the majority, and is distinguished by free institutions, representative government, free elections, guarantees of individual liberty, freedom of speech and religion, and freedom from political oppression.
>
> The second way of life is based upon the will of a minority forcibly imposed upon the majority. It relies upon terror and oppression, a controlled press and radio, fixed elections, and the suppression of personal freedoms.[4]

Speaking shortly after the explosions of atomic weapons on Japan, Albert Einstein depicted a quite different world: "The unleashed power of the atom has changed everything save our modes of thinking, and we thus drift toward unparalleled catastrophes."[5] Implicit in both of these antagonistic perceptions of the world was the crucial role of the United States. Traditional images of American exceptionalism could register in even more persuasive ways, for now the nation could be, according to Truman's Lincolnesque interpretation, the "last best hope of earth," or must, according to Einstein, lead the search for substantive changes necessary for continued human survival.

Heeding the warnings and learning the lessons of these powerful symbols led the CPD and PSR to diametrically opposed perceptions of risk. For the CPD, the degeneration of the American will to sacrifice, the unappreciated threat of the Soviet Union, and the will-weakening fear of nuclear war as fomented by groups such as PSR were leading the nation into the abyss. For PSR, the revival of cold-war fervor and traditional martial enthusiasm, engendered by the CPD, brought about increased interest in the possibility of the use of nuclear weapons, an act that PSR believed would lead inexorably to the destruction of civilization.

The CPD and PSR both understood the nation to be beset by crises of conviction that called for a resuscitation of certain national (or transnational) virtues. Only by awakening to the degenerative processes at work could Americans be led to recognize the true nature of the "present danger" and to enact the different prescriptions of these groups, both of which made use of traditional revivalist declarations of declension and doom as well as expressions of revitalization and restoration. Each group had articulate spokespersons. Members of the CPD occupied influential governmental, academic, and media positions. For PSR, the eloquence of Dr. Helen Caldicott captured the attention of the public.

Each group perceived itself as a significant actor in the great cosmic drama being played out and saw itself working in the "end times," with the current situation perceived as either the latest incarnation of a nightmare that the world had faced before or a new and qualitatively different crisis. In either case, each group was motivated by an apocalyptic view of history. Each tried to awaken people to their spiritual bondage in light of the precarious nature of the present, to outline the proper plan for restoration of the national spirit, and, consequently, to create motivation for that public action crucial for the life of the nation. Each functioned as a restorationist group, designed, as William McLoughlin wrote, "to alter the world view of a whole people or culture."[6]

The Committee on the Present Danger asked Americans to become attentive to the continued existence of the cold-war world described by President Truman. It worked out of certain historical paradigms, sought to revivify old mythologies, and wanted to reconstruct a certain vision of America, a vision necessary as a prerequisite for the resuscitation of American patriotic will. Craving a strength and determination that was perceived to have been lost, its warnings and its corrective program were designed to reverse the process of physical and spiritual degeneration at work in America since the "time of troubles," the 1960s.

Physicians for Social Responsibility took their calling from the warning of Albert Einstein. Sympathetic with people who looked upon the nuclear age as discontinuous with any other and thought that the program of the CPD was itself part of the present danger, PSR sought to make discussion of nuclear weapons issues a part of the common conversation of the nation. Its faith lay in the belief that national security issues could be demystified and democratized and that this would necessarily lead to a recognition of the real present danger—the final epidemic of nuclear war. It sought to awaken people's imaginations to the consequences of nuclear war so as to penetrate what it viewed as a complex layer of defense against thinking about this threat. Using the medical metaphors that came naturally, PSR spoke not of recovering a martial spirit from the American past but of awakening Americans to the disease of thinking about national security in archaic ways and of helping the nation recover from the terminal illness nuclear weapons and preparations for nuclear war had brought about.

Each of these groups set forth a program of cultural restoration that it believed was the last chance for the life of the nation and perhaps for the life of civilization. Both significantly influenced the context in which nuclear weapons issues were discussed and the language of those discussions. Each made a powerful statement about the terms of American recovery in the nuclear age.

The Committee on the Present Danger

By 1950 the bipolar nature of the world was entrenched wisdom in Washington. In that year a joint State-Defense Department analysis of military policy (NSC-68) became the major statement upon which American foreign policy has since been based. The document went much further than George Kennan's celebrated "Long Telegram," which had outlined a policy of containment. NSC-68 stated unequivocally that the Soviet Union was bent upon worldwide conquest, and this threat was projected as an immediate crisis. The Soviet Union was in an "advanced stage of preparation" and could almost certainly attack and overrun Europe and deliver a nuclear attack upon the United States. Despite the ominous revelations of Soviet military might, NSC-68 declared that the real crisis was internal: the nation must learn to maintain vigilance in the face of the enemy, and the nation's "fundamental purpose is more likely to be defeated from lack of the will to maintain" such vigilance.[7]

Responding to this perceived crisis, a group of prominent citizens came together to form the original Committee on the Present Danger in order to help legitimate the goals of NSC-68. Members came from the ranks of government, business, and education. In their initial statement on December 12, 1950, the cofounders of the CPD, James Conant, president of Harvard, Tracy Vorhees, former undersecretary of the army, and Vannevar Bush, who had served during the war as head of the Office of Scientific Research and Development and later as head of the Carnegie Institution, proclaimed that the current crisis and the American response to it were caused by the "aggressive designs of the Soviet Union."[8] Disbanded in 1953 after its members were satisfied that the nation was alerted to the danger, the committee was reconvened in 1976 in the midst of a growing sense of "injured innocence" in America. Unreconstructed cold-war liberals, contemptuous of the McGovernite triumph of 1972, had finally clothed the visceral anti-Communism of the New Right with intellectual respect-ability. The intellectual elite of the CPD consisted of Paul Nitze, a former secretary of the navy, who had been active in government ser-vice since the mid–1940s, Eugene Rostow, former undersecretary of state, and Harvard Sovietologist Richard Pipes. Two journals served as the intellectual organs of the CPD—*The Public Interest,* edited by Irving Kristol and Nathan Glazer, and *Commentary,* edited by Norman Podhoretz.

The dilemmas and frustrations of the postwar world were clear for members of the CPD. They believed that absolute evil, far from being destroyed in World War II, persisted, indeed in an even more hideous form—but could not now be destroyed without cataclysmic effects to American society. The conflict was present, but there seemed no path to an emotionally satisfying ending—the final purification of the world. J. Robert Oppenheimer, the scientific father of the atomic bomb, captured the dilemma in 1953: "We may anticipate a state of affairs in which the two Great Powers will each be in a position to put an end to the civilization and life of the other, though not without risking its own. We may be likened to two scorpions in a bottle, each capable of killing the other, but only at a risk of his own life."[9] The CPD understood that the cold war was now pervasive and that this war was the context within which all life must be lived. Eternal vigi-lance needed to be nurtured in what previously had been called "ci-vilian" life. While the nation must maintain such vigilance toward the enemy outside, it must also demand internal purity against the enemy within.

The memory of post-World War I Europe haunted CPD members. They feared that America was morally tired and militarily weak after its failure of nerve in Vietnam. The committee feared that Americans, desperate for peace, would fail to appreciate the danger from the So-viet Union, an implacable, relentless, and brutal foe whose ultimate aim was the destruction of Western civilization. Failing to realize that the Truman Doctrine provided proper strategic and moral orienta-tion and accurately expressed the terms of the clash between civiliza-tion and barbarism, America had lost its will, and its own innate good-ness—a Billy Budd kind of innocence—kept the country from awakening to the danger. The nation would, then, fall prey to a nuclear-age Munich that would lead either to the "Finlandization" of America or to the terminal war no one wanted.

Consequently, the CPD's purpose was to sound the alarm and awaken the country to the danger and to unwise national security policies (SALT II, for example). But beyond these concerns, this sense of danger touched deep fears among many people that the nation had indeed been victimized—by the war in Vietnam, by the hostage crisis in Iran, and by the Soviet invasion of Afghanistan. For many Americans, the warnings and the prescriptions of the CPD were coherent and allowed them to make use of historical paradigms, such as Munich, that seemed appropriate.

In order to reveal clearly the plan of Soviet "global hegemony," CPD members were successful in influencing the famous Team B National Intelligence Estimate of 1976. Unhappy with CIA figures, conservative military and political elites persuaded President Ford to allow CIA director George Bush to appoint an alternate team from outside the CIA to assess Soviet military strength and intentions. Not surprisingly, Team B claimed clear Soviet superiority in conventional and nuclear weaponry. Leo Cherne, chairman of the President's Foreign Intelligence Advisory Board, commented on the social utility of such revelatory knowledge: "We are in the midst of a crisis of belief and a crisis of belief can only be resolved by belief. 'Will' depends on something most doomsayers have overlooked—crisis, mortal danger, shock, massive understandable challenge."[10] The CPD's "world" was certainly one in which crises were imminent. The external crisis was dangerous not only because of aggressive Soviet intentions but because of the "fallen state" of the United States. Elite members of the CPD began sounding the alarm about the inner disorder the nation faced. Norman Podhoretz, one of the chief theoreticians of the CPD, asked if the nation had become a "culture of appeasement." For Podhoretz, the legacy of Vietnam was a bitter one. As the critical event in the contemporary loss of will in America, it engendered internal disorder and tempted the totalitarian impulse. It led to an insidious pacifism that thought *nothing* worth dying for, and produced a loss of clarity in foreign policy, a loss of confidence in American power, and a "national mood of self-doubt and self-disgust." This "spiritual plague" had moved through the protest of the 1960s, and then found its contemporary home among the "kind of women who do not want to be women and . . . those men who do not want to be men."[11]

These gender confusions—the loss of the masculine principle that was the basis for the will to sacrifice—were important, reminding Podhoretz of the spiritual malaise that swept over post-World War I England and led to a similar abdication of "proper manhood among homosexual writers of the 20's." This abdication had, Podhoretz believed, "an inescapable implication in the destiny of society as a whole."[12] Certainly Podhoretz would have approved of the spirit of a member of the Roosevelt administration who said during the early years of World War II: "In an America grown magnificently male again we have the chance to fight for a homeland. . . . Here is the time when a man can be what an American means, can fight for what America has always meant,—an audacious adventurous seeking—for a decent earth." [13]

For the CPD, the period of détente only contributed to the inner malaise that gripped the country in the post-Vietnam years. Podhoretz spoke contemptuously of "Nixon's doctrine of strategic defeat." Détente, he argued, did not allow for clarity of purpose in a dangerous world. As evidenced by the trauma of Vietnam, it did not allow meaningful sacrifice to inspire the nation to acts of courage. Podhoretz stated that détente took from the Soviet-American conflict "the moral and political dimension for the sake of which sacrifices could be intelligently demanded by the government and willingly made by the people." [14]

The inner confusion brought about by the war and the "spiritual Finlandization" caused by the policy of détente terrified Podhoretz and his contemporaries. In 1978, Eugene Rostow compared the years of détente to the European situation before the world wars, and his perceptions reveal the continued relevance of the Munich paradigm for members of the CPD: "Since the final bitter phases of the Vietnam War, our governments have been preaching with the fear, passivity, and inadequacy which characterized the British and American policy so fatally in the Thirties, and British policy before 1914." [15] This kind of gloom pervaded the ruminations of the CPD. Peter Berger, in the famous *mea culpa* regarding his once-critical stance toward American involvement in Vietnam, looked into the future and saw only a "long, long age of darkness," in which "American society may be swallowed up." [16]

The perceived loss of will and abdication of global responsibility were all the more significant because of the external crisis that was upon the nation. The 1976 policy statement of the CPD declared, "Our country is in a period of danger, and the danger is increasing." [17] The danger was, of course, from the Soviet Union's desire for world domination. As the crisis grew worse, the CPD stated in 1980 that the Soviet Union was pursuing a policy "even more ambitious than Hitler." [18] Nowhere, however, was the reassertion of national will more significant than in the will to nuclear superiority. As Eugene Rostow had declared earlier, unless the strategic deterrent was strong, "unless the adequacy of our second-strike capability is clear—our position in every lesser conflict is in peril." [19] Doubt regarding American will to use these weapons stemmed not only from what the CPD perceived as nuclear inferiority but also from debilitating debate at home. Hence, the CPD was wary of domestic dissent. Verbal policies, its members well understood, could be misinterpreted in the symbolic world of perception that was so crucial to deterrence theory.

Likewise, nowhere was the sense of American weakness greater than in the CPD's analysis of the strategic balance—a weakness (ironically enough) that it chose to proclaim loudly, which could be construed as a destabilizing act in itself. In 1982, the committee stated that the Soviets had a clear margin of superiority and knew how to use it. "The United States has become second best," and a respectable second-strike capability was not forseen until *perhaps* the 1990s.[20] Soviet superiority had immediate implications, Richard Pipes claimed, because the Soviet Union had never followed the philosophy of Mutual Assured Destruction and was making plans to fight to *win* a nuclear war. Further, even if nuclear war never came, Pipes believed that nuclear superiority was part of the Soviet plan of global hegemony. This superiority would be translated into nuclear blackmail—"armed persuasion." In 1984, seven years after writing his celebrated article on Soviet nuclear strategy, Pipes declared that Soviet leaders "believe that nuclear weapons are the means of quick and decisive victory."[21] The chances for change were slim, Pipes believed, because the trouble was in the very roots of Russian culture. The Communist revolution had installed in power the Russian peasant (*muzhik*), and, as Pipes had written in 1977, "the *muzhik* had been taught by long historical experience that cunning and coercion alone ensure survival: one employed cunning when weak, and cunning coupled with coercion when strong."[22]

The message of the CPD went beyond depictions of the internal and external crises that the nation faced. The committee also offered its plan for recovery. The first stage of national rehabilitation was the resuscitation of national courage—the realization that the endless conflict was, perhaps, endless. Podhoretz declared that Americans could no longer simply wish a different world into being. While "liberals are dreaming the dream of a new intellectual order," he complained, the Soviet Union was in a period of "active, imperialist, expansion."[23]

The path toward redemption led through the recovery of the American spirit that had been lost in the 1960s. Speaking before the platform committee of the Democratic party in 1976, Eugene Rostow marveled that slowly, almost intuitively, public opinion "has come to realize that the Cold War is far from over."[24] In that same year, Podhoretz offered a Wilsonian call to righteous battle, declaring that we must "use American power to make the world safe for democracy."[25] In 1980, after the Soviet invasion of Afghanistan, when the Carter administration had reverted to orthodox cold-war anti-Communism, Podhoretz thought it quite likely too late. Perhaps not, he thought, but the country must spend billions more on new nuclear weapons systems "which alone can prevent the Soviets from achieving nuclear superiority and thus an unobstructed road to domination."[26]

For the CPD, commitment to weapons modernization and restoration of moribund systems (the B1, for example) were the unmistakable sign of the recovery of American will. Failure to do this would only bring about Podhoretz's ultimate nightmare, the "Finlandization" of America. In this vision, the Soviet Union would gain economic and political leverage in Western Europe through nuclear blackmail, and U.S. politicians would be forced to work "toward a socio-political system more in harmony with the Soviet model."[27] Podhoretz remained cautiously hopeful, however. He saw the hostage crisis and the invasion of Afghanistan as triggering the end of America's period of self-doubt. He looked to the 1950s as the period that should serve as the paradigm of American patriotism, for this was a time when Americans were willing to "pay the price in blood" to fight Communism.[28] Those like George Kennan who should know enough to look back to this period as a time when perceptions of the enemy were clear and national will inspired blood sacrifice had failed to do so, a sign that they had obviously "grown weary and fearful over the years."[29]

The election of Ronald Reagan, a CPD member, signaled a "new consensus" for the 1980s. In spite of this internal patriotic awakening, the external crisis, according to the CPD, grew more desperate, and Podhoretz's nightmares continued. He envisioned a "Cuban missile crisis in reverse . . . staged in the Persian Gulf, with the Finlandization of the West following inexorably in its wake."[30] Others also constructed invasion scenarios to ensure that the hopeful signs of recovery would not lessen perceptions of the danger. Robert Conquest's *What to Do When the Russians Come* offered a detailed picture of what would happen in America when the Russians invaded. Based on the experiences of Eastern European countries and the postwar occupation of South Vietnam by North Vietnam, Conquest painted a vivid picture of the gradual "Sovietization" of American life—a scenario which would become reality only if the United States became weak militarily and misperceived the intentions of the Soviet leaders. Americans *were* often misled, he believed, but they may "yet wake to the problem."[31] Time, however, was on the side of the Soviet Union, and the bleak scenario he painted was designed to awaken Americans to this present and ominous danger. At the same time as these apocalyptic scenarios were being vividly portrayed, others spoke of the hopeful seeds of recovery: Jeane Kirkpatrick echoed the theme of the rebirth of America, suggesting that the nation's "dark night of the soul" was over; Reagan's election symbolized the end of a "national identity crisis through which the nation has been passing for some ten or fifteen years."[32]

The vision of the apocalypse—descriptions of the terrors that await, the inner degeneration by which the terrors will conquer, but the persistent hope for final recovery—was a part of the awakening process. It motivated the true believer with a sense of missionary fervor; for with the advent of nuclear weaponry, such apocalyptic fantasies were readily believable, and the invigoration of living in the last days provided a sense of cosmic importance to the task of awakening the uninitiated to the end-time crisis.

For the CPD, there were only mutually exclusive choices regarding the future. One may believe that it was better to be "Red than dead" or better "dead than Red," and once the choice was made it governed all future individual value decisions and public policy decisions. Podhoretz's hope for the future rested with the bulwarking of American military might and, with the strength of such martial will in the face of the danger, the eventual breakup of the Soviet Union. Otherwise, he envisioned a gloomy future—an endless war, an "eternity of confrontation . . . without hope of victory in the end." He also foresaw a "universal gulag and a life that was otherwise nasty, brutish, and short." To forestall this process and to bring about the only palatable future, the United States must contain Communism, not just Soviet power, and this meant hearkening back to John F. Kennedy's crusading message: "Let every nation know, whether it wishes us well or ill, that we shall pay any price, bear any burden, meet any hardship, support any friend, oppose any foe, in order to assure the survival and the success of liberty."[33]

The success of the CPD's campaigns lay in its ability to construct a milieu of crisis at a time when the perplexing memories of Vietnam and more current foreign policy dilemmas made Americans susceptible to the comfortable, if not comforting, symbols of the cold war. Sorting out the "proper" perceptions of the enemy at least offered social orientation, and, as the CPD offered the logic of its analysis of the present danger, latent anti-Communism arose quickly. The crisis, some believed, was a time of unprecedented opportunity. Perhaps it *was* possible to resolve the inevitable frustrations of the "scorpions in the bottle" without living forever in a cold-war situation that allowed for no sense of a redemptive ending.

To resolve this unsatisfying balance of terror, the CPD pointed beyond containment to a reassertion of traditional images of heroic war and the renewed power of redemptive sacrifice in a holy cause. A crucial part of the agenda was its attempt to perceive nuclear war as potentially decisive and purifying. As always, this was accompanied by formal denials of fascination with war in American life. Podhoretz wrote: "The idea of war has never been as natural to Americans as it used to be to the English or Germans or French. We have always tended in this country to think of war as at best a hideous necessity." [34] The development of "generations" of nuclear weapons had not—any more than the development of the machine gun—brought humanity to the realization that war might at last be obsolete. The fear of the power of nuclear weapons was matched by the fascination with opportunities for final victory using them. If cold war was intolerable, perhaps the last hot war might bring about the final fundamental transformations that had been dreamed about for so long.

These millennialist fantasies were usually not crudely expressed, except in fundamentalist visions engendered by apocalyptic models in scripture. More often they were construed in the dispasssionate language of nuclear stategists. Nuclear war-fighting scenarios and plans for civil defense were part of the desire for a way out of MAD, for they allowed people to dream once again of freedom, and millennial peace. Colin Gray, consultant to the State Department and member of the General Advisory Committee of ACDA, expressed this hope: "The United States should plan to defeat the Soviet Union and to do so at a cost that would not prohibit U.S. recovery. Washington should identify war aims that in the last resort would contemplate the destruction of Soviet political authority and the emergence of a post-war world order *compatible with Western values*" (emphasis added).[35] The Minuteman was now a missile, but its purpose was apparently the same as that of those original embattled farmers—protection, salvation, and the transformation of the world.

The CPD correctly understood that the debates surrounding nuclear weapons were part of the ongoing debate about what it meant to be an American. For many, Richard Barnet's comments on the early 1960s seemed appropriate: "What characterized America was now its power, and the citizen's sense of belonging was somehow related to the vicarious exercise of national power. More and more an American came to mean someone who identified with the struggle against America's enemies."[36] As one shared in the tremendous power and promise of nuclear weapons—either in fantasies of their use or fantasies of their potential political utility—one presumably shared in the only experience that linked all Americans together. The CPD's call for a revival of the crusading spirit of World War II and the years of the cold war reflected the yearning for a new beginning.

The statements of many CPD members on the character of nuclear war made it clear that nuclear war was perceived as different in degree, but not in kind, from other wars. Hence, because no fundamental discontinuity existed between the nuclear age and previous ages, no fundamental discontinuity existed between war in the nuclear age and other world wars. Richard Pipes, for example, described "realistic" scenarios for nuclear war-fighting and argued that "victory is quite feasible *exactly as it is in any military conflict* [emphasis added], i.e., one side disables the other and inflicts its will upon it."[37] Pipes dismissed arguments that nuclear weapons, by their very nature, precluded rational use in a battlefield situation. These arguments, he believed, served the purposes of the Soviet Union. Pipes believed that the Soviet Union was primarily interested in keeping fear of nuclear weapons at the center of Western thought so that the West would desire good relations with the Soviet Union *above all.* Hence, nuclear anxiety was part of the Soviet plan for global hegemony: "It is designed to translate the natural dread that most people have of war in general and nuclear war in particular into an overwhelming anxiety that paralyzes thought and will."[38] In other words, the rise of fear of nuclear war in American culture in the late 1970s was mainly due to Soviet-constucted anxieties, designed to make Americans think that there was nothing worth dying for. It was *this* insidious degeneration of the will to sacrifice that the CPD feared would lead to the surrender of the West.

It is not entirely clear whether the millennialist ethics of the CPD called for global human sacrifice in the final battle between the forces of good and evil. The justification for global sacrifice had been discussed for some time. In 1961, Sidney Hook declared that "survival at all costs was not among the values of the West."[39] More recently, President Reagan communicated this sense of global sacrifice to the National Association of Evangelicals on March 8, 1983. The message came anecdotally. The president was reflecting on a speech that he had heard a "prominent young man" give on the subject of Communism before a "tremendous gathering" in California during the cold war:

"I love my little girls more than anything—" And I said to myself, "Oh, no, don't. You can't—don't say that." But I had underestimated him. He went on: "I would rather see my little girls die now, still believing in God, than have them grow up under communism and one day die no longer believing in God." There were thousands of young people in that audience. They came to their feet with shouts of joy. They had instantly recognized the profound truth in what he had said, with regard to the physical and the soul and what was truly important.[40]

The CPD's call to recovery seemed to balance precariously between a desire for the final battle in which the national will to preserve sacred principles would be expressed by a willingness to die for them, as a country and perhaps a world, and a desire for a recovery of American will to maintain the contest of wills with the enemy that would continue for the forseeable future. Without question, the CPD called for America to awaken to the dangers that it faced from within and without. The will to nuclear superiority and the stoic determination to sacrifice whatever was necessary were the unmistakable signs of the vitality of cultural renewal.

As the sense of crisis spread, fear of the aggressive intentions of the Soviet Union and the infamous "window of vulnerability" also led to a quite different, but not unrelated, fear—the fear of the growing possibility of nuclear war. While members of the CPD were entrenched in policy-making positions, grass-roots movements began to take issue with their construction of the world and offered quite different terms for American recovery.

Physicians for Social Responsibility

Physicians for Social Responsibility, whose membership had grown to over forty thousand physicians by 1986, had been at the center of the reawakening of American concern over the possibility of nuclear war. It understood the diagnosis and prescriptions of the CPD to be part of the present danger. For members of Physicians for Social Responsibility (PSR), Hiroshima, not Munich, provided the most important historical model. It revealed the nature of a new world, the world since 1945. John Fowler, writing in the *New England Journal of Medicine,* expressed his belief that the growing remoteness of the experience of nuclear war charged physicians with the "absolute responsibility to retain the cultural memory of those events in order to ensure the prevention of further such experiments of human nature."[41] Like the CPD, PSR believed that America was in a fallen state, but the fall was not the result of the degeneration of American will so much as it was a result of technological arrogance, a fall into the final bitter irony, extinction growing out of human technological genius. The attendant spiritual problem was not failure of nerve in the face of an external enemy but an aversion to reach human maturity in the nuclear age. Imagining that wars could now be a rational function of the state was perceived as part of this immaturity, an immaturity pointed to in the words of the former president of PSR, Helen Caldicott, who declared that the United States was like a "beautiful, well fed, six-month old baby holding a hand grenade about to blow up in its face." [42]

PSR was formed in Boston in 1960. It originated in the interest of a small group of physicians in the medical consequences of nuclear war. Skeptical of faith in civil-defense plans and worried about the dangers of radioactivity in the atmosphere, they published an important series of articles detailing the medical catastrophe that would be part of nuclear war, which was published in 1962 in the *New England Journal of Medicine*. To counter the illusion of medical help after a nuclear war, PSR's statement of purpose declared, "The physician . . . must begin to explore a new area of preventive medicine, the prevention of thermonuclear war." [43] This activism was relatively new to the medical profession. Physicians had been involved in studies regarding the safety of radiation lab workers as early as 1942, and two medical teams were sent to Hiroshima and Nagasaki to study the effects of the atomic bomb. With few exceptions, however, throughout the 1940s and 1950s, the medical community emphasized the medical benefits of nuclear energy and the patriotic duty of the medical community to support civil-defense plans. Summarizing attitudes in this period, Paul Boyer wrote, "atomic war would be the ultimate challenge for the American physician, and he must steel himself for it, whatever the odds: any other response would be unworthy and unpatriotic." [44]

Medical activism in the 1960s, like most forms of citizen activism, largely ignored the threat of nuclear war. Not until 1978, in the midst of the crisis of will that also invigorated the CPD, was PSR reborn, animated by a number of issues which brought about increased attention to the nuclear threat—the potential danger of nuclear power dramatically illustrated by the near-tragedy at Three Mile Island, perceived changes regarding the possibility of planning for a limited nuclear war in the latter years of the Carter administration and the early Reagan years, and the impetus provided by widespread citizen activism. The final stimulus might have come from the resurrection of plans for massive civil defense, what for PSR members was the dangerous illusion of survivability. These factors contributed to a remarkable growth in PSR's membership.

In February 1980, PSR held its first public conference on the medical consequences of nuclear war. These conferences were repeated in large and small communities throughout the nation, constituting one of the prerequisites of PSR's plan for national recovery—awareness of what it considered the *real* present danger. The content of these conferences was a sober description of the medical consequences of nuclear war. Often, the effects of a nuclear explosion would be transposed on local community maps in order to bring the message home in a personal way. This message, spread so forcefully by PSR, was soon taken up by a number of other health organizations in the United States, and PSR itself became part of a worldwide movement, International Physicians for the Prevention of Nuclear War, which included medical professionals from thirty-one countries.

The most important public figure—and the revivalist—of the movement was an Australian physician, Helen Caldicott. She wrote of her own awakening to the dangers of nuclear war and nuclear energy at the age of fifteen, after reading *On the Beach:* "It was set in Melbourne, Australia, where I was living at the time, and it frightened the hell out of me. . . . It could have happened that way then; it still could.[45] Motivated by this fear, Caldicott eventually led the successful battles to ban French atmospheric nuclear testing in the South Pacific and to ban the export of Australian uranium. These experiences, especially her successful attempts to awaken uranium miners to the dangers they faced, impressed upon her the power of citizen activism.

Caldicott came to the United States to practice medicine in 1975, became president of PSR in 1978, and in 1980 resigned her dual position at Children's Hospital in Boston and at the Harvard Medical School to devote herself full-time to the work of PSR. She described this as the result of a "deeply religious commitment," because it was not good medicine to "treat children with serious diseases and keep them alive to die in nuclear war."[46] For Caldicott and PSR, the prevention of nuclear war was not merely a problem of crisis management or arms-control negotiations. It was a challenge for preventive medicine. Humankind had fallen victim to the "Last Epidemic." "The planet," Caldicott wrote, "can be compared to a terminally ill patient infected with lethal 'macrobes' which are metastasizing rapidly." Convinced that nuclear war would take place ("a mathematical certainty"), she declared that "time is short. The prognosis is guarded. But the analogy of the terminally ill patient in the intensive care unit who occasionally survives because of dedicated medical, scientific and nursing efforts seems appropriate."[47]

According to PSR, these terminally ill patients—the superpowers—have exhibited the signs of illness by carrying on an unrestrained arms race. Like other terminally ill patients, they have denied that there *was* a problem and, hence, must be moved through the "denial of social death" toward the motivation to change. Consequently, PSR's discussions of the medical consequences of nuclear war were designed in large part to disenchant people—the public as well as policy elites—from a worldview in which nuclear war played a potentially redemptive role in the grand strategy of the superpowers. Once people were disenchanted, their initiation into the realities of the nuclear age could begin, and PSR's program was designed to awaken as well as disenchant, to bring the danger back to the individual level. The goal was to create citizens "so well informed about the dangers of the nuclear arms race that they would be spurred to constructive action."[48]

PSR initially focused on disabusing the public about the role of civil defense in helping a nation recover from nuclear war. Federal Emergency Management Agency (FEMA) officials spoke in words reminiscent of the CPD, declaring "the country that can plan now for survival and recovery is the one that's going to fare best in the long run."[49] Responding to this kind of thinking, Caldicott stated, "They're mad. . . . Uniformly ignorant about the medical, scientific, and ecological consequences of a nuclear war."[50] PSR also tried to disenchant the public from the belief that a nuclear war could be limited—that it was, really, no more than a management problem. Graphic descriptions of the unimaginable power of nuclear weapons were offered at PSR's public meetings. "There is nothing in human experience," declared Dr. Jack Geiger, "that serves as a precedent for such immense destruction."[51] This destruction, it was clear to PSR, would result in death and disease also "on a scale that has no precedent in the history of human existence."[52]

Awakening the public to the *real* present danger—the increasing risk of nuclear war and the common dangerous illusion of survivability—was only part of the process of recovery from this societal illness. Like the CPD, PSR believed that by the early 1980s it had created a climate in which people were awakened to the danger of nuclear war and that this would serve to motivate citizens to work for "improved superpower relations and the achievement of real arms control and disarmament."[53] Like the CPD, PSR prescribed certain actions to counter this societal illness, one of which was a call for a massive reconstruction of both national security policy and personal attitudes toward war, nuclear war, and the Soviet Union. People must, a 1984

PSR report stated, "alter our attitudes and institutions at their roots."[54]

PSR also viewed the present danger as resulting from gender problems—but in quite different terms from the CPD. The need for the "magnificently male" environment proposed by the CPD, in which traditional patriotism could flourish, was exactly what needed to be changed. Caldicott in particular called for women's leadership. If humanity had to evolve to a new maturity, women would lead the way, for they were, Caldicott believed, "closer to the sources of life than men are."[55] This proximity to the sources of life had given women the ability to harness the "instinct to protect and preserve the lives we deliver."[56] The struggles for arms control, for eventual disarmament, and for more mature superpower relationships had to be a women's movement. Robert Jay Lifton, a psychiatrist and an influential antinuclear theoretician, agreed, suggesting that women were "more critical of scenarios of nuclear war which are . . . projected by men and which leave out human beings. . . . They are crucial in the transformation that is before us now."[57]

As PSR awakened citizens to the horrors of nuclear war and some of its leading figures like Caldicott sought to recover the intuitive perception of the sacredness of life that had been lost in the nuclear age, the organization faced the challenge of translating these intuitions into public policy positions. Unlike the CPD, PSR did not constitute a group of official elites who were in positions to have immediate effect on national security policy. Like the CPD, however, PSR recognized the importance of maintaining a climate of perceived risk that would motivate a high level of citizen activism. In their 1984 Annual Report, members of PSR stated that people have indeed awakened to the risks of an arms race and the consequences of nuclear war. Now, however, people demanded more than mere diagnosis of the problem—they wanted treatment. Consequently, PSR "has put forth a complete arms control agenda whose central focus is the Comprehensive Test Ban Treaty." Further, it sought to work with Soviet physicians on the common problem of human survival and to show "our government and the world that East and West may perhaps achieve reasonable understanding."[58] PSR's activities revealed an underlying faith in the power of democratic processes to effect what PSR perceived as beneficial changes in national security policy.

In addition to continued efforts to rescue people from dangerous illusions about nuclear war, PSR sought to demystify nuclear weapons issues: it developed a Policy and Legislative Committee to work with members of Congress; it built a legislative alert network designed to target certain issues like funding for the MX and SDI, CTB, and so on. Members of PSR have gone throughout the country giving policy briefings on these and other issues. A global perspective was also important to this work, and, they thought, "medicine's international network can help to provide it." This global exchange of ideas was promulgated by the International Physicians Task Force, a group charged with examining the psychological effects of the arms race, images of the enemy, and alternative methods of conflict resolution.

The public declarations of PSR made it clear that the struggle to reduce the danger of nuclear war was the issue that transcended all others. Yet, as PSR struggled to awaken the nation to the danger, this primary danger also became just the tip of the iceberg. It opened up other issues for inspection—the nature of war, the need to break away from East-West polarities, the social and economic costs of the arms race, and the nature and role of men and women in the transformation that must take place. Like the CPD, PSR envisioned its work as taking place in the end-times. Invasion fantasies were as important to the group's restorative work as they were to the CPD.

Since the dawn of the nuclear age, PSR argued, nations, particularly the superpowers, have been afflicted with technological hubris, resurgent tribalism, dangerous illusions about managing and winning a war fought with nuclear weapons, and archaic ideas about the function of warfare in the contemporary international system. Beyond the message of doom and degeneration, however, PSR called for a restoration of certain democratic virtues that it believed had been lost and, more ambitiously, called for serious attention to Einstein's "new modes of thinking." PSR assumed that a citizenry, once awakened to the present danger, would try to gain some level of competence in the language and policy-formation process of national security issues. Town meetings all over the nation focusing on the freeze or on civil-defense plans were perceived as unmistakable signs of the dormant virtues of an aroused populace. The degenerations of the times—the mystification of security issues, the long-standing failure to focus on nuclear issues—reflected, according to PSR, political and social deformities peculiar to the postwar world, *not* the essential deformity of the body politic. Further, PSR understood that its own participation in international groups such as International Physicians for the Prevention of Nuclear War was a sign to others that new modes of thinking born out of technological necessity could flourish in nongovernmental channels. In fact, it seemed that the grass-roots programs of people-to-people exchanges, sister-city projects, and so on were the kinds of efforts that could initiate attempts to break down hoary, inflexible, and dysfunctional patterns of communication between governments and peoples.

Finally, PSR perceived its struggle as a way of recovering a sense not only of the transcendent principles embodied by the United States but also of the sacredness of human life—indeed all forms of life on the earth. Awakening to the danger brought with it, potentially, this second grace—the horror would jolt perceptions and consciousness and would allow people to begin to appreciate the gifts of the earth and to work for their survival. Fear of extinction was, according to PSR, potentially redemptive.

CPD and PSR

Both the CPD and PSR set forth powerfully articulate statements about the risks that the nation faced, proper identification of internal and external enemies, and prescriptions for American recovery. Both groups perceived that the moment of truth drew near, and that the restorative work would be the last chance for the nation and for civilization. Both groups made use of the familiar rhetorical patterns of the jeremiad: they spoke both of declension and doom and of revitalization and exaltation. Both began with a tactical revolution of feeling, a required shift of the affections. Each worked out of dominant historical symbols—the memories and lessons of Munich and Hiroshima. PSR, it seems, faced the more difficult task. Munich symbolized only a certain kind of appeasement, international behavior that inevitably leads to war. Most have forgotten, or never learned, what else Winston Churchill said about appeasement: "Appeasement in itself may be good or bad depending on circumstances. . . . Appeasement from strength is magnanimous and noble and might be the surest and perhaps the only path to world peace."[59] Most Americans have not, however, only interpreted the symbol of Hiroshima as the "text" through which life must now make sense in the nuclear age. As recent remembrances of Hiroshima and Nagasaki reveal, the dominant theme to be extracted from the symbol is one of benevolent destruction. It was only this horror, so it is thought, that prevented further horror for the Japanese people and the American troops and that brought the war to an end.

Both groups knew that the recovery would begin with a kind of spiritual discipline: an inner transformation would precede, but be directly related to, the public policy decisions that would spring from a rejuvenated nation. Decisions about the role of nuclear weapons were, for each group, crucial for a successful recovery. For the CPD, willingness to modernize the arsenal and to plan soberly for the possible use of nuclear weapons revealed that Americans had recovered the sense of millennial destiny that they had abandoned only recently. And, ironically, the success of the CPD's program to reawaken cold-war orthodoxy sparked not only fears of the Soviet Union and *their* nuclear weapons but of nuclear weapons in general. Consequently, the origins of the fierce ideological civil war in America can be partly traced to the fervor of the CPD.

PSR asked Americans to look on the cold-war worldview as dangerously archaic and asked that Americans understand that their nuclear weapons, far from being symbols of protection and ultimate salvation, were weapons of absolute destruction. Consequently, PSR asked that citizens abandon the dangerous illusion that nuclear weapons could serve rational ends. It asked that people begin, through the demystification of national security issues, to take part in the gradual evolution of humankind away from war.

Each group was reasonably successful in awakening the unregenerate to the cause, and this success clearly points out the role that perceptions of nuclear weapons play in the bitter civil war being fought in the United States. These perceptions of nuclear weapons, and the ideological positions that have engendered them, will play a significant role in what may seem on the surface to be questions of technological feasibility, strategic wisdom, or political possibility. Fascination with the Strategic Defense Initiative, for example, grafts cold-war fears (the United States must win the battle for space) with the antinuclear's movement hope for a radical transformation of the world (SDI will make nuclear weapons "impotent and obsolete").[60]

Both the CPD and PSR have articulated terms for American recovery and have clashed in policy controversies and popular debate. The intensity of the debate revealed the fervor of the moment, and neither group could content itself with presenting the dilemmas in merely "secular" terms. Both had to work within the framework of American exceptionalism, differently perceived. Both groups, and all others which enter the public forum to shape opinion on these issues, must contend, it seems, with two often-conflicting impulses—the popular desire to be nourished by the patriotic enthusiasms that have given coherence to the postwar world and the fear that these tribal allegiances may lead the nation into the abyss. These clashing contraries continue to set the tone and the terms of American recovery in the nuclear age.

NOTES

1. Nathan A. Scott, "New Heav'ns, New Earth—The Landscape of Contemporary Apocalypse," *Journal of Religion* 53 (1973): 1–35.

2. See Ian Barbour, "Paradigms in Science and Religion," in *Paradigms and Revolutions: Appraisals and Applications of Thomas Kuhn's Philosophy of Science*, ed. Gary Gutting (Notre Dame: University of Notre Dame Press, 1980), pp. 223–45.

3. Columbia Broadcasting System, *From Pearl Harbor into Tokyo: The Story as Told by War Correspondents on the Air* (New York: Columbia Broadcasting System, 1945), p. 296.

4. Carl Solberg, *Riding High: America in the Cold War* (New York: Mason and Lipscomb, 1973), p. 40.

5. Jonathan Schell, *The Fate of the Earth* (New York: Alfred A. Knopf, 1982), p. 188.

6. William G. McLoughlin, *Revivals, Awakenings, and Reform*, Chicago History of American Religion (Chicago: University of Chicago Press, 1978), p. xiii.

7. Jerry W. Saunders, *Peddlers of Crisis: The Committee on the Present Danger and the Politics of Containment* (Boston: South End Press, 1983), p. 43.

8. Ibid., p. 54.

9. Lawrence Freedman, *The Evolution of Nuclear Strategy* (New York: St. Martin's Press, 1981), p. 94.

10. Saunders, *Peddlers of Crisis*, p. 198.

11. See Norman Podhoretz, "The Present Danger," *Commentary* 69 (Mar. 1980): 31; and Podhoretz, *Breaking Ranks* (New York: Harper and Row, 1979), p. 363.

12. Norman Podhoretz, "The Culture of Appeasement," *Harper's*, Oct. 1977, p. 29.

13. Richard Polenberg, ed., *America at War: The Home Front, 1941–1945* (Englewood Cliffs, N.J.: Prentice-Hall, Inc., 1969), p. 3.

14. Norman Podhoretz, "The Future Danger," *Commentary* 71 (Apr. 1981): 38.

15. "Peace with Freedom: A Discussion by the Committee on the Present Danger before the Foreign Policy Association, 14 March 1978," in *Alerting America: The Papers of the Committee on the Present Danger*, ed. Charles Tyroler, II (Washington: Pergamon-Brassey's, 1984), p. 29.

16. Peter Berger, "Indochina and the American Conscience," *Commentary* 69 (Feb. 1980): 39.

17. Tyroler, *Alerting America*, p. 3.

18. "The 1980 Crisis and What We Should Do about It," in Tyroler, *Alerting America*, p. 176.

19. "Peace with Freedom," in Tyroler, *Alerting America*, p. 31.

20. "Has America Become Number 2?" in Tyroler, *Alerting America*, p. 235.

21. Richard Pipes, *Survival Is Not Enough: Soviet Realities and America's Future* (New York: Simon and Schuster, 1984), p. 102.

22. Richard Pipes, "Why the Soviet Union Thinks It Could Fight and Win a Nuclear War," *Commentary* 64 (July 1977): 26.

23. Norman Podhoretz, "Making the World Safe for Communism," *Commentary* 62 (Apr. 1976): 37.

24. Saunders, *Peddlers of Crisis,* p. 195.

25. Podhoretz, "Making the World Safe for Communism," p. 40.

26. Podhoretz, "Present Danger," p. 37.

27. Ibid.

28. Ibid., p. 29.

29. Ibid., p. 40.

30. Podhoretz, "Future Danger," p. 36.

31. Robert Conquest and John Manchip White, *What to Do When the Russians Come: A Survivor's Guide* (New York: Stein and Day, 1984), p. 177.

32. Jeane K. Kirkpatrick, *The Reagan Phenomenon and Other Speeches on Foreign Policy* (Washington: American Institute for Public Policy Research, 1983), p. 12.

33. Podhoretz, "Future Danger," pp. 29–47.

34. Norman Podhoretz, *The Present Danger* (New York: Simon and Schuster, 1980), p. 61.

35. Quoted in Robert Scheer, *With Enough Shovels: Reagan and Bush on Nuclear War* (New York: Random House, 1982).

36. Richard J. Barnet, *Roots of War* (Baltimore: Penguin Books, 1971), p. 255.

37. "Peace with Freedom," in Tyroler, *Alerting America,* p. 34.

38. Pipes, *Survival Is Not Enough,* p. 66.

39. Sidney Hook, H. Stuart Hughes, Hans Morgenthau, and C. P. Snow, "Western Values and Total War," in *American Views of Soviet Russia, 1917–1965,* ed. Peter G. Filene (Homewood, Ill.: Dorsey Press, 1968), p. 364.

40. Ronald Reagan, "Remarks to the National Association of Evangelicals, March 8, 1983," in Strobe Talbott, *The Russians and Reagan* (New York: Vintage Books, 1984), pp. 115–16.

41. John W. Fowler, M.D., letter to the editors, *New England Journal of Medicine* 312 (Jan. 24, 1985): 251.

42. Helen Caldicott, "Nuclear War: This May Be Your Last Christmas," *US Catholic* 46 (Dec. 1981): 22.

43. Quoted in Paul Boyer, "Physicians Confront the Apocalyse: The American Medical Profession and the Threat of Nuclear War," *Journal of the American Medical Association* 254, no. 5 (1985): 642.

44. Ibid., p. 641.

45. D. Milofsky, "Helen Caldicott," *Redbook,* Nov. 1979, p. 228.

46. Caldicott, "This May Be Your Last Christmas," pp. 20–21.

47. Helen Caldicott, "Introduction," to *The Final Epidemic: Physicians and Scientists on Nuclear War,* ed. Ruth Adams and Susan Cullen (Chicago: Educational Foundation for Nuclear Science, 1981), pp. 1–3.

48. Physicians for Social Responsibility, mimeographed material, p. 2.

49. Constance Holden, "Physicians Take on Nuclear War," *Science* 207 (Mar. 28, 1980): 1450.

50. Libby Rosenthal, "Anti-Nuclear Medicine," *Science Digest* 90 (Nov. 1982): 71.

51. Physicians for Social Responsibility, "A 'Limited' Nuclear Attack: Omaha, 1982," brochure.

52. Physicians for Social Responsibility, "The Medical Aspects of Nuclear War," brochure.

53. Physicians for Social Responsibility, mimeographed material.

54. Physicians for Social Responsibility, "Annual Report: 1984," brochure.

55. *New York Times*, May 26, 1982. Caldicott discusses this issue at length in her book *Missile Envy: The Arms Race & Nuclear War* (New York: William Morrow and Company, Inc., 1984). Here, men are seen as captive to the fascination with killing, and a "typical" woman "is very much in touch with her feelings. . . . She innately understands the basic principles of conflict resolution" (p. 294). Consequently, women are the key to survival. It was, in part, Caldicott's emphasis on the gender issue that led to profound differences with others in PSR, and eventually to her resignation as president in 1983. In a speech to the National Women's Studies Association, Caldicott said of her resignation: "Why am I retiring? Partly because men did me in; at PSR there was a male coup. I picked it up intuitively before it happened, but I didn't have the guts to confront the men, even when they lied to me. They stabbed me in the back, and I was so done in emotionally that I resigned" (Peter Canellos, "Nuclear Sadness: The Failure and Retreat of Helen Caldicott," *Boston Phoenix*, Dec. 2, 1986, p. 22). Canellos's article is an excellent retrospective of Caldicott's impact on the antinuclear movement of the late 1970s and early 1980s and of the forces that eventually led to her embittered return to Australia in October 1986.

56. Caldicott, "This May Be Your Last Christmas," p. 22.

57. Robert Jay Lifton, "While There's Life: Can We Still Hope?" *Vogue*, Oct. 1984, p. 227.

58. Physicians for Social Responsibility, "Annual Report."

59. Quoted in Ralph K. White, *Fearful Warriors: A Psychological Profile of U.S.-Soviet Relations* (New York: Free Press, 1984), p. 6.

60. The role of SDI in American culture in this period is examined in Edward Tabor Linenthal, *Symbolic Defense: The Cultural Significance of the Strategic Defense Initiative* (Urbana: University of Illinois Press, 1989).

ALBERT J. RABOTEAU

Martin Luther King, Jr., and the Tradition of Black Religious Protest

On December 1, 1955, a black seamstress named Rosa Parks boarded a bus in Montgomery, Alabama. Buses in Montgomery, the "Cradle of the Confederacy," had always been segregated. Blacks sat in back; whites sat up front. If the bus was full, blacks were required to give up their seats to whites and ride standing in the aisle. Bus drivers insulted black passengers and even made them get off the bus and reenter by the back door after they had paid their fares. The bus system of Montgomery, like others throughout the South, was a daily reminder of the pervasiveness of Jim Crow.

Mrs. Parks found a seat in the front of the section reserved for "Colored" and sat down. As the bus grew crowded with people heading home from work, no seats were available for new passengers boarding the bus. The driver ordered Mrs. Parks and three black passengers next to her to get up and give their seats to whites. The others complied. Rosa Parks stayed in her seat until a policeman came and placed her under arrest. Later accounts would explain that she refused to move simply because she was tired. But the story was more complex. Mrs. Parks had worked for several years as the secretary for the local branch of the NAACP. The Montgomery NAACP had been trying without success to develop a case to test state segregation laws, so Mrs. Parks's arrest occurred in this context of locally planned black protest. News of the arrest spread quickly in the black community. That evening several black women, some of them active in a local Women's Political Council, concluded that blacks should retaliate by boycotting the buses. They broached the idea with E. D. Nixon, director of the NAACP chapter in Montgomery, and he began phoning black ministers and other leaders to mobilize a boycott. For almost a year, blacks in Montgomery stayed off the buses. Despite court injunctions and police harassment, despite threats and bombings, despite the arrest, trial, and conviction of their leaders, they stayed off the buses. And on November 13, 1956, they won: the United States Supreme Court upheld a lower court decision declaring Alabama laws requiring segregation on buses unconstitutional.[1]

Though it was preceded by a successful boycott of segregated buses in Baton Rouge, Louisiana, the more famous Montgomery bus boycott initiated a new era in the struggle of American blacks for racial justice. As the first widely noted mass protest mounted by black people in the Deep South, it signaled and inspired a new militancy among Afro-Americans. Montgomery attracted the attention of the nation and dramatized for more Americans than ever before the reality of segregation. During the boycott, tactics evolved which would be used again and again in the protests of the 1960s. Moreover, Montgomery catapulted to fame the twenty-six-year-old pastor of Dexter Avenue Baptist Church, Martin Luther King, Jr. He, better than any other leader, would articulate the religious meaning of civil rights for the nation. In so doing, he would move thousands of citizens, white as well as black, to revision America.

Montgomery, then, was a watershed. It marked something new in the history of race relations in this country. And yet it also represented something old—the perennial exhortation to the nation to "rise up and live out the meaning of its creed," as King declared at the 1963 March on Washington. Montgomery, and in large part the civil-rights movement that ensued, was a revival, an attempt to reawaken the nation to the ideals upon which it was founded. This revival, like those of the past, echoed the old biblical themes. Once again, the God who had acted in Israel's history was acting in America's. "God had decided to use Montgomery as the proving ground for the struggle and triumph of freedom and justice in America," remarked King in his written account of the bus boycott.[2] The tendency to cast political and social events as scenes in the drama of salvation was familiar to Americans, accustomed to envisioning the United States as God's New Israel and themselves as a chosen people. Over the years clusters of images had formed a complex and powerful myth. Some of these images were scriptural in origin, others derived from the rhetoric of the Revolution and the republican tradition of the Constitution. Whatever their source, these images conveyed the durable belief that America is special. It, of all the nations, has been singled out to save (or help save) the world. Within this myth of exceptionalism, Americans from diverse lands, diverse faiths, and diverse peoples embraced a common identity, invented a common history, and projected a common destiny.[3]

King, and those he spoke for, invoked the national myth. But at the same time, they reaffirmed another set of beliefs which rose out of the profound ambivalence that Afro-Americans felt toward that self-same myth. Denied first freedom and then equality in America, blacks had protested by decrying slavery and discrimination as fundamental violations of American ideals. To the extent that they criticized white Americans for simply failing to live the national creed, they tended to assume the myth of exceptionalism. But as racism proved intransigent and as blacks continued to be defined as aliens in their own land, they began to protest that the myth itself was wrong.

This essay will outline the tradition of black religious protest which King and the civil-rights movement of the 1960s recapitulated and will attempt to show the complex ways in which that tradition has challenged America to recover ideals of freedom, equality, and compassion.

Public black protest began early in the nation's history. As soon as British colonists in North America began to claim that their rights had been violated by England, enslaved Africans took the occasion to claim their right to liberty upon the same grounds. In 1774, blacks in Massachusetts petitioned the governor and the general court to grant them freedom, arguing that "we have in common with all other men a naturel right to our freedoms without Being depriv'd of them by our fellow men as we are a freeborn Pepel and have never forfeited this Blessing by aney compact or agreement whatever. But we were unjustly dragged by the cruel hand of power from our dearest friends and sum of us stolen from the bosoms of our tender Parents . . . and Brought hither to be made slaves for Life in a Christian land." Slavery, they went on to argue, violated not only natural law but also the fundamental commandment of Christianity. "There is a grat number of us sencear members of the Church of Christ how can the master be said to Beare my Borden when he Beares me down with the Have chanes of slavery and [oppression] against my will."[4] This and several more petitions like it were ignored, but in a few years, the Revolution and its aftermath did bring freedom to some slaves. However, for the vast majority, slavery "within a free and Christian nation" would still be the lot of their children's children.

During the late eighteenth century, another revolution held out a promise of freedom to black Americans. The spread of evangelical Christianity, with its emphasis on the necessity of conversion, tended to level everyone in the eyes of God, and, for a while at least, in the eyes of men as well. Social status and racial hierarchy were undercut by the biracial religious communities formed in the Methodist class meetings and the Baptist conventicles. In these gatherings, the poor, the uneducated, and the slaves were encouraged to pray, exhort, and even preach. In the emotional tumult of the revivals, racial barriers were momentarily transcended when whites converted blacks and blacks converted whites. When the Methodists and some Baptists condemned slavery as a moral evil, it seemed that white and black Christians were about to preach the same gospel of freedom. But the evangelical revolution, no less than the political revolution, proved, in the end, to be incomplete. By the turn of the century, Methodists and Baptists had retreated from earlier antislavery positions in the face of stiff opposition from southern Christians. Moreover, the increase in African Methodists and Baptists was disquieting to whites, who began to feel uneasy about worshipping in the company of so many blacks. Seating them in galleries and back pews kept them out of sight, if not out of mind. Even separate black congregations suffered discriminatory treatment from white clergy anxious to keep control over the "brethren in black." Convinced that biracial fellowship really meant white control, black Christians by the 1820s had successfully established their own independent churches.[5]

All evidence to the contrary, Afro-Americans insisted that American liberty and Christian brotherhood were meant to include them. Most refused to believe that America was a white man's country or that Christianity was a white man's religion. When, for example, the American Colonization Society was formed in 1817 to support the emigration of free blacks to Africa, a whole host of black orators protested that America was their native land, bought with the sweat and blood of their ancestors. When white Christians discriminated against them in church or preached that slavery and Christianity were compatible, they built their own churches, if possible, and preached that Christianity and slavery were antithetical. Christianity was not false, the American version of it was.

When whites in the antebellum period spoke of America as a Christian nation and predicted that the millennium would begin on these shores, blacks protested that any Christianity which compromised with slavery corrupted the religion of Jesus. Implicit in this criticism of "slaveholding religion" was the assumption that black Americans were the true disciples of Jesus in the nation. The act of calling America to account for betraying her covenant with the Lord placed the black critics, as they well knew, in the long line of biblical prophets, apostles, and martyrs. The Fourth National Negro Convention claimed as much when it remarked in 1834, "our very sighs and groans like the blood of martyrs will prove to have been the seed of the church." Similarly, the American Moral Reform Society in 1837 exhorted blacks to consider themselves as "so many bibles that shall warn this guilty nation of her injustice."[6] The images varied, but the message was clear: it was the destiny of black Americans to save the nation. Had not the Redeemer Himself come as a "suffering servant"? If so, who in America resembled him more, the master or the slave?

The redemptive mission of blacks clashed with the dominant myth of America. Nothing displays this cultural dissonance more clearly than the image of an American Israel. While white Americans depicted the nation as the New Israel and the country as the Promised Land, blacks asserted that they were the Old Israel, waiting for the Lord to free them from bondage in Egypt land. Slaves heard the story of Exodus, and, as the spirituals eloquently attest, appropriated it to account for their own experience as a people. Free blacks expounded on the analogy between Egypt and America and explicated the similarities between Israel and Afro-America in scores of addresses, sermons, and pamphlets. God, they insisted, would act again, as He had of old, to save His people; their oppressors, He would destroy. In the words of a widely circulated jeremiad published in 1829 by a free black named David Walker: "God rules in the armies of heaven and among the inhabitants of the earth, having his ears continually open to the cries, tears and groans of his oppressed people, and being . . . just and holy . . . will . . . one day appear fully in behalf of the oppressed, and arrest the progress of the avaricious." And in terms strikingly prophetic of the Civil War, Walker warned Americans that God overthrew oppressors by causing "them to rise up one against another, to be split and divided . . . to oppress each other, and . . . to open hostilities with sword in hand."[7]

The war and Emancipation seemed to validate their identification with Israel, but blacks discovered that racial oppression showed no signs of abating. Decades after Emancipation, they still had not entered the Promised Land. During the late nineteenth century, the situation of blacks in America seemed to be worsening instead of improving. Against the background of disfranchisement, lynching, pseudoscientific racism, and institutionalized segregation, blacks struggled to understand what their destiny in America might be. One interpretation explained that God had permitted, but not approved, the enslavement of Africans, so that they could learn Christianity and Western civilization in America before returning to Africa to Christianize and civilize Africans. Though proponents of this interpretation often criticized America as materialist, racist, and militaristic, to the extent that they acknowledged the superiority of Western civilization and Christian democracy they mirrored the dominant national myth.[8]

Another interpretation of black destiny flatly contradicted the myth of the Redeemer Nation. Western civilization, in this view, had been tried and found wanting. The mission of Christianizing the world had passed to others. Walker stated as much in 1829: "It is my solemn belief, that if ever the world becomes Christianized . . . it will be through the means, under God, of the Blacks, who are now held in wretchedness, and degradation, by the white Christians of the world."[9] The fullest statement of this argument was written by an AME clergyman, Theophilus Gould Steward, in 1888. In his treatise, *The End of the World,* Steward intended to debunk Josiah Strong's hymn to the mission of the Anglo-Saxon race published as *Our Country* in 1885. Steward used scripture and history to demonstrate that America had been displaced in the drama of salvation. It was impossible for America to convert the world to Christianity, Steward argued, because America had turned Christianity from a world religion into a clan cult. Americans preached and practiced Anglo-Saxonism, not Christianity. Assessing the militarism, nationalism, and materialism of the times, he concluded that the civilization epitomized by Europeans and Americans would soon destroy itself in fratricidal warfare. A new age was about to begin, during which the darker peoples of the world, long oppressed by Western civilization, would create a raceless, classless, weaponless Christianity that would convert the world and welcome the arrival of "the universal Christ."[10]

James Theodore Holly, a black Episcopalian theologian, agreed with Steward that at the end-time of human history the darker races would replace whites as the agents of salvation. According to Holly, writing in 1884, the "Divine plan of human redemption" unfolds in three historic periods or dispensations. The first dispensation belonged to the Semitic race, whose task it was to formulate, write down, and preserve the word of God. The second or Japhetic phase coincided with the apostolic or evangelical period, the age of the Europeans, who were commissioned to spread the gospel. The Hebrew dispensation ended with the destruction of the temple in A.D. 70. The Japhetic phase will end in warfare, after which the millennium will commence. During this thousand-year reign of peace and justice, the Hamitic race will bring to completion the divine plan of human redemption only imperfectly realized by the Semitic and Japhetic races. To the sons of Ham, "the elect among nations," "the crowning work of the will of God is reserved." The Semites preserved the word of God, the Japhites preached it; during this last and greatest dispensation, the Hamites will finally put the word of God into practice.[11]

By the end of the nineteenth century, the protest of Afro-Americans against slavery and racism had evolved several distinct but related themes which challenged the adequacy of the nation's dominant myth. First, blacks asserted that slavery and discrimination were more than aberrations or anomalies in the overall progress of the national destiny; rather, these were fundamental barriers to the achievement of that destiny. Racism, institutionalized in slavery and segregation, rendered the entire experiment a failure. Second, blacks by criticizing white America assumed a position of moral authority which made them appear to be the true exemplars of Christianity in America. This role blacks symbolized in the image of themselves as Israel, a metaphor which contradicted the image of whites as the American Israel. Third, blacks declared that America was failing its commission to redeem the world. If America would repent, and incorporate the Christ-like virtues of its black people, it might not be too late to construct a just and free civilization. Finally, some concluded that it was already too late. America's apostasy was so great that it had been displaced. The long course of Western civilization was finished and other peoples would at last put into practice the gospel which Americans had only managed to preach.

Starting with an acceptance of the myth of American exceptionalism, black critics in the nineteenth century pressed toward a theory of history in which American exceptionalism was denied. Oscillating between these two poles, the tradition of black protest registered the degrees of black alienation from the dominant cultural nationalism. At the turn of the twentieth century, though some had lost faith in America or Christianity or both, the mind and mood of much of black America was profoundly ambivalent.

Black protest in the nineteenth century had been predominantly religious. Many of the leaders of protest were ministers. Churches served as major forums for organizing and expressing protest, and the primary symbols of protest were religious ones. During the first decades of the twentieth century, new variations on the traditional themes of protest emerged. Though some scholars have claimed that protest was secularized during this period, the black church remained more political and protest more religious than some have thought. The involvement of clergy, for example, in the organization of such "secular" protest organizations as the National Association for the Advancement of Colored People and the Universal Negro Improvement Association, especially on the local level, was extensive. Although neither the NAACP or the UNIA developed any formal relationship with religious bodies, they did justify their goals by appealing to religious ideals. It was republican or civil, rather than biblical, religion, however, on which they based their appeal. In its long struggle to desegregate the nation, the NAACP attempted to get the republic to practice its faith by using the guardians of that faith, the courts of law. To the degree that it succeeded, the NAACP preserved the religion of the republic for black citizens still denied full participation in the civic rituals of voting and public education.

Marcus Garvey, architect of the largest mass movement Afro-America has ever seen, founded his Universal Negro Improvement Association on the principles of democracy and Christianity, which he hoped to embody in an African republic, a black nation destined to unite the scattered Africans of the world. Garvey denied that his movement was antiwhite and professed unwavering faith in the brotherhood of man and the fatherhood of God. Though Garvey and his followers despaired of achieving justice for blacks in America, they remained loyal to the ideals of America and sought to transport them to their Republic of Africa. Garveyism inspired civic piety among the black masses and structured their piety around symbols appropriate for a black civil religion. The UNIA offered black Americans a cultural nationalism of their own, freed of ambivalence and alienation. To this end, Garvey's movement developed its own hymnal, creed, catechism, and baptismal ceremony.[12]

While the Garveyites sought to replace the American civil religion with one of their own, some black Americans began to formulate for themselves an entirely new religio-racial identity, divorced from American mythology. As noted earlier, blacks had generally adhered to Christianity while attacking the behavior of white Christians as a travesty of true Christian doctrine. Some, however, found it impossible, in the face of white Christians' racism, to distinguish between true and false Christianity and condemned the entire religion as white man's propaganda. For them, the tension involved in holding the same religion as the oppressor proved too great. Christianity was a religion for whites. In the early twentieth century, esoteric versions of Judaism and Islam laid claim to the allegiance of blacks. In these "new religions" black Americans embraced the alienation forced upon them by the intransigence of racism in Christian America. Spiritually, if not physically, they abandoned America to search for citizenship and acceptance in a different world. Particularly in the Nation of Islam, led by Elijah Mohammed and publicized by Malcolm X, the alienation of black Americans took on mythic form. The black Muslims turned American exceptionalism on its head: America was special all right; America was Satan!

Black protest in the twentieth century, then, has not been as "secular" as some have thought, nor has the black church been as quiescent about protest as is sometimes claimed. Black clergy played active roles in the Garvey movement, the NAACP, and in local political affairs, not only in the North but in the South as well. Granted, much of their political activism would not appear "radical" from the perspective of the 1960s, but demonstrations of protest did occur. In 1935, for example, Martin Luther King, Sr., led several thousand black demonstrators on a march from Ebenezer Baptist Church to the city hall of Atlanta in support of voting rights for blacks. And even earlier, Reverend Adam Daniel Williams, the younger King's maternal grandfather, organized rallies at Ebenezer to protest a municipal bond issue that contained no plans for high school education for black youth.[13] The activism of some black ministers, as well as the legal struggles of the NAACP and the Urban League, laid the groundwork for the movement that began in Montgomery,[14] in which the themes of black religious protest found their most eloquent expression.

As the son, grandson, and great-grandson of Baptist ministers, Martin Luther King, Jr., was shaped by the black church. Though he briefly considered careers in medicine and law, he decided as a teenager that he too would enter the ministry. Already it was apparent that he was, as his father commented, a magnificent preacher. Throughout the civil-rights movement, King remained a preacher. He, and others, perceived his leadership as fundamentally religious. His style of speaking, the cadence of his voice, the choice of words and images, all echoed his church background and evoked, no less than the substance of his message, the rich tradition of black religion. In King, social justice and religion seemed inseparable. It was important that this connection be made because many whites and some blacks felt that civil rights was really a political rather than a religious issue. Christian ethics were personal, not social. King was a living contradiction of that position.[15]

His own commitment to social justice came early. Though his childhood was emotionally and economically secure, he personally experienced several instances of discrimination. He was shocked and hurt by them, and, like most black children, he never forgot them. During his college years at Morehouse in Atlanta, King began to reflect systematically upon race in America and came to see that racial and economic oppression were linked. He read and reread Thoreau's "Essay on Civil Disobedience" and appropriated the notion that noncooperation with an evil system is a moral duty. Later at Crozier Seminary in Pennsylvania, King was influenced by the works of the Social Gospel advocate Walter Rauschenbusch. By the time he reached maturity, he was deeply convinced that Christianity required Christians to work actively for social justice.

His concern for social justice, as well as his intellectual interests, led him to study the social philosophies of the major thinkers in Western philosophy as he pursued graduate degrees at Crozier and at Boston School of Theology. Though strongly attracted to the academic world, King decided that his commitment to social activism for racial justice could best be fulfilled in pastoral ministry in the South. So he accepted the call to pastor the Dexter Avenue Baptist Church in the shadow of the Confederate capitol in Montgomery. As he recalled later, "When I went to Montgomery as a pastor, I had not the slightest idea that I would later become involved in a crisis . . . I neither started the protest nor suggested it. I simply responded to the call of the people for a spokesman."[16] As spokesman for the boycott, King hammered out for himself and for the public, hostile and friendly, a philosophy of black protest. The necessity of protest, he proposed, flowed directly from the principle of noncooperation with evil. For black people passively to accept the unjust system of segregation was tantamount to cooperating with the system. Disruptive as demonstrations, marches, rallies, boycotts, and sit-ins were, they were necessary tools for breaking down the complacency of a false social order. Peace in a segregated society was a false peace in which the oppressed merely accepted their subordination out of fear. Black protest did not create disorder, but revealed the disorder already there in American society, lying just below the surface.

To create such tension that whites could no longer ignore the issue of race, to arouse such conflict that whites were forced to negotiate, these were King's goals in city after city, their names a veritable litany of protest: Montgomery, Albany, Birmingham, Washington, Selma, Chicago, Memphis. To those who argued that the time was not ripe for protest, King replied that "we have waited for more than 340 years for our constitutional and God-given rights" and "we are tired—tired of being segregated and humiliated; tired of being kicked about by the brutal feet of oppression."[17] The time to protest is now. To those who objected that demonstrations encouraged lawlessness, King answered that sometimes allegiance to a higher law required breaking an unjust law and suffering the consequences. Besides, the reaction of whites to black protest revealed the true source of lawlessness. When white police attacked unarmed black demonstrators with clubs, cattle prods, fire hoses, and police dogs, the lawlessness of racism stood revealed, captured on film for the entire nation to see. (And thousands at home and abroad were shocked that such things could happen in America.)

Demonstrations, then, were directed not just at local patterns of discrimination but at racism in the nation at large. Even when they resulted in minimal local gains, they dramatized the plight of blacks in a segregated society and created pressure for change. Moreover, demonstrations were rituals of revival, powerful exhortations to the nation to repent. They were the means for achieving the goal of the movement, at least as King and the Southern Christian Leadership Conference saw it: "to save the soul of the nation." The soul of the nation, King and the demonstrators were saying with their bodies as well as their words, is tied to the struggle for racial justice. In his most famous defense of protest demonstrations, "Letter from Birmingham Jail," King eloquently restated the relationship between black freedom and the American myth: "We will reach the goal of freedom in Birmingham and all over the nation, because the goal of America is freedom. Abused and scorned though we may be, our destiny is tied up with America's destiny. Before the pilgrims landed at Plymouth, we were here. Before the pen of Jefferson etched the majestic words of the Declaration of Independence . . . we were here. . . . We will win our freedom because the sacred heritage of our nation and the eternal will of God are embodied in our echoing demands."[18] In 1963, then, King's dream for black Americans was still "deeply rooted in the American dream."

But just as it had in the nineteenth century, the linkage between Afro-American destiny and American destiny kept slipping. The fit was not exact. The demonstrators graphically illustrated the distance between the ideal image of America and the reality perceived by blacks. In fact, the distance between image and reality was measured precisely by the gap which stretched between black and white America. The demonstrations revealed how wide the separation really was to many Americans who had not even suspected it was there. A gap so wide was bound to call into question the myth of American identity. Was there one America or were there two?

The society revealed by the demonstrations was not simply divided, it was in conflict. Just as King and the demonstrators intended, their protests brought to the surface the underlying conflict between America's deeds and her principles, and so proved to many Americans for the first time that civil rights was indeed a moral struggle, not simply a political dispute with extremists on both sides. Aided by men like Bull Connor and Jim Clark, the demonstrators embodied the conflict between good and bad, but in this drama the old color symbols were reversed. Black was on the side of right and white on the side of wrong. King made it clear: the KKK and White Citizens' Councils were "protesting for the perpetuation of injustice," the civil rights activists "for the birth of justice."[19] The demonstrations provoked a crisis of conscience. Americans had to choose, as the freedom song put it, "Which side are you on?" If whites wanted to be on the side of right, they needed to join the cause of blacks. The soul of the nation depended on it.

Once again, the nation was reminded that her destiny lay in the hands of black people. As King told a packed audience on the eve of the Montgomery boycott, "If you will protest courageously, and yet with dignity and Christian love, when the history books are written in future generations, the historians will have to pause and say, 'There lived a great people—a black people—who injected new meaning and dignity, into the veins of civilization.' This is our challenge and our overwhelming responsibility." "The Negro," he concluded, "may be God's appeal to this age—an age drifting rapidly to its doom."[20]

According to King, blacks had to save the nation through nonviolence. "The spiritual power that the Negro can radiate to the world comes from love, understanding, good will, and nonviolence."[21] King's first contact with the theory of nonviolence came from reading Thoreau, but a lecture by Mordecai Johnson, president of Howard University, on the life and thought of Mahatma Gandhi inspired King to study the Indian leader and to commit himself to nonviolence. Nonviolence, he thought, was the perfect method for translating the love ethic of Christianity into social reform. With the advice of Bayard Rustin, a black veteran of the pacifist Fellowship of Reconciliation, King fitted a theory of nonviolent resistance to the tactics of the civil-rights movement. He also preached that nonviolence was not just a tactic but a way of life.[22]

As King outlined it, nonviolence requires active resistance to evil instead of passivity; it seeks to convert, not to defeat, the opponent; it is directed against evil, not against persons; it avoids internal violence, such as hatred or bitterness, as much as external violence, because hatred depersonalizes the individual. Nonviolence, according to King, is based upon the belief that acceptance of suffering is redemptive, because suffering can transform both the sufferer and the oppressor; it is based upon loving others regardless of worth or merit; it is based upon the realization that all human beings are interrelated; and it is grounded in the confidence that justice will, in the end, triumph over injustice. Belief in redemptive suffering was crucial to King as *the* rationale for nonviolent direct action. By accepting the violence of the oppressor, without retaliation and even without hatred, the demonstrators, he taught, could transform the oppressor's heart.[23] King's doctrine of redemptive suffering awakened old themes within Afro-American religious culture, in particular the theme of the suffering servant with all its associations in the slave past. The prayers, sermons, and especially the traditional songs "brought to mind the long history of the Negro's suffering," he noted.[24] A simple reference to freedom as the "Promised Land," for example, stirred racial memories and triggered religious emotion. The biblical quotations and allusions which studded King's speeches served to locate the protestors in the long train of prophets and martyrs. The civil-rights movement was heir to the early Christian movement, King suggested by writing two epistles in the style of the New Testament, "Letter from Birmingham Jail," and "Paul's Letter to American Christians."[25]

The demonstrations themselves took on the feel of church services. Invariably, they began with rallies in the black churches (primary targets for white terrorist bombings therefore). These rallies followed a pattern consisting of song, prayer, scripture reading, discussion of goals and tactics, and an exhortation that frequently sounded like a sermon. From the churches, the demonstrators moved out into the public arena to bear witness with their bodies to the gospel of freedom and equality. Some gave their lives.

Just as in the nineteenth century, twentieth-century black protest claimed that the moral leadership of the nation had passed to blacks. And blacks in both centuries asserted this claim in biblical and messianic terms. Once again the redemptive mission of blacks contradicted the national myth. But this was not to say that Afro-Americans had simply created a black version of Anglo-Saxonism. King, and others, realized that there was something universal about the black experience and they said so. The particular history of black Americans represented the suffering of the poor and oppressed everywhere. And the lesson of black history for the world was that suffering could be redemptive. Nothing expressed this universal dimension of black protest as well as the spirituals. Gandhi himself had once commented that the slave spirituals got to "the root of the experience of the entire human race under the spread of the healing wings of suffering."[26] King touched on this universalism when he ended his "I have a dream" speech with a vision of the day "when all of God's children, black men and white men, Jews and Gentiles, Protestants and Catholics, will be able to join hands and sing *in the words of the old Negro spiritual,* 'Free at last! free at last! Thank God almighty we are free at last!'"[27]

With King, as with earlier black protest leaders, reflection on black destiny in America seemed inevitably to push beyond the boundaries of America. In part this was due to his concept of nonviolent love. Love recognized the interrelatedness of all people and impelled one to break down all barriers to community. There is a "network of mutuality" binding all communities, all states, all peoples, King explained to an interfaith committee of ministers who demanded to know why he, an outsider, was demonstrating in Birmingham. "Injustice anywhere is a threat to justice everywhere," he told them.[28] The philosophy of nonviolence tended to corrode the myth of American exceptionalism, in King's thinking.

In addition to nonviolence, the independence struggles of darker peoples around the world influenced King, and many black Americans, to place the civil-rights struggle in an internationalist context. In 1958 he wrote that "This determination of Negro Americans to win freedom from all forms of oppression springs from the same deep longing that motivates oppressed people all over the world. The rumblings of discontent in Asia and Africa are expressions of a quest for freedom and human dignity by people who have long been the victims of colonialism and imperialism. So in a real sense the racial crisis in America is a part of the larger world crisis."[29]

For King, the heaviest blow against the traditional vision of America's role in the world was delivered by the Vietnam War. Against the wishes of many of his advisors, King began to speak out against the war in 1967. In his most famous antiwar speech, delivered at Riverside Church in New York City exactly one year to the day before his assassination, King described America in terms that Theophilus Gould Steward and James Theodore Holly would have found familiar a century earlier. First, he attacked "the deadly Western arrogance that has poisoned the international atmosphere for so long." Then he accused the nation of being on the wrong side of the revolutions against poverty and injustice taking place all over the world. The only hope for America, he argued, was for the nation "to undergo a radical revolution of values." "We must rapidly begin the shift," he asserted "from a 'thing-oriented' society to a 'person-oriented' society," if the "great triplets of racism, materialism, and militarism" are ever to be conquered.[30]

Finally, King's concern about the relationship between racism and economic injustice, which had troubled him since his youth and which led him to organize the Poor People's Campaign in the last year of his life, caused him to focus increasingly on the need for structural change, if the glaring disparity between wealthy and poor was ever to be closed. To attack these problems, a new universalist perspective must prevail, King argued: "Every nation must now develop an overriding loyalty to mankind as a whole." In the "long and bitter—but beautiful—struggle for a new world," everyone dedicated to peace and justice must take on a new role. They must become for Americans the voice of the others—the aliens, the enemies, the poor, the oppressed:

> Beyond the calling of race or nation or creed is this vocation of sonship and brotherhood, and because I believe that the Father is deeply concerned especially for his suffering and helpless and outcast children, I come tonight to speak for them. This I believe to be the privilege and the burden of all of us who deem ourselves bound by allegiances and loyalties which are broader and deeper than nationalism and which go beyond our nation's self-defined goals and positions. We are called to speak for the weak, for the voiceless, for victims of our nation and for those it calls enemy, for no document from human hands can make these humans any less our brothers. . . . Here is the true meaning and value of compassion and nonviolence when it helps us to see the enemy's point of view, to hear his questions, to know his assessment of ourselves. For from his view we may indeed see the basic weakness of our own condition, and if we are mature we may learn and grow and profit from the wisdom of the brothers who are called the opposition.[31]

Though King attracted widespread support from the local black churches, it was never unanimous. Some clergymen disagreed with his philosophy of social activism because they believed that Christian ethics was a matter of personal morality and salvation. Society would be changed by obedience to God, not by political agitation. The most cogent critic of King's theory of nonviolent resistance came from outside the Christian churches. Malcolm X rejected King's tactics and insisted that blacks use any means necessary to achieve freedom, including violence. Malcolm, and the Nation of Islam for whom he spoke, scorned integration as a misguided fantasy and condemned nonviolence as detrimental to black self-worth. Malcolm's critique was made all the more powerful because of his eloquence and integrity. During the last years of King's life, disappointment over the slow pace of change and disillusionment with the tactics of nonviolence led some black activists to adopt a more militant stance and to raise a demand for "black power." For them, King's assassination seemed to seal the demise of nonviolent resistance as a viable means of achieving equality for blacks in America. In some quarters, the rejection of nonviolence was coupled with strong criticism of the black church as a detriment to black liberation. Integration yielded to goals of liberation, self-determination, and community control. Black pride and the re-covery of black cultural identity represented a new mood of independence, which some called separatism, among Afro-Americans. Black clergy in white churches founded separate black caucuses to deal with questions of black identity and power within white-controlled denominational structures.

Responding in part to the militant criticism of the church and in part to their own agenda, black churchmen began in the late 1960s and early 1970s to develop a black theology which stressed that God's presence is to be found primarily among the poor, the oppressed, and the outcast. It is the voice of these voiceless which black liberation theology seeks to speak. Entering into dialogue with third-world theologians from Latin America, Africa, and Asia, these theologians are—in a sense—the heirs of the vision of Walker, Steward, Holly, King, and the tradition of black religious protest.[32]

The continuous tradition of black protest in the United States has, in turn, called America to live up to her mythic vision of herself, has contradicted that image, and has argued that an entirely new vision was needed. Some Americans, white as well as black, have, over the long years, listened to the voices of black protest. They have realized, against all appearances, that the nation has need of the wisdom of the invisible men and women who were called slaves and niggers, if Americans are to recover their ideals, admit their failures, and develop a chastened but mature identity as a people. But, sadly, many looked and saw nothing, or looked and saw only distorted images of themselves.

NOTES

1. Martin Luther King, Jr., *Stride toward Freedom: The Montgomery Story* (New York: Harper & Row, 1958), pp. 34–35, 43–70; Howell Raines, *My Soul Is Rested: Movement Days in the Deep South Remembered* (New York: Viking Penguin, 1983), pp. 37–61; Aldon D. Morris, *The Origins of the Civil Rights Movement: Black Communities Organizing for Change* (New York: Free Press, 1984), pp. 42–63.

2. King, *Stride toward Freedom*, p. 70.

3. See Conrad Cherry, ed., *God's New Israel: Religious Interpretations of American Destiny* (Englewood Cliffs, N.J.: Prentice-Hall, 1971).

4. To Gov. Thomas Gage and the Massachusetts General Court, May 25, 1774, *Collections of the Massachusetts Historical Society*, 5th ser., vol. 3 (1877), pp. 432–33.

5. See Albert J. Raboteau, "The Slave Church in the Era of the American Revolution," in *Slavery and Freedom in the Age of the American Revolution*, ed. Ira

Berlin and Ronald Hoffman (Charlottesville: University Press of Virginia, 1983), pp. 193–213.

6. *Minutes of the Fourth Annual Convention for the Improvement of the Free People of Colour . . . New York, June 2–12, 1834* (New York, 1834), pp. 27–30; *Minutes and Proceedings of the First Annual Meeting of the American Reform Society* (Philadelphia, 1837), rpt. in *Early Negro Writing, 1760–1837,* ed. Dorothy Porter (Boston: Beacon Press, 1971) p. 203.

7. David Walker, *Appeal to the Coloured Citizens of the World,* 3d ed. (Boston, 1830), rpt. in *One Continual Cry,* ed. Herbert Aptheker (New York: Humanities Press, 1965), pp. 65–66.

8. Absalom Jones, *A Thanksgiving Sermon Preached January 1, 1808, in St. Thomas's or the African Episcopal, Church, Philadelphia: An Account of the Abolition of the African Slave Trade . . .* (Philadelphia, 1808), p. 18; William Miller, *A Sermon on the Abolition of the Slave Trade: Delivered in the African Church, New York on the First of January, 1810* (New York, 1810), p. 4; George Washington Williams, *History of the Negro Race in America,* 2 vols. (New York, 1883), vol. 1, pp. 113–14.

9. Walker, *Appeal to Coloured Citizens,* p. 81 n.

10. Theophilus Gould Steward, *The End of the World; Or, Clearing the Way for the Fullness of the Gentiles* (Philadelphia, 1888), pp. 119–27.

11. James Theodore Holly, "The Divine Plan of Human Redemption, In Its Ethological Development," *AME Church Review* 1 (Oct. 1884): 79–85.

12. Randall K. Burkett, *Garveyism as a Religious Movement: The Institutionalization of a Black Civil Religion* (Metuchen, N.J.: Scarecrow Press, 1978) and *Black Redemption: Churchmen Speak for the Garvey Movement* (Philadelphia: Temple University Press, 1978).

13. Martin Luther King, Sr., with Clayton Riley, *Daddy King: An Autobiography* (New York: William Morrow, 1980), pp. 84–87, 95–102.

14. See Morris, *Origins of the Civil Rights Movement,* pp. 1–16.

15. Stephen B. Oates's *Let the Trumpet Sound: The Life of Martin Luther King, Jr.* (New York: Harper & Row, 1982) is the most comprehensive biography of King so far. I have depended upon it and King's own writings for the sketch of King that follows. John J. Ansbro's *Martin Luther King, Jr.: The Making of a Mind* (Maryknoll, N.Y.: Orbis Books, 1982) is a helpful analysis of King's thought.

16. King, *Stride toward Freedom,* p. 101.

17. Ibid., p. 61.

18. Martin Luther King, Jr. *Why We Can't Wait* (New York: New American Library, 1963), pp. 92–93.

19. King, *Stride toward Freedom,* p. 62.

20. Ibid., pp. 63, 224.

21. Ibid., p. 224.

22. Ibid., pp. 90–101.

23. Ibid., pp. 101–7.

24. Ibid., p. 86.

25. "Letter from Birmingham Jail" is reprinted in *Why We Can't Wait;* "Paul's Letter to American Christians" in *Strength to Love* (Philadelphia: Fortress Press, 1981), pp. 138–46.

26. Cited in Howard Thurman, *With Head and Heart: The Autobiography of Howard Thurman* (New York: Harcourt, Brace, Jovanovich, 1979), p. 134.

27. Oates, *Let the Trumpet Sound*, p. 262. Italics added.

28. King, *Why We Can't Wait*, p. 77.

29. King, *Stride toward Freedom*, p. 191.

30. This speech is most easily accessible in *A Testament of Hope: The Essential Writings of Martin Luther King, Jr.*, ed. James M. Washington (San Francisco: Harper & Row, 1986), pp. 231–44.

31. Ibid., pp. 237, 240–41, 243.

32. See *Black Theology: A Documentary History, 1966–1979*, ed. Gayraud S. Wilmore and James H. Cone (Maryknoll, N.Y.: Orbis, 1979).

CHARLES REAGAN WILSON

"God's Project":
The Southern Civil Religion, 1920–1980

In *Broken Covenant: American Civil Religion in Time of Trial* (1975), Robert N. Bellah suggested that scholars look beyond the American civil religion to alternative visions of American destiny. Among other possibilities, he offered the experience of the South, although he noted that the region's sentimentalization of the past and its militarism tempered its realism and its willingness to look critically at national life. The South's history has been, though, notably different from the national experience, and in considering the possibility of American recovery of meaning one should look carefully at the lessons of the southern past. The period from 1920 to 1980 is revealing, in particular, because it witnessed the profound transformation of a southern civil religion. Noting that "civil religions have come into being in America and passed away again," historian John Wilson has asked in *Public Religion in American Culture* (1979) whether "a public religion once substantially depleted in a democratic society can be revitalized." Examination of the southern civil religion in the twentieth century offers the opportunity to observe the adaptation of one such public religion to new social and cultural conditions.[1]

In the years from 1920 to 1980 the southern civil religion evolved from a public faith celebrating the virtues of a religiously sanctioned regional culture to preoccupation with what the region's new destiny was on the national and indeed universal human scale. The term "civil religion" can be used to describe the post–1920 effort of southerners to place their historical experience in cosmic perspective. The new visions that southerners offered of their destiny may now provide visions for America's renewal. The transformation of an earlier civil religion also provides the hope that America's mythic structure can be refocused on humane concerns that will still reflect the best of the nation's heritage.

Historians have never been able to agree on when a southern identity, a regional consciousness, emerged, but it is clear that the Civil War experience and Confederate defeat gave a new meaning to that identity as a separate southern people within the American nation. It now had mythic dimensions. Historian George Tindall has described myths as mental pictures summing up a people's experience, and he argues that the South is especially given to myths because they appeal to the southerner's love of concrete images and dramatic stories. Out of the experience of defeat came the myth of the Lost Cause, which centered on the efforts of southerners to come to terms with defeat, embodying the idea that the South had been destined to lose because of the sheer force and power of the North. Much of this effort involved trying to justify the actions of the South and of southerners. Long after the war ended, political leaders like Jefferson Davis wrote books still insisting that secession was legally defensible. Military leaders wrote books explaining that their military maneuvers during the war had been correct and the real blame lay elsewhere.[2]

There were also religious efforts to deal with the war and defeat. Ministers and churches during the war had insisted that the Confederacy was a crusade against the evil empire of the Yankee. It was a holy war, but how does one come to terms with losing a holy war? In *Baptized in Blood: The Religion of the Lost Cause* (1980), I discussed the way the Confederate experience led southerners to see their historical past in transcendent, cosmic terms. Southerners came to believe that God had not abandoned them but instead had chastized them, in preparation for a greater destiny in the future. The South has given rise, of course, to many myths—the Old South, New South, Reconstruction, the savage South of violence, the decadent South of Tennessee Williams, and now the Sunbelt. The unique aspect of the myth of the Lost Cause in the late nineteenth century was the structure that existed around it. It became the basis for what anthropologists would see as a functioning religion. It was not a formal religion; no First Church of the Lost Cause ever existed. But it was the focus for a complex of religious phenomena.

The Lost Cause had icons, including pervasive images of Robert E. Lee, Jefferson Davis, and Stonewall Jackson—the Lost Cause Trinity. The Confederate heroes were portrayed as saints, prophets, and martyrs. Their images were found in schools and on the stained glass windows in selected churches. Southerners had their sacred artifacts, such as the Confederate battle flag, the song "Dixie," and the ubiquitous Confederate monuments. There were distinctively southern rituals, such as Confederate Memorial Day, the dedication of Confederate monuments, the funerals of Confederate veterans, and the reunions of living veterans. These ritual events were the focus for prayers, sermons, and speeches recalling the Cause and the failed Confederacy. Institutions gave the Lost Cause an organizational structure. Southerners could join the United Confederate Veterans, the

United Daughters of the Confederacy, the Sons of Confederate Veterans, and the Children of Confederate Veterans. The Protestant churches were crucial in keeping alive a religious interpretation of the Lost Cause. The Baptists, Methodists, and Presbyterians remained regionally organized after the Civil War, and their ministers played an active role in nurturing the idea that the South's past had continuing spiritual significance. The Episcopalians were even more prominently involved as leaders of southern society.

These were not unrelated parts but aspects of a well-organized spiritual movement, a cultural revitalization movement emerging out of the fear that the South would not survive as a distinct entity after its military and political defeat in the Civil War. Two key theological concepts were at the heart of the religious interpretation of the Confederate experience—southerners were a Chosen People but they were also a Tragic People. They had been destined to crusade with honor for a cause they saw as right, but they had been destined to lose and suffer.

The Lost Cause became a popular movement, and through its various activities, southerners in the late nineteenth and early twentieth centuries were regularly taught to retain a sense of southern identity. Southerners were told that they were different and that that difference had spiritual significance. Historian C. Vann Woodward has written that southerners came to have a tragic view of life because of their historical experience. The southern people of the late nineteenth century did indeed know this because their culture embodied it for them in a culture religion, or, more accurately, a civil religion, which saw religious significance in the Confederate nationalist experience in particular and in regional culture in general.[3]

The Lost Cause as an organized movement had a long history; indeed, it still exists. Yet the vitality of the movement had begun to ebb by World War I. That war represented a landmark in the reincorporation of the South back into the Union, and the Lost Cause increasingly seemed out of date. What happened to the "religion of the Lost Cause," to the belief that the Confederate nation, in retrospect, had spiritual meaning? Consideration of the topic offers a way to examine the decline and transformation of one variety of civil religion in America. The decline of the Lost Cause as an explanation of southern mission set the stage for the emergence of new dreams of southern destiny.[4]

In sociological terms, the religion of the Lost Cause failed to make the transition from cult status to denominational status. It gradually declined in cultural significance as a popular movement, as those associated with the Confederacy died. The veterans themselves had been a constant reminder to southerners not to forget their past, but as the ranks of the veterans thinned out, southerners as a people had less reinforcement for remembering the war. As time went on, the Lost Cause ceremonies and activities were less likely to evoke spiritual feelings. The pattern of life had changed in the South, and it seemed that the issues that the Lost Cause addressed were no longer of central concern to southerners. Lost Cause activities became less and less full community events. To be sure, the forms were still followed, but without the same spirit and community importance. Confederate Memorial Day still exists and the faithful still honor it, but it is no longer a community event; the Fourth of July is more likely to be a social and community happening. Lee's birthday is still a holiday, but newspapers rarely publish editorials about it anymore. Confederate monuments still dot the landscape, but the young have little sense of what they mean. Young southerners are much like youthful Americans across the country. They know more about John Travolta than about Robert E. Lee, thanks to the media and to modern cultural ideals.[5]

Although the ritualized, institutionalized spiritual aspects of the Lost Cause religious movement have been eclipsed since 1920, the Lost Cause, the memory of Confederate defeat, has played a role in regional and national life. It has been used in many ways by different kinds of southerners. The first phase of the modern southern civil religion was the literary Lost Cause. The years from 1920 to 1950 witnessed the Southern Literary Renaissance, a flowering of culture such as the South had never seen. The great Confederate novel did not come out of this, although many Civil War novels and biographies of Confederate leaders did appear. Writings of the period certainly praised the virtues of the Confederates. W. J. Cash in his classic work, *The Mind of the South* (1941), lauded their "honor, courage, generosity, amiability, courtesy." Southern writers also, however, explored the tragic meaning of the southern experience. There is a sense of brooding about the past in much of this writing. The Lost Cause all along had been to southerners more than just the story of romantically going off to war. The words themselves give the clue. The Lost Cause was the memory of defeat itself, of struggling with every ounce of heroic effort, and then failing and having to live with the results of the past. In this era it was no longer just a regional story. As poet Allen Tate said, these modern southern writers converted the memory of the regional past "into a universal myth of the human condition."[6]

Southern writers such as William Faulkner and Robert Penn Warren had profound things to say about the South, about its grandeur and its tragedy. Some scholars argue that southern literature and history have been used "as sacramental acts," intended by writers to counter the instability and chaos they perceive in the modern world. "By such an interpretation," C. Hugh Holman writes, "literature ultimately becomes a religious act, and the distinctiveness of southern writing rests not on its view of social structures or the facts of history but upon the religious orientation of the region."[7] The writers of the Southern Literary Renaissance, then, in one sense extended the religion of the Lost Cause. They converted the southern experience into high art, into parables of the human condition, conveying the southern experience to the rest of the world.

Claiming the Confederate legacy, the belief that the southern past still offered meaning for the region and the nation, was not easy, perhaps no easier for southern intellectuals of the 1920s and 1930s than it had been for the post-Civil War generation. Their efforts should be seen in the context of the 1920s. This was a decade when the region appeared to the world as the "Benighted South," to use George Tindall's phrase, the savage South of the Ku Klux Klan, chain gangs, lynchings, the Scopes trial, and hookworm and pellagra. On the other hand, the internal leadership of the South was in the hands of the boosters, the forces of modernization. Southern intellectuals and artists, including writers, generally faced an identity crisis, caught between the older South and a newly emerging one, neither of which they fully approved. Southerners of the post-Civil War era had turned to the southern past, to the Lost Cause, to help cope with their identity crisis as a defeated people, and now, in the 1920s and 1930s, southern intellectual leaders again turned to the past.[8]

Allen Tate perhaps best embodied the southern identity crisis and the belief that the South of the Lost Cause still had meaning. Born in Winchester, Kentucky, Tate attended Vanderbilt University and came away a self-conscious intellectual, firmly aware of and committed to the latest modernist literary outlook and assumptions. He gravitated to New York City and its sophisticated Greenwich Village scene. But eventually he came to reassess his southern heritage. In the fall of 1926 he began work on "Ode to the Confederate Dead." This poem expresses the frustration of a modern young southerner standing at the gate of a Confederate cemetery. He thinks of the "inscrutable infantry rising" and of the battles fought. He envies the Confederates their convictions, their knowledge of why they fought and what they believed. The modern southerner knows too much, in effect, for simple convictions. He doubts and questions, making it impossible to regain the faith and wholeness of the past.[9]

Tate immersed himself in the Lost Cause in the hope of somehow regaining the traditional southern faith. He wrote biographies of Stonewall Jackson, Jefferson Davis, and Robert E. Lee. He read southern history, studied genealogy, and toured battlefields. He bought an antebellum home with columns and porches, and he kept a loaded rifle and a Confederate flag over his mantelpiece. All the while, he clung to the image of the Old South as a unified, religiously oriented society, like the Middle Ages. In his essay "Remarks on the Southern Religion" in *I'll Take My Stand*, Tate asks, "How may the Southerner take hold of his Tradition?" His answer is "by violence." By this he meant by an act of the will, and he tried to do this in his own life.[10]

In this period he was obsessed with the southern past and the Lost Cause, but it was not the South of Confederate defeat, it was not the tragic South that had played such a great role in the rhetoric and rituals of the Lost Cause movement of the late nineteenth century. Back then, southerners lived with the tangible results of the tragedy of war and could not deny it. Tate was interested in the Lost Cause for other reasons—because it offered a vision of southern crusaders, the Chosen People, battling for a way of life they believed in.

In spite of Tate's passionate interest in it, the Lost Cause was no longer a popular movement. He and his literary colleagues were largely without influence with the masses of the southern people themselves. The tragic view of life that many of these writers expressed had once been embodied in the activities of the Lost Cause movement, but in the modern South it seemed that most southerners preferred to forget the tragic lessons of the Civil War and to think in more upbeat ways. Tate attended a Confederate memorial service in Clarksville, Tennessee, and was told by a local Baptist minister that Confederate defeat was simply God's ordained way to bring about industrial development in a New South. Factories in Clarksville—that was what the war had been about. This was, in fact, a standard interpretation for many southerners in the 1920s, but it was frustrating to someone like Tate, who saw deeper meanings to the southern experience in war.

Tate's alienation from this common interpretation of the war reflected the alienation of southern writers from their community and people. They had grown up at a time in the early twentieth century when they could see the truly distinctive South before later changes; they had also lived outside the region and were involved in modernist intellectual currents. They were transitional figures. They saw spiritual meaning in the southern experience, a deeper meaning than southerners themselves wanted to hear.[11]

Regional writers kept alive, though, the idea of the South as a potentially redemptive community. Critic Lewis P. Simpson has argued that "the Southern writer has tended to be a kind of priest and prophet of a metaphysical nation," who has endeavored to "represent it as a quest for a revelation of man's moral community in history." Writers increasingly placed the South's experience in the broadest possible perspective, making their greatest achievements when, as Simpson says, "they became sufficiently aware that the South is a part of the apocalypse of modern civilization." As among the most sensitive chroniclers of the South's spiritual destiny, the literary community would play a crucial role in refocusing the southern civil religion on concerns beyond the Lost Cause.[12]

In the 1950s and 1960s, Confederate symbolism reemerged in the segregationist Lost Cause, a popular movement in response to the civil-rights movement. Spokesmen for the Lost Cause organizations, and especially ministers in them, had rarely discussed racial issues in the post-Civil War era. Perhaps they simply did not have to do so because the southern white consensus on racial supremacy was so great. In any event, to earlier generations of southerners the Lost Cause symbols had taught complex lessons, including spiritual lessons of human limitation, suffering, the heroic sacrifices of the Confederates, and finally their tragic defeat. But in the 1950s, the Confederate symbols took on a harsher racial meaning. Segregationists used the symbols of the Lost Cause, and they became explicitly, almost exclusively, tied in with white supremacy in a way they had not been before. Whether at Central High School in Little Rock in 1957, at Ole Miss in 1962, or at Selma in 1965, segregationists displayed the Confederate battle flag and played "Dixie." After Central High School was integrated at bayonet point, a local official in Forest, Mississippi, told the high school band there to play "Dixie" before football games instead of the "Star-Spangled Banner." During the riot in Oxford in 1962, students pulled down the Stars and Stripes from the flagpole and raised the Confederate flag. This was powerful symbolism a hundred years after the Civil War. The Ku Klux Klan had made that Confederate flag a central symbol in the early twentieth century, the White Citizens' Councils used it in the 1950s, and in the minds of many Americans that is now its prime association. Writer Walker Percy explained the historic shift in meaning of Confederate symbolism, pointing out in 1961 that "racism is no sectional monopoly. Nor was the Confederate flag a racist symbol. But it is apt to be now. The symbol is the same, but the referent has changed. Now when the Stars and Bars flies over a convertible or a speedboat or a citizen's meeting, what it signifies is not a theory of government but a certain attitude toward the Negro."[13]

This phase of the Lost Cause ebbed in the 1970s, with adjustment to the end of legal segregation and less explicit expression of racism. As a result of the 1950s' linkage with racial confrontation, the South has seen a decline of Lost Cause symbolism. Most southern universities dropped the playing of "Dixie" during sporting events, a practice that was once common throughout the South. The University of Mississippi, however, retains "Dixie" as a school song, and some public schools and private academies still use the flag.[14]

The third phase of the modern Confederate memory was the Civil War centennial in the early 1960s. The centennial was a national fad, the kind of modern American event that advertisers love to take advantage of—"If General Lee could have had an automobile, he would have wanted a Chevy." To be sure, it also occasioned the display of more Lost Cause symbolism and brought much interest in battle reenactments. Newspaper editorials appeared and southerners bought national books and magazines and even wrote many themselves. Shelby Foote's magnificent multivolume narrative history of the Civil War began appearing, and interest in military history—always strong in the South—reached a high point. It was all tied to the southern passion for genealogy and social activities. Faulkner had anticipated this. In *Requiem for a Nun* (1951), he wrote that "the old deathless Lost Cause had become a faded (though still select) social club or caste," and that was indeed what had happened. But the striking fact is that southerners as a group in this era showed little interest in being reminded of defeat. Southerners were interested in the Confederacy of 1861, in the fighting itself, not in the South of 1865. Nor did the war occasion many southern reflections upon the idea of the region's destiny. Those twin concepts of the older Lost Cause—the Chosen People, the Tragic People—were, then, rarely mentioned during the centennial. Again, it seemed that the spiritual meaning, the religious significance, of defeat, which southerners had once dwelled upon, had been forgotten.[15]

Two perceptive literary southerners, Robert Penn Warren and Walker Percy, did see deeper meaning in the Civil War centennial. To them, the Civil War was an ongoing process in their own age. The Civil War had produced great leaders and noble deeds, but the South of their own age produced neither. "Even now," Warren wrote in *The Legacy of the Civil War: Meditations on the Civil War Centennial* (1961), "any common lyncher becomes a defender of the southern tradition, and any rabble-rouser the gallant leader of a thin gray line of heroes." Warren argued that the modern southerner's protests against racial changes were "nothing more than an obscene parody of the meaning of his history." The Confederates offered the lesson that human dignity and grandeur are possible, even amid human weakness and vice, but the actions of contemporary southern leaders were a debasement of the southerner's history, "with all that was noble, courageous, and justifying bleached out, drained away." He found it inconceivable to picture General Lee, a symbol of integrity, shaking hands with Orval Faubus.[16]

Walker Percy made the same point about the modern South. "When Lee and the Army of Northern Virginia laid down the Confederate flag in 1865, no flag had ever been defended by better men. But when the same flag is picked up by men like Ross Barnett and Jimmy Davis, nothing remains but to make panties and pillowcases with it." That is a prophecy that has come true. The Lost Cause souvenir industry, which seems to operate out of Taiwan, turns out Confederate flag beach towels, cigarette lighters, oversized T-shirts, and, perhaps the best, the southern yuppie version of the Lost Cause—Confederate flag jogging shorts.[17]

Percy's novel *The Last Gentleman* (1966) can be read as an ironic commentary on the centennial. The protagonist, Will Barrett, is a modern southerner suffering cultural amnesia. He can remember bits and pieces from the past but they have no coherent meaning. The novel is filled with Civil War references—battles, forts, and generals. Barrett admires the Confederates but he can find no leader in his own age worth following. Even Barrett cannot bear to face the realities of the Lost Cause in the modern age. Barrett reads Douglas Southall Freeman's biography of General Lee, but eventually he gives it up. "He was tired of Lee's sad fruitless victories and would as soon see the whole thing finished off for good." Barrett was another centennial-era southerner who could not accept the deepest meaning of the Lost Cause.[18]

Most recently, the Confederacy has served as the basis for a popular-culture Lost Cause—the Lost Cause as entertainment. This has sometimes involved nonsouthern attempts to market the South. "Dukes of Hazzard" on television, for example, includes a souped-up automobile called the General Lee, with a Confederate flag on its roof. But southerners themselves have made Lost Cause symbolism a part of a cultural revitalization movement in the late 1970s and 1980s. One sees it in sports, for example, and especially in college football. The god of southern football is a tribal god, a god of the Chosen People. When Alabama played Notre Dame in the 1970s southerners from many states waved the flag and rooted for their legions against the Yankees. The evangelical fervor of the South met squarely the Catholic crusaders. In his last years, and especially after his death in 1983, Bear Bryant was as close to a southern saint as the modern South has produced, with frequent comparisons to General Lee. One also sees a renewed southern spirit in country music, another form of indigenous southern culture. Charlie Daniels consciously evokes the image of a Rebel and uses Confederate symbols as he sings "The South's Gonna Do It Again"; Hank Williams, Jr., sings "If Heaven Ain't a Lot like Dixie, Then I Don't Want to Go"; the group Alabama displays the Confederate flag on virtually every record album and their latest song is "If It Ain't Dixie, It Won't Do." Bob McDill's song, "Good Ole Boys," recorded by Don Williams, evokes a whole series of southern images, recalling his youth when a picture of Stonewall Jackson was above his bed at night.[19]

The popular-culture use of the Confederate symbolism is good-natured. If young southerners do have an image of the Lost Cause, it is probably this one. The Confederate symbolism does not seem as racially charged as it did in the 1960s, but neither is it historically as meaningful. After analyzing a 1971 North Carolina public opinion survey, sociologist John Shelton Reed concluded that, although the flag and "Dixie" still bring to mind the Confederacy, these symbols have become simply "badges of regional identification and objects of conventional piety for many white southerners, regardless of whether the beholder has any particular interest in the history that they represent." When faced with the Confederate symbolism, most blacks thought not of the Confederacy but of the more recent white resistance to racial equality. In both cases, the meaning of the Civil War historical experience itself, and especially any spiritual significance in it, seems to be of little interest or importance to modern southerners. Lost Cause symbolism has not disappeared, but it certainly lacks the tragic dimension it once had for southerners.[20]

Although the Confederate past no longer seems to evoke profound sentiments on the part of modern southerners, there have been serious efforts to show the continuing relevance of the southern past. The two concepts of the Chosen People and the Tragic People have survived, although not always in association with the Confederate memory itself. The religious dimension of the Lost Cause all along had addressed the issues of who the southern people were, what their distinctive identity was, and whether they had a destiny under God. The evangelical churches have at times suggested that the South's destiny is to be a great evangelical empire, eventually conquering the nation and the world. Southerners represented, in this interpretation, the last stronghold of pure religion. Segregationists of the 1950s argued that the South's destiny was as one of the last defenders of racial purity in the Western world.[21]

Two dreams of the South's destiny seem to be enduring because they are rooted in the region's distinctive history and represent a continuing critique of dominant American patterns. The southern Agrarians of *I'll Take My Stand* (1930) embodied one variety of the southern civil religon—the antimaterialist South. The Agrarians believed that southern identity had religious significance. As Richard Weaver wrote, "Being a Southerner is definitely a spiritual condition, like being a Catholic or a Jew." But, as mentioned earlier, the Agrarians lived during the time of a regional spiritual crisis, which was an identity crisis. Louis D. Rubin, Jr., has suggested that the Agrarian manifesto "was an *assertion of identity,* an assertion made necessary precisely because the identity was, in part at least, no longer present." All southerners had to face this, but by the 1920s, for the first time in southern history, the traditionalists were on the defensive. In the New South, business-industrial advocates were ascendant. The booster outlook seemed triumphant and, unlike the New South advocates of the late nineteenth century, these boosters had little use for the past.[22]

The Agrarians were thus embattled. They saw industrial advocates within the region as their enemy, but they continued the tradition of regional defensiveness by focusing their fears upon the abiding external enemy, the North. Frank Owsley wrote of the northern "war of intellectual and spiritual conquest" against the South, and John Shelton Reed argues that *I'll Take My Stand* was "the opening salvo of a counterattack in this spiritual and intellectual war." He sees the Agrarians as cultural nationalists trying "to rejuvenate a culture." The civil religion issue was central to their efforts because religion, along with rural living, was the key to their defense of the region. Their advocacy of the religiously based agrarian way of life had a dignity to it that reinforced lagging southern self-esteem at the end of the 1920s. The religion of the Lost Cause in the post-Civil War era had provided a mythic reassurance of southern worth, in spite of the reality of defeat, and the Agrarian manifesto had a similar psychological origin and function. "It even suggested that the South might be a beacon, an example for the rest of the world to emulate," writes Reed. Instead of the New England city on a hill, the Agrarians, in effect, pictured a farm on a hill to be admired and copied.[23]

The rejuvenation of southern culture was important not only to southerners but to the world. The Agrarians saw the South's destiny in terms of the decline of Western civilization. The South was thus potentially the savior for a disturbed world, because it was the last Western embodiment of a society that had escaped the dehumanization and instability of modern industrial life. This vision of the destiny of the southern chosen people was one grand dream of the southern civil religion, a conservative humanist vision. It hoped the South would profit from its tragic history. Forced by the war into generations of deprivation, the South had gained a spiritual superiority to the North, a superiority that it had to use wisely.[24]

Another twentieth-century vision of the South's destiny rooted in the past was that of the biracial South. It was a southern liberal dream, stated succinctly in 1961 by Leslie W. Dunbar, director of the Southern Regional Council: "I believe that the South will, out of its travail and sadness and requited passion, give the world its first grand example of two races of men living together in equality and with mutual respect. The South's heroic age is with us now." Southern white liberals had, in fact, expressed this idea often during the years of segregation. They insisted that southern blacks and whites understood one another better than their counterparts in the North.[25]

The southern liberal dream of the South's destiny was rooted in regional evangelical religion. Advocates of the biracial South were generally from evangelical backgrounds, and they came to believe that racial segregation was a violation of basic Christian ideas. They had had conversion experiences, converting to the belief in brotherhood. They used religious language and spoke of "the regeneration of the South." They saw segregation as a moral problem and used the simple ethical teachings of the Sermon on the Mount as their guide, rather than sophisticated theology. Like the good southerners they were, they had grievances against northern liberals, whom they saw as morally complacent about northern society and "holier than thou" toward the South. The hope was that out of the South's history of suffering and tribulation would come the realization that the suffering had been a shared suffering, black and white, and that the South's destiny was as one society, not two. The end of segregation would free the white southerner and the black for great achievements.[26]

The ideas of Reinhold Niebuhr helped to shape the vision of the biracial South. On a personal level Niebuhr contributed time and energy to such southern liberal religious efforts as the founding of the Highlander School in 1932 and the Fellowship of Southern Churchmen in 1934. Niebuhr was the preeminent theologian of Neoorthodoxy, which called into question human institutions, and many southerners found this religiously based questioning an effective approach to criticizing racial segregation. C. Vann Woodward explicitly applied Niebuhr's outlook to the South in essays such as "The Irony of Southern History" and "The Search for Southern Identity."[27]

The vision of a biracial South was also put forward by southern blacks, especially during the civil-rights movement. Martin Luther King, Jr., spoke of the movement's national and international significance for black liberation, but he also spoke often of the specifically southern context. Achieving racial justice would contribute, he said, to individual moral health, national political life, the nation's prestige in the world, and "our cultural health as a region." He spoke of "our beloved Southland" and lamented its "tragic attempt to live in monologue rather than dialogue." In a 1961 interview he characterized the South as a land "that has some beauty, that has been made ugly by segregation." "There is an intimacy of life that can be beautiful if it is transformed in race relations from a sort of lord-servant relationship to a person-to-person relationship," he said. He predicted that the nature of life in the South "will make it one of the finest sections of our country once we solve this problem of segregation." Like southern white liberals, King saw regional manners and informal relationships as the source of hope for achieving the biracial South. Noting that southern blacks and whites had the kind of personal contacts that northerners lacked, King predicted in 1963 that once segregation ended, "I think you'll have a beautiful relationship in terms of brotherhood." He added that "when you find a white southerner who has been emancipated on the issue, the Negro can't find a better friend."[28]

King used the language of the late nineteenth-century Lost Cause, speaking of suffering, tragedy, honor, the need for virtuous behavior, the need of a defeated people to achieve dignity, and the search for group identity and destiny. He compared traditional southern white values and those of black freedom protesters in 1963, noting that "the virtues so long regarded as the exclusive property of the white South—gallantry, loyalty, and pride—had passed to the Negro demonstrators in the heat of the summer's battles." King suggested that the compensation for black physical deprivations was a spiritual maturity—exactly the argument white southerners had made about their defeated region in the late nineteenth century. King hoped to release "spiritual power" and "soul force" that would transform the South and, from there, the nation and the world. King's "I Have a Dream" speech in 1963 portrayed a redemptive South that would be the scene for national salvation. Reflecting a traditional southern concern for place, he argued that the nation's transformation would not be in some disembodied location, but in a specific locale, the South. The region had been the center of black suffering and of flawed humanity, but ultimately the virtue of blacks and decent whites would lead to reconciliation. One day "on the red hills of Georgia," blacks and whites would "sit down together at the table of brotherhood." In the coming day of redemption, even the state of Mississippi, "a state sweltering with the heat of injustice, sweltering with the heat of oppression, will be transformed into an oasis of freedom and justice."[29]

King and other civil-rights leaders dreamed, then, southern dreams as well as American dreams. Much has happened since to encourage this vision and much to discourage believers in it. In terms of the South's intellectual life, this remains today perhaps the South's predominant idea of its distinctive regional destiny. Jimmy Carter articulated it in his presidential campaign of 1976 and the national media even suggested the dream was being achieved—a pronouncement that was a bit premature, to say the least. The South has generated yet another mythic view of itself—the myth of the biracial South.[30]

The individual who most fully explored the relationship between the two visions at the heart of the modern southern civil religion was James McBride Dabbs. Born in South Carolina to a family that had been in the state since the colonial era, educated in the South at the University of South Carolina and out of the region at Clark University and Columbia University, a soldier in France during World War I, Dabbs was, at various times, a college teacher, a leader in the southern Presbyterian church, president of the reformist Southern Regional Council, and, for most of his life, a practicing farmer at the family plantation, Rip Raps. In a series of books and in articles in the *Christian Century* and denominational journals, Dabbs brooded upon the southern past. He regarded much of it as shameful and he examined southern guilt over it, yet he remained very much a southerner proud of his family ancestry, identifying with his people, and unwilling to repudiate the past. He was prophetic, castigating "the racial sins the white South has committed," which made understandable "the justice of its being defeated and thwarted" in the Civil War. God himself had willed "that defeat and the great lessons it spread before us." He became an active supporter of the civil-rights movement, yet retained his influence among his fellow white southerners. His attempt to take in all of the southern past was reflected symbolically in his own home. Dabbs kept on his living room wall a plaque of recognition from the Detroit NAACP; hanging below it were two crossed Confederate rifles.[31]

Dabbs urged southerners, black and white, not to accept "the straight American religion" and forget the past. "It seems to me sheer waste to throw away so much only to gain—more shares in General

Motors!" The southern experience has been a tragic one, but he believed it had meaning, not only for southerners but for others as well. He argued that the South had been "a pilot project learning—at terrible expense it is true, but learning doesn't come easy—how to do within a limited area what now has to be done if civilization is to survive." The land itself had been "God's gift to the South," but it became "the Southerner's chief temptation." Southerners exploited the land and tainted it with the sin of slavery. Dabbs understood that, nonetheless, the modern South had lessons to teach on the necessity of preserving the land and of ecological sanity. The southern experience at its best had nurtured an awareness of nature. Southern whites and blacks had been farmers, attuned to nature's ways. Dabbs's first writings were on farming and later in life he frequently quoted the nature poet, Wordsworth, and came under the influence of Thoreau. For Dabbs, farming had religious significance because it nurtured an awareness of the mysteries of life. "The basic religious fact about farming," he wrote, "is the farmer's sense of dependency." Reflecting the Agrarian vision, Dabbs believed that southern farmers, black and white, despite deprivation, had led a deeply integrated life, where spiritual and material values were intertwined, where the meaning of family and work were tied intimately together. Industrialism and its attendant problems threatened the South and the nation. The South needed "men who know that machines are for human use," and that human beings "are here to live, and that life is now, infusing both the means and the ends." Dabbs projected into the future the wisdom of the southern farmer, who had continually learned nature's lessons and respected its rhythms, in a call for redemption of the land through respect for the environment. "This is my religion," he announced in a 1934 article, "the universe throbbing with life gives of this life, carelessly indeed but lavishly, to those who know and are fortunate."[32]

The South's attempt to build a biracial society had taught related lessons. Dabbs pointed out that the "Entity called the South was hammered out by black man and white man working together." The land was the setting for building a biracial community, which was at the heart of the southern way of life. The traits that distinguish those in the South as southerners, he observed, "are chiefly the result of this basic productive pattern: Whites and Negroes farming, in some sense, together." "Through the processes of history and the grace of God we have been made one people," he wrote, and now "there is no telling what great age might develop in the South." The South was destined to show the way to the rest of the world.[33]

Dabbs repeatedly reiterated "the religious significance of the Southerner's experience." If indeed the South had experience and perhaps even wisdom that might be of use to the nation, "this has happened because of the grace of God. The South has been God's project." The world itself, in a broader sense, is "God's project," he admitted, "only God's hand is more evident in the South than in most other regions." The southern church had a special responsibility to embody this understanding. The church must "make use of the cultural similarity between the races in its attempt to unveil the vision of the religious significance of race relations: to interpret the biracial South as God's Project." Writing in 1964, he charged the church with recognizing "the tragedy of Southerners," which had led, through God's grace and mercy, to the creation of "a common bond between Southern Whites and Negroes."[34]

Southerners have not, to be sure, always understood the experiences that Dabbs explored, and this is another lesson the southern civil religion can offer the nation as it sets about its renewal. The Agrarians, for example, as historian F. Garvin Davenport has pointed out, lacked a sense of irony, lacked enough detachment from the southern experience to see its true significance. Convinced of the essential virtue of the southern past, they were unable to explore fully its deeper meanings. The southern experience has been tragic, but, as Dabbs says, "there is a world of difference between failure interpreted as the experience solely of oneself or one's group and therefore implying injustice, and a failure interpreted as the human lot." The South has been aware of failure in the first sense, and that led to what Robert Penn Warren calls the Great Alibi, by which southerners have used their history as an excuse for failure to face their problems and deal with them, for nurturing arrogance and resentment.[35] The myth of a biracial South finally recognizes that the southern tragedy is symbolic of the human condition. Southern white narcissism—and American pride—must be repudiated in favor of the awareness of its common lot with the rest of humanity.

The American people as a people are notoriously ahistorical—looking toward the future, progressive, optimistic. But southerners have had a deep historical sense, which remains a valuable national resource. Robert Penn Warren has observed that a people with no sense of history "can have no sense of destiny. And what kind of society is it that has no sense of destiny and no sense of self?" The visions of the Agrarian South and the biracial South are not directly related to the myth of the Lost Cause, which once had been the source for the southern civil religion. In the course of the twentieth century the memory of Confederate defeat has been eclipsed by new dreams, which represent potential southern contributions to national recovery. Southerners who lived through the social upheaval of the civil-rights movement in the 1950s and 1960s had to struggle to seize meaning from a complicated past. To a large degree, there has been a "recovery," a reinterpretation of the spiritual meaning of southern history. Southerners who have reflected on the meaning of the South's experience when placed in transcendent perspective increasingly hope the southern past can be a resource toward not only racial reconciliation but also national ecological health. Howard Zinn long ago argued that the distinctiveness of the South was in embodying in extreme form certain national tendencies, mostly negative.[36] It may be that the South, the scene of the most dramatic changes in race relations and a radical transformation, with the move from farming to urban industrialization, in the relationship to the land, can distill its concentrated experiences into a national resource.

Robert Bellah's original article on the American civil religion pointed toward an emerging world order. Since then he has argued that a new vision of mankind, a new sense of human connection and possibility in an international context, would emerge in the late twentieth century. The modern southern civil religion suggests that the American recovery of meaning must not overlook regional and local resources as well. The American environmental and social justice crises of the late twentieth century are part of a broader international crisis of meaning. The South's struggle to build a biracial society, in particular, will be of special meaning as Americans approach the Third World. Martin Luther King, Jr., while founding his vision on the experience of Montgomery and Selma, nonetheless understood the relationship between the civil-rights movement in the South and the liberation movements in the developing nations. Such blendings of localism and universalism have continuing relevance in American life. As southern blacks and whites have created elements of a common culture in the South despite the residue of segregation, the story of that attempt to forge a biracial society, out of fear and suffering, despite greed and exploitation, and with sacrifice and inevitable struggle, may help American society recover a sense of meaning as it faces the future and faces the world.

NOTES

1. Robert N. Bellah, *The Broken Covenant: American Civil Religion in Time of Trial* (New York: The Seabury Press, 1975), p. 145; John Wilson, *Public Reli-*

gion in American Culture (Philadelphia: Temple University Press, 1979), pp. 20, 21.

2. George Tindall, *The Ethnic Southerners* (Baton Rouge: Louisiana State University Press, 1976), p. 23.

3. Charles Reagan Wilson, *Baptized in Blood: The Religion of the Lost Cause, 1865–1920* (Athens: University of Georgia Press, 1980); C. Vann Woodward, *The Burden of Southern History* (Baton Rouge: Louisiana State University Press, 1960).

4. The religion of the Lost Cause was the most important manifestation of regional religious patriotism in the South, but the full history of the southern civil religion would include such topics as the founding of Jamestown, the myth of a colonial Eden, the southern role in the American Revolution, the sectional-national antebellum dichotomy, the southern role in national wars, and southern ideas on regional destiny.

5. Wilson, *Baptized in Blood,* chap. 8; John Shelton Reed, *Southerners: The Social Psychology of Sectionalism* (Chapel Hill: University of North Carolina Press, 1983), pp. 85–91.

6. W. J. Cash, *The Mind of the South* (New York: Alfred A. Knopf, 1941), p. 392; Allen Tate, *Essays of Four Decades* (Chicago: Swallow Press, 1968), p. 592; Thomas L. Connelly and Barbara L. Bellows, *God and General Longstreet: The Lost Cause and the Southern Mind* (Baton Rouge: Louisiana State University Press, 1982), pp. 107–13, 121–27; C. Hugh Holman, *The Immoderate Past: The Southern Writer and History* (Athens: University of Georgia Press, 1977), p. 39; Daniel Aaron, *The Unwritten War: American Writers and the Civil War* (Oxford: Oxford University Press, 1973), pp. 327–42.

7. Holman, *Immoderate Past,* p. 96.

8. Tindall, *Ethnic Southerners,* pp. 43–58.

9. Allen Tate, "Ode to the Confederate Dead," in *Poems: 1928–1931* (New York: Charles Scribner's, 1932), p. 50.

10. Allen Tate, "Remarks on the Southern Religion," in Twelve Southerners, *I'll Take My Stand: The South and the Agrarian Tradition* (Baton Rouge: Louisiana State University Press, 1930), p. 174.

11. Daniel Joseph Singal, *The War Within: From Victorian to Modernist Thought in the South, 1919–1945* (Chapel Hill: University of North Carolina Press, 1982), pp. 232–60; Fred Hobson, *Tell about the South: The Southern Rage to Explain* (Baton Rouge: Louisiana State University Press, 1983), pp. 204–5; Louis D. Rubin, Jr., *The Writer in the South: Studies in a Literary Community* (Athens: University of Georgia Press, 1977), pp. 91–93; Connelly and Bellows, *God and General Longstreet,* p. 137.

12. Lewis P. Simpson, "Southern Spiritual Nationalism: Notes on the Background of Modern Southern Fiction," in *The Cry of Home: Cultural Nationalism and the Modern Writer,* ed. H. Ernest Lewald (Knoxville: University of Tennessee Press, 1972), pp. 190, 206.

13. Walker Percy, "Red, White and Blue-Gray," *Commonweal,* Dec. 22, 1961, p. 338; Walter Lord, *The Past That Would Not Die* (New York: Pocket Books, 1967), pp. 31, 63, 134, 137, 178; James W. Silver, *Mississippi: The Closed Society*

(New York: Harcourt Brace and World, Inc., 1963), p. 5; Connelly and Bellows, *God and General Longstreet*, pp. 117–19; Numan V. Bartley, *The Rise of Massive Resistance: Race and Politics in the South during the 1950s* (Baton Rouge: Louisiana State University Press, 1969), third illustration.

14. The University of Mississippi never officially adopted the Confederate battle flag as the school symbol, but its use was encouraged from 1948 on, especially after the home economics department there made the largest battle flag in the world in 1949.

15. William Faulkner, *Requiem for a Nun* (New York: Vintage Edition, 1975), p. 212; Connelly and Bellows, *God and General Longstreet*, pp. 113–19.

16. Robert Penn Warren, *The Legacy of the Civil War: Meditations on the Centennial* (New York: Random House, 1961), pp. 54, 57.

17. Percy, "Red, White and Blue-Gray," p. 338.

18. Walker Percy, *The Last Gentleman* (New York: Farrar, Straus and Giroux, 1966), pp. 236–37; J. O. Tate, "Civility, Civil Rights, and Civil Wars: Walker Percy's Centennial Novel," in *Perspectives on the American South*, ed. James C. Cobb and Charles R. Wilson, vol. 4 (New York: Gordon and Breach, 1985).

19. See Reed, *Southerners*, pp. 86–87; Connelly and Bellows, *God and General Longstreet*, pp. 137–48; Thomas L. Connelly, *Will Campbell and the Soul of the South* (New York: Continuum, 1982).

20. Reed, *Southerners*, pp. 87–91.

21. Samuel S. Hill, Jr., Edgar T. Thompson, Anne Firor Scott, Charles Hudson, and Edwin S. Gaustad, *Religion in the Solid South* (Nashville: Abingdon Press, 1972), p. 29; Lord, *Past That Would Not Die*, pp. 77–78; Silver, *Mississippi*, pp. 26, 27.

22. Richard M. Weaver, "The South and the American Union," in *The Lasting South: Fourteen Southerners Look at Their Home*, ed. Louis D. Rubin, Jr., and James J. Kilpatrick (Chicago: Henry Regnery Co., 1957), p. 64; Rubin, *Writer in the South*, pp. 91–92.

23. Frank Lawrence Owsley, "The Irrepressible Conflict," in *I'll Take My Stand*, p. 66; John Shelton Reed, "For Dixieland: The Sectionalism of *I'll Take My Stand*," in *A Band of Prophets: The Vanderbilt Agrarians after Fifty Years*, ed. William C. Havard and Walter Sullivan (Baton Rouge: Louisiana State University Press, 1982), pp. 46, 48, 54.

24. Reed, "For Dixieland," p. 57; Hobson, *Tell about the South*, pp. 329, 333; Richard M. Weaver, *The Southern Tradition at Bar: A History of Postbellum Thought* (New Rochelle, N.Y.: Arlington House, 1968), p. 391.

25. Leslie W. Dunbar, "The Annealing of the South," *Virginia Quarterly Review* 37 (Autumn 1961): 507; Morton Sosna, *In Search of the Silent South: Southern Liberals and the Race Issue* (New York: Columbia University Press, 1977), pp. 201, 207; Charles L. Black, Jr., "Paths to Desegregation," *New Republic*, Oct. 21, 1957, p. 15.

26. Sosna, *In Search of the Silent South*, pp. 173–74, 201, 197, 208–9. These liberals frequently had conversion experiences, born again into the belief in brotherhood. See Will D. Campbell, *Brother to a Dragonfly* (New York: Continuum, 1980), pp. 98–99.

27. Richard H. King, "Stoking the Fires or Polishing the Pinnacles," in *Perspectives on the American South,* ed. John Shelton Reed and Merle Black, vol. 2 (New York: Gordon and Breach, 1984), pp. 61–72; Woodward, *Burden of Southern History,* pp. 3–26, 187–212.

28. Martin Luther King, Jr., *The Wisdom of Martin Luther King: In His Own Words* (New York: Lancer Books, 1968), pp. 41, 23, 64, 75; Martin Luther King, Jr., *Why We Can't Wait* (New York: Harper & Row, 1963), p. 80.

29. King, *Why We Can't Wait,* p. 116; King, *Wisdom of King,* p. 77; *New York Times,* Aug. 28, 1983, p. 16.

30. See John Shelton Reed, "Up from Segregation," *Virginia Quarterly Review* 60 (Summer 1984): 378, 391–93; "The South Today: Carter Country and Beyond," *Time,* Sept. 27, 1976.

31. James McBride Dabbs, *Who Speaks for the South?* (New York: Funk and Wagnalls, 1964), pp. 343–44; Robert M. Randolph, "James McBride Dabbs: Spokesman for Racial Liberalism," in *From the Old South to the New: Essays on the Transitional South,* ed. Walter J. Fraser, Jr., and Winfred B. Morre, Jr. (Westport, Conn.: Greenwood Press, 1981), pp. 254–56; Hobson, *Tell about the South,* pp. 335–52; Charles P. Roland, *The Improbable Era: The South since World War II* (Lexington: University Press of Kentucky, 1976), p. 191.

32. Dabbs, *Who Speaks for the South?* pp. 369, 371; Dabbs, *Haunted by God* (Richmond: John Knox Press, 1972), p. 40; Dabbs, "The Religion of a Countryman," *Forum* 91 (May 1934): 305–9; Dabbs, "The Land," in Rubin and Kilpatrick, *Lasting South,* pp. 79–80, 83.

33. Dabbs, *Who Speaks for the South?* p. 368; Dabbs, "The Land," p. 78; Dabbs, *The Southern Heritage* (New York: Alfred A. Knopf, 1958), pp. 267–68.

34. Dabbs, *Who Speaks for the South?* pp. 371–73, 377.

35. F. Garvin Davenport, Jr., *The Myth of Southern History: Historical Consciousness in Twentieth-Century Southern Literature* (Nashville: Vanderbilt University Press, 1967), p. 188; Dabbs, *Who Speaks for the South?* p. 370; Warren, *Legacy of the Civil War,* pp. 54–58.

36. Robert Penn Warren, *Democracy and Poetry* (Cambridge: Harvard University Press, 1975), p. 56; Howard Zinn, *The Southern Mystique* (New York: Simon and Schuster, 1964).

Roland A. Delattre

Supply-Side Spirituality:
A Case Study in the Cultural Interpretation of Religious Ethics in America

This essay is addressed to more than one kind of recovery, but primarily to a recovery of neglected resources and patterns of religious ethics among Americans, by recognizing their cultural importance and by drawing them into visibility as part of the account we give of religious ethics in American society. A cultural approach to religious ethics will give attention to dimensions of American culture and features of religious ethics sometimes overlooked or underestimated by more philosophical or theological, more sociological or more strictly historical approaches. It must begin by characterizing the essential features of the cultural interpretation through which to contribute to the recovery of a richer account than heretofore of religious ethics in the life of Americans.

Because it will take more than a single essay to make good on the promises represented by that program for cultural interpretation, the bulk of this essay will concentrate on a single case study as an illustration of the approach, focusing upon the emergence of what might be called "supply-side spirituality"—an important kind of religious response to the expectation, the experience, and the imagination of abundance that comes, in the course of the nineteenth century, to gain huge cultural force among many Americans and to gather around itself such a powerful cluster of other cultural themes that one can properly speak of a culture of abundance. Both the culture of abundance and supply-side spirituality have, in the course of the twentieth century, gained rather than lost significance as powerful crystallizations of values and commitments among at least the dominant two-thirds of American society. Ralph Waldo Emerson will figure prominently in this portion of the account, for he is still a benchmark figure on the American cultural landscape and remains the most representative voice for a kind of spirituality that informs the way millions of Americans today no less than yesterday are reflective—when and as they are reflective—about the moral life.

I

In order to recover a richer sense of the place of religious ethics in the lives of Americans, the range of what counts as religious ethics needs to be broadened. Toward this end, one might apply to religious ethics an analogy invoked by Larzer Ziff in a recent study of American literature: "Just as [in physics] mass is finally inseparable from its field of forces because it is fundamentally an intense form of the energy that surrounds it, so, I believe, literature is a particular concentration of cultural forces continuous with, rather than apart from society." [1] In the same spirit, religious ethics can be seen as continuous with and as an intense form of the cultural energies that surround it—energies that may already be charged with religious meaning. Those energies are embodied in socially available systems of significance upon which people draw as they seek to make sense of their world and of their own experience, often modifying those symbolic resources in the process.

What culture is about is making sense, something people do individually and collectively with only more or less success. For Americans as for others in the world, success in this sense-making enterprise is complicated by the plurality and sometimes considerable diversity of the several cultural worlds or universes of meaning through which each must make a way. To the extent that one is more rather than less successful, what the process yields is orientation and a framework of interpretation. Alternatively, one is left more or less in a state of disorientation and with little perspective on our experience. The work of cultural interpretation is simply to press that sense-making process a little more deliberately and systematically. Ethics—religious or otherwise—is concerned with the moral dimensions of this sense-making process, and it proceeds by critical reflection upon what it is that renders morally persuasive particular versions of reality and humanity, particular modes of orientation in the world.

Many of the most powerful and socially available systems of significance and cultural themes upon which Americans draw to make sense of their lives and inform their behavior are at least tinged if not saturated with religious meaning. Ethics is a critical feature of both religion and culture insofar as people are reflective about their lives. As Clifford Geertz observes, the heart of a religious perspective is "the conviction that the values one holds are grounded in the structures of reality. . . . What sacred symbols do for those to whom they are sacred is to formulate an image of the world's construction and a program for human conduct that are mere reflexes of one another." [2]

In offering a cultural interpretation of religious ethics, I use "culture" here in this Geertzian sense of the symbolic forms and processes upon which people draw in developing a more or less articulate sense of how things are (call it a "sense of reality") and of what it is to be properly human (call it a "sense of humanity"), together with ritual action through which they render affectively persuasive the correspondence between their sense of reality and of humanity. Culture, then, operates very much in performative terms as a process of attunement, as strategy, as continual negotiation of a passage through the world. Ritual takes on a high priority for both cultural interpretation and religious ethics in this, for it is very largely in ritual performance and gesture that a people renders articulate the life of feeling and the structures of feeling that lie beneath both thought and action, conception and behavior, and renders affectively persuasive the sense that the way they do things is in accord with the way things really are, accomplishing all this through—to use Suzanne Langer's fine definition of ritual—"the disciplined rehearsal of right attitudes."[3]

The cultural interpretation of religious ethics proposed here involves asking at least four kinds of questions—questions about cultural geography, cultural aesthetics, cultural politics, and cultural embodiment—and these four kinds of questions bear some explanation.

1. *Cultural geography* involves approaching the regions of experience as cartographers, asking: What is the lay of the symbolic landscape? What are the significant boundaries and how are they symbolized and negotiated—boundaries, for example, between sacred and profane, private and public, masculine and feminine, production and consumption, leisure and work? What are the major landmarks or benchmarks on the symbolic landscape that provide orientation? How are the various regions of experience related to one another? Which among those regions of experience are most culturally powerful? And where are the role models for the well-lived life? What narratives are being enacted and told by those who occupy this cultural place? And what cultural features shape the choreography or flow of human activity? By what rituals do people mark out significant times and places and occasions?

2. *Cultural aesthetics* recognizes that all experience has an aesthetic component, not just discrete "aesthetic" or artistic experience. It attends to the life of feeling and the affections as fundamental to the moral life, as essential to the capacity for valuation, and asks: How do people feel about and evaluate themselves and their circumstances? What are the culturally available ways of registering and of channel-

ing feelings? What are the culturally prominent and formative patterns of negative and positive affections? Of appreciation and depreciation? Cultural aesthetics includes an erotics of culture, asking, for example, what arouses interest and attracts attention? What generates excitement and mobilizes energies?

3. *Cultural politics* recognizes that power as well as meaning is at stake in cultural affairs, that symbolic activity involves the attribution of power to persons, places, things, times, events, or situations. It asks how is power, especially sacred power, envisaged? How is the play for power and influence culturally evident? How are the symbols of power and authority distributed, and who has access to them, and how?

4. *Cultural embodiment* is a subject for which there is no conventional term like geography, aesthetics, and politics, but it is an essential subject for both cultural interpretation and ethics. Cultural processes are not disembodied or free-floating, but are physically embodied in human bodies, in the natural world as that is marked by human presence, and in the artifactual world of things we make and use and enjoy. Without minimizing the importance of the ecological connection with the natural world or of the social fabric in this context, it is important nonetheless to emphasize—because they are more commonly neglected in religious ethics—the embodiment of culture in human bodies and in artifacts and to ask in what ways the human body of moral agents participates in the fabric of meaning? What is the body's share in the costs and benefits of a particular cultural version of reality and of being human? How are cultural values and commitments incorporated—that is, taken into or imposed upon and expressed through bodies? And finally, how is a culture articulate in and through its artifacts—its buildings, vehicles of transportation and communication, clothing, foodways, and so on?

These sets of interpretive questions must be kept in mind, for they are at least implicit in the following discussion of supply-side spirituality, and they return more explicitly as a cultural interpretation of religious ethics in America proceeds.

II

"Supply-side spirituality" is a powerful but often overlooked cluster of cultural themes that have been drawn upon and developed in quite diverse but kindred ways for a broad range of religious options among Americans. The most important and distinguishing of those themes is the assumption that abundance (variously interpreted) rather than scarcity, plenty rather than poverty, is the destiny of Americans (when religiously interpreted) as spiritual children of God. Although it has some affinities with supply-side economics, the inspiration for the phrase "supply-side spirituality" is rather the prominence of the term "supply" in the vocabulary of some of those to whom the phrase can be applied.

It is not until the early twentieth century that there appears a professional economist, Simon Patten, whose entire career as an economist is based on the assumption of abundance rather than scarcity.[4] One would expect the "dismal science" to be slow to take abundance as an assumption, but by the mid-nineteenth century the assumption of abundance as something to be expected as normal, if one but took advantage of the opportunities presented by conditions in America, was becoming a major theme in the dominant—not uncontested, but dominant—cultural version of what America was all about. By the end of the nineteenth century, that culture of abundance was rapidly becoming also a culture of consumption—one in which the critical symbolic resources for personal orientation were more a function of one's relation to the activities and processes of consumption than to those of production. Supply-side spirituality represents in part— though at its center—a religious appropriation and amplification of themes that were developing also, though sometimes quite differently, in the wider and socially dominant culture of abundance. It is incomprehensible apart from that cultural context, though it is not simply or solely a function of that culture.

Supply-side spirituality makes for a good case study in the cultural interpretation of religious ethics in America, for while it does find expression in highly institutionalized forms, it more commonly manifests itself as a part of a strong American tradition of extra-institutional, minimally institutional, and even anti-institutional spirituality and piety. It takes a cultural interpretation to draw such forms of spirituality into visibility and to portray adequately their place in the sometimes inarticulate but deeply felt set of moral commitments of people attracted by some variety of supply-side spirituality. Recovery of awareness of how these people and movements have sought to make religious sense of their experience and to provide spiritual guidance for themselves and others will enrich our understanding of the dynamics of religion in American life. If properly undertaken, the inquiry may also contribute to American moral and spiritual resourcefulness by illuminating both the possibilities and the liabilities of a religious ethic grounded in supply-side spirituality.

A wide variety of moral and ethical as well as spiritual options are opened up by commitment to the assumption of abundance as a birthright, depending upon which of the other themes, among the set of themes called "supply-side spirituality," are appropriated and developed in association with the central one of abundance. Among these other themes are a positive rather than a negative image of humanity, an attention to physical as well as spiritual health, energy, and power, and a recommended way of life that is affirmative, optimistic, expectant, energetic, and confident.

Some of the ingredients of supply-side spirituality have a much longer history, as part of quite different cultural patterns, but I wish to concentrate here on a mode of spirituality that begins to challenge previously dominant cultural and religious patterns only during the past 150 years, with selective attention paid to its most striking nineteenth-century versions, which run across a broad spectrum from the highly individualistic New Thought movements[5] to Mormonism and the utopian socialism of Edward Bellamy. Versions of more contemporary origin also range widely, from *est* (Erhard Seminars Training)[6] and evangelist Robert Schuller's "possibility thinking"[7] to the quite-different "creation spirituality" of the Dominican Matthew Fox.[8] As these examples suggest, the range of cultural themes and religious options which can be included under "supply-side spirituality" is broader than those Sydney Ahlstrom refers to so aptly as "harmonial religion"[9] or than those Donald Meyer associates with the "positive thinkers" from Mary Baker Eddy to Norman Vincent Peale and Oral Roberts,[10] though supply-side spirituality involves both the harmonial vision and the positive psychological strategies to which Ahlstrom and Meyer direct attention. Furthermore, supply-side spirituality appeals in various ways to millions of Americans who do not identify with any of these benchmark figures and movements, answering their fears and hopes and informing their piety in significant ways, whatever may be their institutional religious location (if any).

The fountainhead of supply-side spirituality is Ralph Waldo Emerson, who sets forth its themes in protean forms that multiply already in his own mind and continue to provide inspiration to his spiritual descendants for generations. One cannot reduce Emerson to the terms of supply-side spirituality, of course, because he is, after all, the inspiration for so much, but he does contribute in a decisive way to this tradition. Emerson lived in expectation of an abundant supply to meet both the spiritual and material needs of the new nation, if it would but seize the opportunity opened up for nation and individual by the American experiment. He sought to break the intimidating grip of received creeds and institutions, asking that people recognize and affirm with confidence their own importance and the readiness of the environing universe to respond to the dazzling possibilities for fulfilment that are the birthright of every American individual. The greatness of Jesus, Emerson informed the graduating class at Harvard Divinity School in 1838, was that "alone in all history he truly estimated the greatness of man."[11] It was man's potential for divinity rather than his inclination to sin that Emerson asked them to go forth and preach. And that potential lay immediately to hand, for it was within every individual—a resident source of power and spiritual realization identical with divinity, with God. To the self-reliant soul an inexhaustible supply of possibilities and satisfactions is open, precisely because such true self-reliance is really God-reliance. The great long-kept secret is out: the highest power of the universe dwells as a liberating and creative power within every soul.

Early and late, in "Nature" (published in 1836) as well as in *The Conduct of Life* (lectures from the 1850s published in 1860), and especially in the lecture on "Wealth" included in the latter volume, Emerson displays a conviction of humanity's entitlement to abundance—to a vast supply of spiritual abundance from within and a corresponding cultural and material abundance drawn from nature by the masterful application to it of the human spirit—that is, of the divine spirit that dwells in every individual. Emerson never entirely shakes off a profound ambivalence about the transformation of his society into a commercial market economy, but the ascending note in Emerson is one of spiritualized celebration of our entitlement to abundance. As is true of other subjects as well, Emerson's importance here is his extraordinary gift for rendering articulate—both reflecting and nourishing—the emergence of supply-side spirituality as an important theme in American culture.

This is clear even in a consideration of only two texts mentioned, "Nature" and "Wealth." The title of the former is "Nature," but the subject is the triumphal celebration of the prospects of enjoying an affirmative and prosperous as well as an "original relation to the universe." Positioning himself in the woods, openly delighting in the natural world, Emerson confesses: "I become a transparent eyeball; I am nothing; I see all; the currents of the Universal Being circulate through me; I am part or parcel of God." What he gives in one phrase, he takes back in the next, and accordingly quickly adds "that the power to produce this delight does not reside in nature, but in man, or in a harmony of both." That harmony, what he later calls "that wonderful congruity . . . between man and the world," is said to subsist because man is "the head and heart" of the world and therefore its lord, through whom the world, "a remoter and inferior incarnation of God," comes into its own. "The Supreme Being," Emerson tells us, "does not build up nature around us, but puts it forth through us." And in that enterprise we are "nourished by unfailing fountains" and have at our disposal "inexhaustible power." "Who can set bounds to the possibilities of man?" so conceived, he asks, and in the concluding paragraph of the essay, having reminded the reader that "the world exists for you," Emerson invites him to "build therefore your own world. As fast as you conform your life to the pure idea in your mind, that will unfold its great proportions. A correspondent revolution in things will attend the influx of the spirit," culminating in the prospect of "the kingdom of man over nature . . . a dominion such as now is beyond his dream of God."[12]

The lecture on "Wealth" is in the same spirit, but more explicit. No man, the audience is told, can "do justice to his genius without making some larger demand on the world than a bare subsistence. He is by constitution expensive, and needs to be rich." Indeed "he is born to be rich." Explicitly rejecting the advice of those like Thoreau who sought well-being by reducing their wants, Emerson proceeds to celebrate the man who "is tempted out by his appetites and fancies to the conquest of this and that piece of culture, until he finds his well-being in the use of his planet, and"—in a rhetorical flourish that is ominously prophetic of a later century—"of more planets than his own." "Man was born to be rich, or inevitably grows rich by the use of his faculties; by the union of thought with nature." "Open the doors of opportunity to talent and virtue and . . . property will not be in bad hands. In a free and just commonwealth, property rushes from the idle and imbecile to the industrious, brave and persevering. . . . The level of the sea is not more surely kept than is the equilibrium of value in society by the demand and supply; and artifice or legislation punishes itself by reactions, gluts and bankruptcies." The doctrine and the promise are of course spiritualized. The essay concludes: "The true thrift is always to spend on the higher plane; to invest and invest, with keener avarice, that he may spend in spiritual creation and not in augmenting [mere] animal existence."[13]

The most successful of several New Thought movements to embody this doctrine of abundance was the Unity School of Christianity, founded by Charles and Myrtle Fillmore in 1889.[14] Unity has not sought to develop in the conventional pattern of an institutional structure with local congregations, though there are by now several hundred local Unity Centers with regular services of worship. But Unity has developed primarily through its ministry of prayer and publications and retreats, served by a large staff at its headquarters in Unity Village near Kansas City, Missouri. Its magazines, including *Thought* and *Unity*, and its monthly devotional guide, *Daily Word*, reach hundreds of thousands if not millions of Americans regularly, and thousands correspond every day or join in prayer through a program called Silent Unity. Unity teaches that goodness, health, and prosperity rather than sin, pain, and poverty are the natural condition of humanity and the companions of true spirituality. As one sympathetic interpreter (James Freeman) said of Charles Fillmore, "he felt it is as right for men to have an alert mind, a healthy body, and prosperity in their affairs as it is for them to be spiritual. He felt that men are meant to live abundantly on all levels of their being; that it is God's will for them to be strong and vigorous and rich and successful and happy." [15]

Two themes are central to Unity's teaching and practice—health and prosperity. Each day at the Unity School a special period of prayer is devoted to healing and another to prosperity. Unity teaches that a proper consciousness, an awareness of God as the source of all supply, is the key to realizing perfect health and prosperity. Similarly, a typical day's reading in *Daily Word* begins with the affirmation "God has established perfect health in man; I am renewed, energized, and made well," followed by a prayer or set of further affirmations on the theme of "perfect health" (4 Jan. 1984). The next day's devotion begins with the affirmation "God is doing a good work for me; I am prospered and enriched," followed by a prayer or set of affirmations on the theme of "prosperity." Sometimes the subject of the prayer/affirmations for a day is "Supply," beginning with an affirmation such as this one: "The flow of God's supply is inexhaustible, unending," which continues in part, "When we are in the flow of divine supply we are not anxious about our lives and affairs. We have faith in God to provide our needs. . . . for our heavenly Father knows our needs. We are to seek first the kingdom of God and His righteousness. As we seek the kingdom of God within us, we feel our oneness with the divine source of all that appears. We are enriched and prospered" (21 Sept. 1984). Another reading on the theme of prosperity says in part: "I think of myself as a child of God, heir to all the riches of the kingdom. This is the truth about me. I know that I am worthy of abundance. I am willing to act in faith to claim that which the Father has already provided for me. I am uplifted and happy right now, and my prosperity is assured" (3 Nov. 1982). The form of these prayers is more affirmation than petition and, of course, requires action in conformity with what is affirmed. But affirmations are the key to right action. [16]

One of Charles Fillmore's most popular articles, often reprinted in

Unity magazine and then as a pamphlet, was "Overcoming the Poverty Idea," in which the biblical David is portrayed as slaying the Goliath of giant errors with five stones of truth, of which the last three are these affirmations:

> My own shall, by the sure and certain law of God, come to me, and I now welcome it in the presence of this clear perception of Truth.
> I am under obligations to no one. God, my opulent Father, has poured out to me all resource, and I am a mighty river of affluence and abundance.
> My bounty is so great that men marvel at its sumptuous abundance. I own nothing selfishly, yet all things in existence are mine to use and, in divine wisdom, to bestow upon others.[17]

There is some ambiguity throughout these texts about the relation between spiritual and material abundance and supply. But what is interesting and what justifies the rubric "supply-side spirituality" is the conviction that abundance rather than scarcity is natural, that anything less is an unnatural condition that can be overcome through the right application of a spiritual power, and that such power is at human disposal.

If Unity is the most successful movement of its kind, Ralph Waldo Trine is the quintessential supply-sider of a kindred spirituality, among the first in what is by now nearly a century-long line of enormously popular writers of optimistic inspirational literature. He hit full stride in 1897 with the publication of his classic statement, *In Tune with the Infinite*, subtitled *Fullness of Peace, Power and Plenty*. It is addressed, as he tells us in the preface, to the fears and hopes of all who "in this busy work-a-day world of ours, would exchange impotence for power, weakness and suffering for abounding health and strength, pain and unrest for perfect peace, poverty of whatever nature for fullness and plenty."[18]

Trine's message is that "there is a divine sequence running throughout the universe" and that "to come into harmony with it and thereby with all the higher laws and forces . . . is to come into possession of unknown riches, into the realization of undreamed-of powers." This is possible because one's real life is identical with the life of God, the "Spirit of Infinite Life and Power" which is "the great central fact of the universe." To the degree that people come into a "vital realization of our oneness with this Infinite Life" and "open ourselves to this divine inflow we are changed from mere men into God-men," and "no one can set limitations to a man or a woman of this type." In a chapter on "Fullness of life—bodily health and vigor" the reader is assured that "full, rich, and abounding health is the normal and the natural condition of life. Anything else is an abnormal condition, and abnormal conditions as a rule come through perversions. God never created sickness, suffering, and disease; they are man's own creations. They come through his violating the laws under which he lives." But he who is not perverse, who lives in the realization of his oneness with "the Spirit of Infinite Plenty, the Power that has brought, that is continually bringing, all things into expression in material form . . . becomes a magnet to attract to himself a continual supply of whatsoever things he desires." Indeed, a chapter on "Plenty of all things—the law of prosperity" announces that "Opulence is the law of the universe, an abundant supply for every need if nothing is put in the way of its coming. The natural and the normal life for us is this,—To have such a fullness of life and power by living so continually in the realization of our oneness with the Infinite Life and Power that we find ourselves in the constant possession of an abundant supply of all things needed." [19]

Trine's message presupposes and gives spiritual validation to a conviction of entitlement to abundance, something to which Americans in the late nineteenth century were increasingly responsive, despite fears and apprehensions that they themselves as individuals would not be among its beneficiaries. Trine specifically attacks the notion that godliness and poverty somehow belong together. Such a notion has no basis in fact, he says, and is, like the idea of asceticism, the product of an age in which it was believed that "there was necessarily a warfare between the flesh and the spirit." On the contrary, he assures, "opulence is the law of the universe," and when the demand is rightly and wisely made, "the supply is always equal to the demand." [20] Such is the power of true spiritual consciousness and the effectiveness of the law of attraction. All of this, of course, is quite different from the conception of entitlement built into the Protestant work ethic.

The dominant forms of supply-side spirituality are highly individualistic, but there are more communitarian and even collectivist versions as well. Of these, two—a major religious movement, the Mormons, and an influential author, Edward Bellamy—are illustrative of the range of those in nineteenth-century America who assume and find spiritual authority for the assumption of an entitlement or birthright to abundance, both spiritual and material, for the saints, variously identified.

The Mormon departure from Christian orthodoxy is no less radical than that of Emerson, and it is no less impossible to imagine it emerging out of any other context than that of early nineteenth-century

Protestant America. And, like Emerson, who scandalized even the Unitarians at first and yet came to be embraced as the chief spokesman for a powerful stream of American spirituality, so also, though in a quite different way, the Mormons began by scandalizing nearly everyone around them and yet came by mid-twentieth-century to be widely respected by non-Mormon Americans as an admirable if not indeed quintessential embodiment of a whole cluster of convictions and behavior patterns regarded as central to the mainstream of American culture. The relation of Mormonism to American culture in general is fascinating and complex, and has been the subject of several recent books. Here the focus is on only one aspect of that relationship, having to do with supply-side spirituality.[21]

According to Mormon theology, God is not the creator of the world but its master, and God's mastery of himself and of his world sets the pattern for the saints who are called to follow the path of God, who is envisaged in radically anthropomorphic terms. Every individual is free to follow that path of perfectibility, a path of self-improvement, mastery, and organization of the natural world, following a trajectory that Thomas O'Dea has described as a "spiritualization of materialism" and a "transcendentalism of achievement."[22] Nothing short of deification is the ultimate promise to those who persist in faithful application of knowledge, energy, and perfect will, for, as Joseph Smith himself announced in April 1844: "God himself was once as we are now, and is an exalted man, and sits enthroned in yonder heavens! That is the great secret. If the vail were rent today . . . you would see him like a man in form. . . . God . . . was once a man like us . . . and you have got to be Gods yourselves, and to be kings and priests to God, the same as all Gods have done before you, namely by going from one small degree to another, and from a small capacity to a great one."[23] That drama of salvation, which began before birth into this world, will continue beyond life in this world, and the prospect for abundant realization and entry into the Kingdom is assured by the pioneer achievement of God and the example of Jesus Christ, "which is the power of God unto salvation."[24] This is but one aspect of the Mormon religion, but it is an important one, and it represents a significant and powerful expression of supply-side spirituality.

Edward Bellamy's utopian novel, *Looking Backward: 2000–1887*, published in 1888, represents another exemplary case of supply-side spirituality. The spiritual vision to which it gives expression is quite different from that of New Thought and the Unity School of Christianity, yet it bore sufficient kinship with them for Charles Fillmore to include excerpts from it in the new magazine he launched in 1889 called *Modern Thought*. Bellamy's vision is of a world in which self-reliant individualism is displaced by a socialized conception of self realizing its full humanity and its "solidarity with the universe" through social solidarity. Already in 1874 Bellamy had formulated his thoughts on such themes as this in an unpublished essay on "The Religion of Humanity."[25] *Looking Backward* became, as Cecelia Tichi puts it in her introduction to a recent edition of the book, "an American cultural landmark, a book that speaks directly to the anguish and the hopes of its own age, and which also embodies the sustaining myths of the nation of its origin."[26] In his novel, Bellamy expresses a vision of a Christian socialist America in which material abundance and leisure are placed on a par with social harmony and full employment. Indeed, thanks to the efficiency of a well-managed industrial army and an egalitarian social system assuring a steady flow of abundance to all and immoderate possession to none, the focus of the novel is upon the wonders of a consumer paradise of leisure, recreation, and enjoyment, facilitated by giant department stores, garden cities, credit cards, and electronic communication (even sermons) brought into the home. Recognizing that the ancient demand for "bread and circuses" is a "wholly reasonable demand" and that if bread is the first necessity of life, recreation is a close second, provision is made, through a triumph of scientific management, efficiency, and the cultivation of appropriate social sentiments, for normal retirement from productive labor at age forty-five in order to "renew our youth" and enjoy a citizen's birthright—the leisure to "devote ourselves to intellectual and spiritual enjoyments and pursuits which alone mean life."[27] Bellamy's novel is significant as a manifestation of supply-side spirituality because it was so enthusiastically received by millions of readers, many of whom were led to form Bellamy clubs across the nation and to follow Bellamy into the reform politics of the Nationalist movement and Populist party.

III

To those who do not share their faith, these varieties of supply-side spirituality may seem strange and exotic, but here the interest is less in their distinctiveness than in their connections with major currents in American culture. Those connections are substantial and supply-side spirituality enters in some measure into the lives and figures in the moral reflections of a good percentage of those in the dominant two-thirds of American society—those who share in the culture of abundance and consumption. A cultural interpretation brings out the broad connection posited here among the five figures and movements offered as representative of some of the varieties of supply-side spirituality: Emerson, Unity School, Trine, the Mormons, and Bellamy. They are in some ways quite diverse, but they have in common a spiritual development of the cultural assumption and expectation of abundance. Because some form of that cultural theme of abundance and its spiritual development plays a part in the lives of millions of Americans who do not associate themselves with these five figures and movements, studying them can illuminate a much wider cultural and religious landscape, and can yield a keener sense of the possibilities and liabilities of a way of approaching and doing religious ethics that is persuasive in some significant measure for many Americans.

The connections as well as the diversity among these figures and movements may be made more evident by taking up the four kinds of questions identified as important for a cultural interpretation of religious ethics, questions which have not been dealt with explicitly in the preceding sketches. What light do those questions shed on the representative variety of supply-side spirituality just presented? With these questions as a guide, it is possible even in this brief essay to expand upon the earlier suggestion that among the themes commonly associated with the central one of abundance by supply-side spirituality are a positive rather than a negative image of humanity; attention to physical as well as spiritual health, energy, and power; and a recommended way of life that is affirmative, optimistic, expectant, energetic, and confident.

Cultural geography: All five versions of supply-side spirituality move within a cultural landscape rich with the promise of abundance, and in their different ways envisage a physical landscape marked by human activity and transformed thereby into a domesticated place of habitation—whether a desert wilderness irrigated and cultivated into a garden, something Emerson envisaged and the Mormons practiced, or an urban paradise à la Bellamy. Both Unity School and Trine, like other New Thought movements, have been most persuasive among those who faced the promise and the perils of a growing urban middle class. It may be worth noting that Charles Fillmore's worldly success, uneven as it was, came as a real estate developer in Kansas City.

All five of these figures and movements articulate a vision of abundance symbolically related to a powerful cultural and religious theme about America as a special place—a new and sacred place, a new world, a setting in which to do new things in new ways, a place for spiritual renewal and for a new way of life flowing out of that renewal. Emerson's writings reflect a deep commitment to this theme. For Mormons, sacred time is restored in the age of latter-day saints, and sacred space comes to be centered around the temple at Salt Lake City, the New Jerusalem, through which now passes, by divine dispensation, the *axis mundi*. It comes naturally to Bellamy to imagine a secularized version of the heavenly city as a transformed Boston at the end of the twentieth century. And it seems no less natural and appropriate to the Fillmores that Unity School of Christianity and its activities be centered in and near Kansas City, on the great heartland plains of America.

The moral and spiritual landscape of supply-side spirituality is charted by all five figures and movements in ways that reflect a readiness, first and most audaciously expressed by Joseph Smith and by Emerson, to break loose from traditional orthodox Christian language and symbols. The *Book of Mormon* addresses the reader in the diction of the Bible and mobilizes the symbolism of ancient Israel, but the center of the drama of salvation has shifted to the new world and the message has departed as radically from that of Christianity as the message of the early Christian churches and the New Testament had from the scriptures and practices of the people of Israel.[28] Both Unity School and Trine, like Emerson before them, continue to invoke the figure of Jesus as a model of true spirituality and to appeal to the moral and spiritual witness of prophets and psalmist. But these are witnesses rather than formative authorities, and the appeal to their words and example is sometimes matched by appeal to sacred scriptures, prophets, and seers from other nonbiblical religious traditions.

With the qualified exception of the Mormons, the benchmarks for orientation on the spiritual landscape across which the drama of salvation moves are not so much moments of fall and redemption as they are moments in a struggle—variously interpreted—upward along a path of spiritual development from lower to higher spiritual ground, from immature to mature stages of spiritual refinement. The qualification to keep in mind with respect to the Mormons refers to the moments in the Mormon vision of sacred history when episodes of apostasy and fall from grace do not lead to a restoration of spiritual progress. Still, the dominant image for Mormons is of life as always presenting opportunities for spiritual progress along a path pioneered and prescribed by God. And that is an image shared across the spectrum of supply-side spirituality.

Cultural aesthetics: What supply-side spirituality feels like as a way of life is affirmative, optimistic, expectant, energetic, and confident. Even in the face of physical hardship, personal anxiety, and social or economic adversity, supply-side spirituality affirms an ultimate harmony between sacred reality and one's own humanity—variously interpreted—a harmony that can be made manifest also in the relations between humanity and the environing world of natural and artifactual conditions. The harmonial spirit of supply-side spirituality is generally not a simple achievement, though it sometimes finds expression in ways that virtually deny the reality of pain, suffering, and evil. More commonly it rests upon faith in a higher reality and power and a commitment to an appropriate piety and a disciplined pattern of life which, by conforming itself to that higher power, is brought into an affirmative (if not an original) relation with the divine harmony. The individual is encouraged to affirm and experience a sense of his or her importance and worth and to feel and act upon a sense of confidence about the prospects and possibilities of life. Emerson is characteristically imprecise about the features of reality upon which rests his confidence in the "wonderful congruity . . . between man and the world," but the Mormons are very clear about the grounds for the exhilaration and energy, as well as the systematic discipline, which inform their personal and corporate life. And both Trine and Unity School are no less clear about the grounds for the expectant attitude and affirmative feelings which infuse the pattern of life they recommend. Bellamy's quite different vision and the felt quality of life as he envisages it is also confidently harmonial.

The harmonial promise of supply-side spirituality is realized through one of two general approaches—by letting go or by mastery and control. The achieved sense of harmony is in each case quite different, and the differences have to do with issues to be returned to in the final section of this essay. There is something of both strategies evident in Emerson: the self-reliant individual seeks mastery and control of self and circumstances insofar as lies within his powers, but with a willing spirit lets go of all that is beyond his personal powers, affirming by faith an overriding harmony not clearly evident in all particulars of experience. For both Unity School and Trine as well, we participate in and contribute to the harmony of all things, not so much by mastery and control as by letting go and conforming our minds and hearts to (in Trine's words) "the divine sequence running throughout the universe."

For the Mormons and Bellamy, on the other hand, the divinely proffered harmony will be actualized rather by taking hold than by letting go. It is by control, organization, and management that Mormons imagine the kingdom of God will be achieved and the spiritual mastery of all creation realized. And Bellamy envisages a world in which scientific, rationalized management and cooperative organization of productive activity will liberate humanity to live in conflict-free harmony enjoying the fruits of abundance and the freedom of creative leisure activity. In all of these varieties of supply-side spirituality, it is not the transcendence and otherness of God but the immanence and availability of divine power that is felt.

What most powerfully mobilizes energy and generates excitement for these varieties of supply-side spirituality? For Emerson it is openness to the vision of infinite possibilities and powers resident in each individual and now recognized as one with the powers of the universe, the divine soul. For Unity School and for Trine in a closely related way, it is the challenge and promise of abundance, together with the confirming experience of well-being and the renewal of energy and confidence nourished by the appropriate practice of piety and by success in the application of the principles taught by Unity School and by Trine. For Mormons, energy is mobilized by the challenge of achievement, both spiritual and material, through a lifetime of disciplined living that is nourished, emotionally, intellectually, and spiritually, by the complex fabric of family, church, and community, the support of which transmutes duty into pleasure, discipline into satisfaction, individual achievement into mutual support and affirmation. What Bellamy finds exciting is the prospect of postindustrial abundance managed so efficiently and humanely that energy is not exhausted in production but is reserved for the enjoyment of leisure and creativity in an environment of cooperative relations and material abundance. To participate in such a cooperative venture is to participate in the sacred power which he identifies with socialized humanity.

Cultural politics: Supply-side spirituality is essentially apolitical or nonpolitical and even antipolitical. All five varieties which I have considered share a distaste for politics, though they express that distaste differently. For Emerson, the self-sufficient individual is only reluctantly and minimally a citizen of the state and a political participant— in sharp contrast with the Calvinist and Puritan vision of the ideal saint as political citizen. True, the Mormons envisage a Mormon state, but their civil as well as their ecclesiastical polity is more administrative than political. Power in the church is hierarchically organized and distributed, with the critical power assigned to men—and generally to men who have made their mark in business and in administrative or management roles. Women as well as men participate from an early age in the elaborately institutionalized life of the church and have opportunities to rise through carefully calibrated echelons of leadership within their own parallel organizational channels, but without the same power as is available to male saints. Participation is very widespread, but power is hierarchically centralized and patriarchal. Bellamy, too, places his greatest confidence in administrative and managerial skills. He entrusts his utopian society to experts in management—not to politically generated leadership but to managers whose roles are modeled after those of generals of the army.

Unity School and Trine are essentially apolitical or nonpolitical in a quite different and more passive way. Collective life and political participation are not matters to which they direct any attention. It is as though, for them, power is essentially available only from its divine source directly to the individual. Unity School does, of course, make much of the collective mobilization of divine power for healing and for prosperity by joining in the shared life of prayer through Silent Unity. But this has to do with spiritual power, which is not understood in political terms by either Unity School or Trine.

On the whole and across the spectrum of its varieties, supply-side spirituality tends to see power in economic rather than political terms, either celebrating leadership on the corporate model rather than a political model (the Mormons, Bellamy) or giving their tacit support to such models of leadership and of the well-lived life (Unity School and Trine). Their voices are heard in affirmative even if sometimes nervous concert with the voices of the corporate world emerging in the latter half of the nineteenth century—a corporate world which is by then well on its way to becoming the governing instrument of production and the dominant instrument for the distribution of abundance.[29]

Cultural embodiment: It is characteristic of all varieties of supply-side spirituality that they assign great importance to physical as well as spiritual health and emphasize the intimate relation between the two, attending with care to the well-being and prosperity of the body as well as the spirit. Supply-side spirituality commonly sets itself over against the darkness and negative attitude toward sinful humanity which is perceived as an essential feature of orthodox Protestant Christianity in the surrounding culture. A healthy body and physical pleasure are regarded as important values in the light of their positive attitude toward life and their conviction that true spirituality enlists the affirmative more than the negative affections and shapes a way of life characterized by joy. The particulars of this positive concern for physical health vary across the spectrum of supply-side spirituality.

Mormon attitudes toward the body are informed by a distinctive metaphysic according to which spirit is refined matter rather than a different order of reality, as in the commonsense dualism of spirit/matter and mind/body that informs so much of the surrounding culture. For them, it is not simply that the body is to be seen as a temple of God and, therefore, to be kept holy and pure against defilement. It is rather that spirit and body are of a single order of reality, so that care for the body and its health is integral to care for the spirit and its health. Abstinence from certain activities and substances is encouraged or enjoined, not in the first place because they are perceived as sinful but, rather, because they are perceived as unhealthy. So Mormons abstain systematically from coffee and tea, tobacco, and alcohol. More affirmatively stated, Mormon life is characterized by simplicity and wholesomeness, centered around the values and activities of family, church, and daily productive activity.

But the absence of frivolity does not mean a lack of physical activity and pleasure. Physical development and achievement is an important part of personal formation among Mormons and is of a piece with their respect for and enjoyment of artistic achievement. Who has not heard and enjoyed the Mormon Tabernacle Choir or the superb organ music broadcast nationally every Sunday morning? Less well known, perhaps, but no less important to the Mormon way of life is their celebration of the more manifestly physical art of dance and of performance in sports. Mormon culture is distinctive for its encouragement and enjoyment of dance as both a participant activity and a performance art. Brigham Young University is perhaps the only university in the United States with a permanent professional resident dance company. Physical discipline is important to both bodily health and spiritual advancement, but it is also valued intrinsically as an ingredient in the well-lived life and as essential to full enjoyment of life among the latter-day saints.

Bellamy's concern for the body and the reality of embodiment seems minimal, especially in contrast with the Mormons. His interest in the body has to do primarily with relieving it of the burdens imposed upon it by the irrationalities and inefficiencies and brutalities of industrial society in late nineteenth-century America. With those burdens relieved in Bellamy's ideal society of the year 2000, the body does not figure prominently in his portrayal of the most attractive features of life among its inhabitants, where intellectual and "spiritual" pursuits are evidently most prized—music, literature, fine sermons, intelligent conversation, and leisurely pleasures—and it seems sufficient satisfaction to the body that it be relieved of heavy labor and have a share in the life of ease.

Unity School places health as well as prosperity at the center of its concern and addresses issues of physical as well as spiritual health through prayer and the modification of behavior in accordance with prayer and simplicity of life. Both Unity School and Trine reflect participation in a network of New Thought movements[30] in which physical health was a significant problem for many of the participants and leaders. They assign great importance to physical as well as spiritual health, but their attention is commonly focused on the mind or spirit as the determinant of physical health. They give little attention to physical culture or to the artistic and athletic development of the body. Health seems rather a gift of right spirituality than of physical practice. Unity School teaches about exercising one's "God-potential" but does not speak directly about exercising one's physical capacities. Real healing is spiritual healing. A typical meditation in *Daily Word* is entitled "The Christ life expresses itself as health and wholeness in me" and reads in part: "I pour out a very special blessing upon my body as I appreciate and give thanks for the healing, restoring Christ life within me. . . . I cooperate with the healing, restoring life of Christ within me by thinking positive thoughts and by expressing a healthful attitude in word and action" (3 Dec. 1985). Elsewhere in the readings for the same month come these affirmations: "Any time I open myself to the flow of God's power, strength surges through me" (17 Dec. 1985). And when "I see myself with an inner vision, as God sees me, . . . every cell of my being vibrates with health and wholeness. I have a real sense of my abundant potential to be all that God created me to be" (26 Dec. 1985).

Supply-side spirituality is not to be identified straight-out with the religious movements and writers discussed here as representative of it. There is more to each of them than this. Yet none of them seems plausible apart from the emergence of the cultural experience and expectation of abundance among Americans. One might say that it is abundance and questions about how to respond appropriately to it in a religious way that set the agenda for supply-side spirituality.

Furthermore, it is important to keep in mind that here the effort has been to locate and identify supply-side spirituality culturally rather than socially. This does not mean that it has no social location, only that it is primarily to be found among Americans as an ingredient in the symbolic processes and fabric of meaning upon which they draw in making sense of their lives and their world. It is more characteristically present as a coloring in the cultural and spiritual atmosphere than in the form of socially distinct religious institutions. So, for example, Unity School's *Daily Word* claims about two and a half million subscribers, the vast majority of whom are active members of those various Protestant denominations which are their social locations. However, the perspective taught by Unity School contributes significantly to the way they interpret their lives and find guidance for their action in the world.

IV

One does not need to be a close student of American culture to recognize in these commitments and values of supply-side spirituality distinctive concentrations of ingredients widely diffused through American culture—ingredients upon which a broad spectrum of Americans draw in making spiritual and moral sense of their lives and in providing guidance for their action. Supply-side spirituality and the culture of abundance are, of course, still very much alive in America, contributing to both the circumstances of the moral life and the resources for religious ethics. Most of those Americans who have not found supply-side spirituality to offer them, at least in some measure, a persuasive religious response to the conditions and possibilities of a world of abundance, nonetheless do inhabit—most of them even more completely than did their nineteenth-century predecessors—a culture of abundance.

That culture of abundance, now grown more powerful than ever in ways that are often quite independent of and even antithetical to supply-side spirituality, has become also a culture of consumption—a culture in which orientation and identity is achieved at least as much by virtue of one's relationship to processes of consumption as to those of production.[31] It now faces problems shared to some extent by a number of other advanced high-technology societies, problems to which at least some versions of supply-side spirituality offer, if not answers, at least resources for thoughtful religious ethics. One example may, in conclusion, serve to illustrate the relevance—beyond historical knowledge and self-understanding—of recovering acquaintance with some of the options developed by supply-side spirituality.

As pointed out earlier, the harmonial promise envisaged by supply-side spirituality is realized through one of two general approaches— one by letting go, the other by mastery and control—and the achieved sense of harmony is in each case quite different. Mormons, for example, embody a supply-side spirituality interwoven with Protestant cultural norms of the work ethic and collective discipline among the saints, while Unity School embodies a supply-side spirituality more closely allied with and receptive to cultural therapies of self-fulfilment and possessive individualism. The strategy of mastery and control, of taking hold rather than letting go, has some kinship with the dynamics of the culture of abundance as that has developed during the twentieth century into being also a culture of consumption. Among the definitive features of the culture of consumption is dependence upon acquisition as a ready solution to almost every problem. Americans are encouraged to believe—and many have come to at least behave in accordance with a belief—that nearly every felt need can be met by some kind of acquisition.

A fix by fortunate acquisition has become a powerful pattern of addictive dependence in a culture which nourishes and even seems to require dependence upon an enormous variety of addictive substances and activities. Addictive dependence upon acquisition is evident throughout the culture of consumption in which most Americans participate, however uneasily, but nowhere more dramatically than in the extraordinary high levels of personal debt and national debt and international trade deficits—all of which have reached dramatically new levels in recent years in spite of much rhetoric about balanced budgets. The most dangerous manifestation of this culture of procurement—to give it a suitably ugly name—is the escalating commitment to military procurement as the primary basis of national security and, even more important, the high tolerance and even support for that approach on the part of a society in which the same logic of addictive dependence upon acquisition or consumption is an essential feature of the dominant culture.

To the extent that this diagnosis of the dominant culture of American society is correct, then the second strategy for realizing the harmony envisaged by supply-side spirituality—the strategy of letting go—offers resources and guidance for recovery. The twelve-step program of Alcoholics Anonymous, Alanon, and related programs addressed to spiritual renewal and recovery from various addictive dependencies and patterns of codependency constitutes the most impressive and successful manifestation of this kind of supply-side spirituality.[32] While it has its origins in the experience of bottoming-out by its alcoholic founders in the 1930s, it has much in common with other versions of supply-side spirituality, including its assumptions about abundance. What makes the twelve-step program important in the present context is that it embodies and articulates a cultural alternative and a religious ethic addressed to addiction, which is understood as a pathological manifestation of the culture of abundance and consumption, while yet sharing enough of the convictions and assumptions of the culture of abundance that it can speak effectively for a spiritual and moral alternative within the terms set by that culture. In its simplicity; in its focus on individual freedom and personal growth, health, and responsibility; in its nondoctrinal spirituality; in its minimal institutionalization—in all of these respects it is a characteristically American movement. It offers a spiritually grounded pattern of life characterized at once by letting go and by personal responsibility in a way best suggested by the "serenity prayer" so central to the program: "God grant me the serenity to accept the things I cannot change, the courage to change the things I can, and the wisdom to know the difference."

The Alanon program, a slightly modified version of AA, is designed to meet the needs of individuals for recovery from a wide range of addiction-related dependencies. It offers a model—not a complete one, but a promising point of departure—for addressing the demands of a situation more complex than that of an addictively dependent individual. One problem is that, like other versions of supply-side spirituality, it is essentially nonpolitical or apolitical. The hope that such a program for spiritual renewal can be given a more political edge is rendered at least plausible by observing that Reinhold Niebuhr—the quintessentially political Christian ethicist of the twentieth century—is the author of the serenity prayer[33] which has been embraced by many people, but none more systematically than those who seek daily guidance from repetition and reflection upon it as a resource for recovery and spiritual growth according to the twelve-step program of AA and Alanon.

If there were space to examine this twelve-step program, it would be useful to invoke also the spirit and perspective of William James.[34] That most characteristic of American philosophers, a celebrant of the energetic life as the life worth living, described the critical moments in the religious life in terms of the mobilization of personal energy—of taking hold—but he also understood the process of religious conversion in terms of a shift from a morality of control to a spirituality of letting go. For now, this illustration of a strategy of letting go within the tradition of supply-side spirituality will suffice to suggest one of the ways in which a recovery of that tradition's development in American culture might also serve a pressing contemporary need for recovery from the excesses of the culture of abundance and consumption and from addictive dependence upon procurement as the principal way of responding to felt needs and threats.

NOTES

1. Larzer Ziff, *Literary Democracy: The Declaration of Cultural Independence in America* (New York: Penguin Books, 1981), p. xx.

2. Clifford Geertz, *Islam Observed* (New Haven: Yale University Press, 1968), p. 97.

3. Suzanne K. Langer, *Philosophy in a New Key,* 3d ed. (Cambridge: Harvard University Press, 1957), p. 153.

4. See Simon N. Patten, *The New Basis of Civilization* (1907; Cambridge: Harvard University Press, 1968); also Daniel M. Fox, *The Discovery of Abundance: Simon N. Patten and the Transformation of Social Theory* (Ithaca: Cornell University Press, 1967).

5. On New Thought see Charles S. Braden, *Spirits in Rebellion: The Rise and Development of New Thought* (Dallas: Southern Methodist University Press, 1963).

6. On *est* see Steven M. Tipton, *Getting Saved from the Sixties* (Berkeley: University of California Press, 1982), pp. 176–231.

7. Among his many publications see Robert Schuller, *Tough Minded Faith for Tender Hearted People* (1983; New York: Bantam Books, 1985).

8. Matthew Fox, *Original Blessing: A Primer in Creation Spirituality* (Santa Fe, N.Mex.: Bear and Company, 1983).

9. Sydney E. Ahlstrom, *A Religious History of the American People* (New Haven: Yale University Press, 1972), pp. 1019–36.

10. Donald Meyer, *The Positive Thinkers: Religion as Pop Psychology from Mary Baker Eddy to Oral Roberts* (New York: Pantheon, 1965; reissued, with new preface and conclusion, 1980).

11. Ralph Waldo Emerson, "Divinity School Address," in *Selected Writings of Emerson,* ed. Brooks Atkinson (New York: Modern Library, 1940), p. 72.

12. Emerson, "Nature," in *Selected Writings,* pp. 3, 6, 7, 35, 36, 37, 42.

13. Emerson, "Wealth," in *Selected Writings,* pp. 694, 695f., 701, 705, 716.

14. See Braden, *Spirits in Rebellion,* pp. 233–63.

15. James D. Freeman, *The Household of Faith: The Story of Unity* (Lee's Summit, Mo.: Unity School of Christianity, 1951), p. 9.

16. *Daily Word* (Unity Village, Mo.: Unity School of Christianity), published monthly.

17. Charles Fillmore, "Overcoming the Poverty Idea," reproduced in Freeman, *Household of Faith,* pp. 246–50; my quotation at p. 250.

18. Ralph Waldo Trine, *In Tune with the Infinite: Fullness of Peace, Power and Plenty* (New York: Thomas Y. Crowell, 1897), preface.

19. Ibid., preface and pp. 11, 18, 17, 82, 176, 192.

20. Ibid., p. 177.

21. On the Mormons see Klaus J. Hansen, *Mormonism and the American Experience* (Chicago: University of Chicago Press, 1981); Jan Shipps, *Mormonism: The Story of a New Religious Tradition* (Urbana: University of Illinois Press, 1985), Thomas F. O'Dea, *The Mormons* (Chicago: University of Chicago Press, 1957); and Marvin S. Hill and James B. Allen, eds., *Mormonism and American Culture* (New York: Harper and Row, 1972).

22. O'Dea, *Mormons,* p. 150.

23. Quoted in ibid., p. 55.

24. President Joseph F. Smith in 1916, quoted in Shipps, *Mormonism,* p. 143.

25. Reproduced in *Edward Bellamy: Selected Writings on Religion and Society,* ed. Joseph Schiffman (New York: Liberal Arts Press, 1955), this essay was not published in Bellamy's lifetime.

26. Cecelia Tichi, "Introduction" to Edward Bellamy, *Looking Backward* (New York: Penguin Books, 1982), p. 8.

27. Bellamy, *Looking Backward,* pp. 148–51.

28. For a full development of this interpretation, see Shipps, *Mormonism.*

29. For an illuminating analysis of these developments see Alan Trachtenberg, *The Incorporation of America: Culture and Society in the Gilded Age* (New York: Hill and Wang, 1982).

30. See n. 5, above.

31. See Richard Wightman Fox and T. J. Jackson Lears, eds., *The Culture of Consumption* (New York: Pantheon Books, 1983).

32. See Ernest Kurtz, *Not-God, A History of Alcoholics Anonymous* (Center City, Minn.: Hazelden, 1979). The twelve-step program is not easily rendered in a capsule and is easily misrepresented. For example, step one reads: "We admitted we were powerless over our addiction, that our lives had become unmanageable." But the point—and the success—of the program is precisely personal empowerment over addictive dependence. See *Twelve Steps and Twelve Traditions* (New York: Alcoholics Anonymous World Services, Inc., 1953), second only in importance among AA publications to "The Big Book," *Alcoholics Anonymous,* 3d ed. (New York: Alcoholics Anonymous World Services, Inc., 1976).

33. On Niebuhr's authorship of the serenity prayer, see Richard W. Fox, *Reinhold Niebuhr: A Biography* (New York: Pantheon Books, 1985), pp. 290–91.

34. On the significance of William James to the founders of Alcoholics Anonymous, see Kurtz, *Not-God.*

L. SHANNON JUNG

The Recovery of the Land:
Agribusiness and Creation-Centered Stewardship

The transformation of land from a combination of humus and animal life into a matter of credit sources and price supports can be dated from 1933. Things on the farm had been grim for three years. In March of 1933 Congress passed the Agricultural Adjustment Act. Cotton farmers were paid to plow their cotton under; wheat and corn and hog farmers were also being paid not to produce. By September, farm mailboxes were full of government checks which provided the first substantial money farmers had had in nearly two years. After observing the check-writing machine and having its purposed explained to him, a Russian visitor exclaimed, "Good Lord! This is a Revolution."[1] Indeed it was.

The revolution under scrutiny here is the process by which agriculture became agribusiness, or more particularly how that intricate mix of soil, sweat, and sun—agriculture—has changed into an aggregate of interest rates, commodity futures, and tax shelters—agribusiness. My contention is that concern for the economic efficiency of agriculture undermined the traditional stewardship ethic as the ascendancy of the business ethic obscured the intrinsic value of land. This essay subsequently makes the case that there are resources in the American and Christian traditions which can refurbish the stewardship ethic and lead to a recovery of the value of land.

To demonstrate these claims, my argument begins by describing the processes by which the agrarian tradition of agriculture gradually lost ground to the efficiency tradition of agribusiness. The significance of this transition becomes clear when one realizes that human values are tied to land and to its economic distribution and organization. The second section of the argument asserts that the stewardship ethic has been unable to resist that deleterious transformation, for reasons both internal and external to the moral tradition. Thus what is needed is a recovery and refurbishing of that ethic along the lines of a creation-centered tradition rooted in American and Christian sources, rooted, in short, in distinctively American resources. My conclusion will suggest some of those resources and some directions of mind and sensibility which will enable Americans to effect that recovery.

The Metamorphosis: Agriculture to Agribusiness

Even a perfunctory examination of the history of American farm policy from 1933 to the present reveals that a focus on efficiency and productivity has almost driven out the values of land care and quality of life. (The fact that in other areas "quality of life" has become inextricably associated with quantity of income for Americans makes the point vividly.) This is a national trend which—it should come as no surprise—affects the agricultural sector no less than any other. The origin of the trend in agriculture can be identified with Franklin Roosevelt's signing of the Agricultural Adjustment Act, which was passed in a desperate economic situation in order to allow all owner-operated family farms to survive. The fact that almost all farms were of this type in 1933 should not escape notice. Far from achieving that goal, however, by 1939 Roosevelt had to admit that about half of the nation's farms were not commercially viable.[2] Although that legislation was intended to be only a temporary measure, its main features continue today in a vastly different situation, and the result of our national policy has been to benefit those who have the most land or produce the most bushels, just as Roosevelt's act benefited those who had the most acres to plow under or hogs to kill. The determinates of efficiency and productivity have come to dominate the values both of rural and farm life and of the careful nurture and use of the land.

Rather than detailing the succession of legislative enactments that benefit most those farmers who need them least, I want to focus on U.S. intellectual and social currents as they interact with and influence cultural events.[3] In that way, the sometimes hidden or subtle forces that have overwhelmed the stewardship ethic become quite vivid.

The ascendancy of the values of efficiency and productivity has been noted by various sources, among them Earl Heady, who writes that

> Changing values of farm operators and families . . . may create new attitudes toward farming in the next twenty years. In the past, farm families highly valued the farm operator per se. Using the partial equity obtained by inheritance or related means, the family worked industriously to maintain an acceptable standard of living, retire the farm's mortgage, live on its rental value in old age, and pass it down through the family. Today fewer young farmers view farming in this light. Their

income and management goals are more comparable to those of a me-
dium-sized corporation or of the president of a manufacturing firm.
The focus is now less on the farm as a physical entity and more on it as
a business generating cash flows and capital gains.[4]

In general terms, there have been two major value traditions
operating in American agriculture: the agrarian tradition and the
efficiency, production, or business tradition.[5] The agrarian tradition
roughly corresponds to the Jeffersonian "independent yeoman-
farmer" or farming-as-a-way-of-life view of agriculture. Briefly described, this tradition has seen agriculture as a primary contributor to
democracy, to social virtue, and to economic prosperity—effects, it
was assumed, stemming from *the intrinsic goodness* of working with the
land.[6] Agriculture was held to be the nation's basic industry, the one
responsible for American economic self-sufficiency. Thus it supported
a democratic way of life and promoted the virtues of independence,
freedom, honesty, moral integrity, and dependability. The agrarian
tradition elevated the view of farming as a way of life because the
idealized farmer represented in microcosm those social virtues which
America "stood for" in macrocosm. On both the micro- and macro-
levels, it was the land which anchored the nation and generated
strength and virtue.

The efficiency tradition corresponds to the Horatio Alger drive for
success or farming-as-a-way-of-making-a-living view of agriculture.
This view is variously labeled the "productivity," "business," or "entre-
preneurial" tradition. Its primary belief is that "waste is somehow sinful and any self-respecting [person] is duty-bound to combine effort,
skill, and substance in such a way as to get the most possible from
every resource at hand."[7] The land, and farming as an occupation,
are viewed as *instrumentally good* in terms of what they contribute to
material well-being. The value of industry as leading to success, epitomized by Ben Franklin in *Poor Richard's Almanac*, is clearly integral to
this tradition, as is the stress put on "making something of oneself."
In this tradition the land is viewed as a resource to be employed efficiently in promoting the best possible future for oneself and also for
the nation, beneficiaries whose fortunes are assumed to proceed in
lockstep. Forgotten in this tradition is the independent standing of
the land and the way in which *it* challenges and questions human
beings.

It is almost indisputable that both traditions have coexisted in
America since Governor Bradford and Squanto raised their first ears
of corn back on the Plymouth Plantations. Indeed, William Cronon

suggests that changes in the land resulted from the interaction of the English colonists with the Indian population. The "key causal agent" for ecological changes was the colonists' "perception of how the resources of the New England landscape might be made useful to those who could possess them"—in short, market demand.[8] He quotes Richard Hakluyt's 1584 description of fish, fur, and timber as "merchantable commodities."[9] The point here is that Western agriculture has long been both an enterprise and a way of life. Both of these traditions have deep roots in American cultural life. Practically, it is clear that farmers have always had to be concerned about making a living; concomitantly, the abundance of land and natural resources in America supported the agrarian tradition. In a wider cultural sense, each of the traditions has expressed something of the American experience and validated elements of the image that Americans hold of themselves and the nation. The weight or significance of each tradition in their combination has varied, however. This adjustment perhaps reflected cooperation during the period when much of the nation was rural; it has become competitive with the dominance of urban life. Although most Americans still retain an affection for the agrarian tradition, the efficiency or business tradition has all but supplanted its former partner.

In an important sense, then, the agrarian and business traditions have long existed side by side, with subsequent cultural shifts and movements ineluctably compounding the power and reach of the tradition of efficiency. By now, the ideas of size and efficiency have become their own compelling tradition. "Ever since the 1890's," writes Gilbert C. Fite, "efficiency has been a key concept in American business and government. It would have been unrealistic to assume that agriculture could have escaped the same trends."[10] What is perhaps remarkable is that the rhetoric of the agrarian tradition has survived as long as it has.[11] That it has is indicative of some values which we Americans wish to conserve; I will return to the question of those values.

At present, however, the question is how this transition occurred. A number of elements enter into the story of the particular transformation of agriculture. The rapid expansion of technology and scientific methods which occurred in the 1940s enabled the individual farmer to plant more acreage and harvest the greater yields which his scientifically developed seeds produced, and the advent of fertilizers, pesticides, and herbicides further accelerated the farmer's potential productivity and, not incidentally, his sense of control. Concomitantly, the specialization that had come to characterize other industries changed the nature of farming from a diverse multiculture to a monoculture. By the late 1950s most commercial producers were concentrating on one or two main crops.[12] Farmers, more absorbed in the cash and credit economy, now bought at the grocery much of what their fathers had grown. Increasingly, the farmer was dependent on cash, credit, and good management; technology and specialization are expensive. It is hardly surprising, then, that farmers *wanted* to increase their efficiency and income. Land-grant colleges, banks, seed companies, and farm equipment manufacturers also encouraged these trends toward large-scale, capital-intensive, petrochemical farming.

The drive toward greater productivity, efficiency, and wealth on the farm was entirely consistent with national values.[13] National values seemed captive to rationalization[14]—the rational application of means to ends—which could be taken as a synonym for efficiency. The rise of scientific methods in agriculture as in many other realms of cultural life appears oriented to efficiency of production, in agriculture, or results, in other realms. Thus the values to be found in the integrity of working with and appreciating the land were overshadowed by the drive for efficiency of results. (Ironically the emerging negative consequences of conventional agriculture geared to efficiency are beginning to suggest the need for alternative farming methods.)

As a result of all of these developments, farming grew increasingly utilitarian. The emphasis on usefulness and practicality for which farmers were known declined; they lost a sense of pride in knowing their land, an ability to fix their own equipment, and the knowledge of how to care for stock and plants. These virtues have come under external management as American culture increasingly values expert opinion. Practicality and usefulness, as defined by the media and banks, have come to mean "bottom line," by whatever means. The tendency toward quantification aided and abetted this movement, and the era of electronic agriculture will surely sever the farmer from the land to an even greater degree.

Also feeding the transition was the emergence of single-issue politics, with its resultant fragmentation. When farming was really perceived as everybody's bread and butter, the agrarian tradition retained the force inherent in its democratic and economic elements. When "farming is everybody's bread and butter" becomes merely a political slogan of one group clamoring for its own self-interest, however, the efficiency/business tradition has clearly become more powerful. The acquisitive potential of farmers was not restrained by the sense of contributing to the public interest. Consumer groups and urban interests came to be seen as competitors and farmers as only one constituency among others.

Three dynamics hastened this transition. The first was the beginning of extensive governmental intervention into agriculture. With that intervention a change in viewpoint began to take place. Farmers who had valued their land as good in itself and as part of their *homes* started to see the products of the land as *commodities* subject to price supports and set-aside arrangements. A second dynamic, more gradual in its development, promoted the instrumental view of land as leading to other benefits. The arrival of monoculture cash crops contradicted the tradition in which the farm produced the food served at the family's dinner table and undermined the obvious nexus between land and life reinforced in the agrarian model. However, as farmers became consumers along with the remainder of the population, they began to see themselves solely as businesspeople efficiently pursuing adequate incomes. Third, farmers have become more and more subject to bank loans and policy decisions, subject also to the prices set by manufacturers of seed and chemicals and equipment. When banks establish the conditions which farmers have to meet before their loans are approved, when farmers become dependent on the level of target prices set by the government, their perception is—accurately—that they have lost control over their operations. They begin to peg decisions about the land to external factors and loan payments which further erode intrinsic values and reinforce instrumental goals.

This transition is entirely compatible with the perspective of the wider culture, as American values have shifted toward instrumental goals. Farm operations simply reflect the more general cultural move to economic definition. But the point is not to single out the farmer as more blameworthy than others so much as it is to suggest how certain value perspectives have been obscured and ultimately lost in the process. Particularly vivid is the loss of the sense of the inherent dignity of farming as a vocation and of the family farm as contributing to the good life (defined in noneconomic terms). The love of the land as an American communal heritage and respect for the farmer as the caretaker of the collective environment is in retreat. What is decidedly more troublesome is that the present structure of U.S. agriculture has operated against the well-being of the nation—the majority of farmers in this country, against the interests of the public at large, and against the health of the land, air, and water.

Such a bold evaluation of the collective losses entailed in the transition from agriculture to agribusiness is founded on the demonstrable perniciousness of the trend. If the costs of that development were minor or merely sentimental, then the inadequacy of the stewardship ethic would become an eminently forgettable bit of social history, but those costs have been anything but trivial.

The transition to agribusiness has operated against the majority of farmers, literally by forcing them off their farms. In the thirty years from 1919 to 1949, the number of rural farm families dropped from 6.5 million to 5.7 million; in the period from 1949 to 1979 the drop was from 5.7 million to 2.3 million. The number of farm families has continued to decline since then; in 1984 alone five thousand Minnesota farms were lost. The average size of the American farm has more than doubled in the past thirty years. As farming became a commercial industry, it became less and less possible to farm in relation to natural factors and more and more necessary to farm in relation to price supports, loan rates, and credit sources.

Of course farmers need to practice good management; reports are, however, that good management is no longer enough. Prize-winning farms are going under. Unlike other businesses, farmers buy at retail and sell for whatever the going price or commodity credit is. They have little control over either the price they pay or the price they receive. For no other product has the price received been in decline for the past five years as it has been for wheat, for instance. And yet the price of food at the supermarket has not declined. Explaining this anomaly is the vertical integration of corporate farms with processing and distributing companies. Giant food companies, verging on monopolies, control the price of "raw" commodities and make their profits from processing, packaging, and distributing food stuffs. It is, baldly put, corporations and economic elites for whom a "cheap food" agricultural policy promoting small numbers of large producers is designed. These "plutocracies masquerading as agribusinesses"[15] have contributed to the small farmers' dilemma. Extensive studies reveal that small farmers do not consume as well or support the economy as munificently as large operators, and documentation also indicates that this trend, steered by government, is not unintentional.[16]

The trend toward ignoring the economy of households in favor of a national "money" economy alone is threatening rural communities as well. Most obviously, the fact that there are fewer farmers means that small town businesses and organizations suffer or fail. (Statistically, the loss of six farms leads to the loss of one business.) A classic study by Walter Goldschmidt, replicated recently with similar results, demonstrated that a community of small farms enjoys a higher "quality of life" (measured in terms of number of voluntary organizations, income, businesses, higher retail sales, better schools, and more citizen participation) than one with few but large farms.[17] In short, the move to agribusiness bodes ill for the survival of small towns and for the sense of community in those that survive.

Not only rural people, however, are affected. City-dwellers feel the tide of rural migration as it swells unemployment lines and floods welfare offices. This puts pressure on urban jobholders. Moreover, as food monopolies develop, prices go up and quality goes down. Unlike the moderate-sized farmers, vertically integrated contractors can command high prices for their product by controlling availability. They do not operate under the stress of having to sell at the going price or store their products at high prices. The quality of the food that urban people consume is also deteriorating. Vegetables that are chemically preserved for transportation or genetically manipulated for easy packaging (for example, the square, hard tomatoes one buys in supermarkets) are neither as healthy nor as appealing as the products of patient horticulture. The diet of the American people has declined with the rise of agribusiness; the consumption of staple foods has dropped with the popularity of fabricated foods. Dairy products, vegetables, and fruits have given ground to soft drinks, sugar products, and chips. Many researchers are convinced that the rising incidence of many diseases and physical ailments—among them heart disease, diabetes, some forms of cancer, and hypertension—are linked to our declining national diet.[18] Finally, the concentration of the farm-and-food industries undercuts the democratic principle of the dispersal of power, leads to urban decay, and promotes the regionalization of agriculture.

The quality of our soil is also threatened. Studies of the amount of wind and water erosion in the Great Plains reveal that current levels exceed those of the Depression era. The use of pesticides, herbicides, and fertilizers whose long-term properties are unknown is a haunting reality. Every so often the effects are immediate and visible (paraquet, EDB) and the ensuing commotion is considerable. But, the now-conventional method of petrochemical farming demands more of the land than it is capable of protecting and of regenerating. High debt loads demand higher yields from farms than are ecologically responsible. Amish and organic methods of farming receive little attention since they require fewer chemicals and less consumption. Furthermore, conventional farming cuts into petrochemical reserves in a way that simply cannot be continued into the long-term future.

Even in terms of efficiency, defined as it often is solely in monetary terms, it is debatable whether the agriculture system realizes an "economy of scale." In 1973 the USDA completed a study of "The

One-Man Farm." Noting that "the claim of efficiency is commonly used to justify bigness," the report said that "when we examine the realities we find that most of the economies associated with size in farming are achieved by the one-[family] fully mechanized farm. Farms larger than 'optimum' are essentially multiples of the optimum farm, and are technically no more efficient than the one-[family] farm." Other studies suggest that economies of scale are reached with a relatively small number of acres. Still others have concluded that smaller farms are *more* efficient.[19]

In all these ways, then, the business or efficiency tradition has failed, and the overall problem is simply that our culture has come to value efficiency and money as *primary rather than secondary* goals, thus losing sight of other values. One fading central value has been the place of the common good. More specifically for the farmer, the underlying *cause* of the problem is the split between nature and culture, the estrangement of human beings from the ways in which they are natural, the way their minds and bodies interpenetrate and act conjointly. Instead, Americans tend to think of themselves (culture) technically, as dispassionately analyzing and controlling and mathematically/scientifically deciding, and of nature as being analyzed, controlled, decided about, inanimate—to see themselves as *techne*, not *poiesis*, in Erazim Kohak's sense.[20] Abstracting the human self from nature and forgetting the material kinship with, and dependency on, nature, *techne*—precise and analytic rationality, a valuable part of the human—has become the whole. But it is no substitute for the equally important *poiesis*—the emotional, visionary, visceral aspects of the self. In short, the transition in the American view of the land reflects a deeper erosion in the American self.

The Pernicious Effect of Stewardship

The stewardship ethic has proved incapable of resisting this transition, if in fact it has not reinforced it. That ethic, espoused by virtually all of the Judeo-Christian bodies in the United States, has been the primary lens through which religion has viewed human responsibility to nature. There is a secular version of this view and, even though the task here precludes significant attention to it, it deserves brief recognition.

The reason for attending to the secular as well as the religious value system has to do with the way public morality in the United States is shaped. Drawing on the political and moral thought of Montesquieu, James Sellers has suggested that the public morality of the

U.S. is shaped by the interaction of its civil laws and its public "morals and manners."[21] The legal pole—legislative enactments relating to agriculture—interacts with those institutions which shape public "morals and manners"—religious organizations, educational institutions, professional groups, businesses, and civic clubs. Law, economics, politics, and religion stand in a complementary relationship when it comes to shaping human conduct. Margaret Mead put it this way: "This way in which people behave is all of a piece, their virtues and their sins, the way they slap the baby, handle their court cases, and bury their dead."[22] It should be expected, then, that secular and religious morals and manners influence each other in the interflow which always characterizes cultural existence.

The secular equivalent of the stewardship ethic is the ethic of soil conservation. Not only are there agencies of the U.S. Department of Agriculture devoted to that end, but also it would be difficult to find any conscientious citizen who does not—with some degree of commitment—support soil conservation. Furthermore, the stewardship and the soil conservation ethics mutually reinforce each other, though they rest on different ideological bases. One key to their complementarity is that both see the sphere of nature as essentially unrelated to that of human identity; the material world is segregated from the human essence of mind and spirit.[23] Both have emphasized the separateness and distinctiveness of people from nature and the material world, almost to the extent of obscuring the fact that human beings are natural and material beings themselves. Thus even the relationship of dependence that exists between people and land has become hidden, and it has become much easier to use land and other natural beings carelessly. The health of the land becomes a secondary consideration in the process of decision-making. Remedial action requires taking account of the impact of this separation of the material and human worlds.

Though the relationship between sociopolitical and religious values is a complex one, it seems clear that both the transition from the agrarian to the business tradition and the arrival of the secular ethic related to this matter have been abetted by the religious thought and activity of the Judeo-Christian tradition in the United States. As the primary belief of those bodies in regard to environmental responsibility, it is the stewardship ethic itself whose impact requires investigation.

The stewardship ethic has claimed that God created the world good, that human beings are responsible for its care, and thus that human beings are accountable to God as stewards. At the outset, then, men and women are differentiated from nonhuman nature and told to "subdue and dominate" as well as to "till and keep" the earth.[24] The stewardship ethic is basically hierarchical: the rest of creation is acknowledged as the sphere over which human beings serve as stewards. With this implicit model of human beings as superior to nature, the upshot is that, if there is a conflict between the interests of people and the land, then the nonhuman counts for little more than zero in the equation. Nature finally is for the benefit of humans, and the only reason for its care and conservation is its utility for future (human) generations.

In conjunction with the contemporary scientific worldview which embraces a mechanistic and instrumental interpretation of nature, the stewardship ethic can easily conceive of nature as desacralized. Influenced by these dynamics, the ideal of stewardship provides little resistance to those contingencies which threaten its degeneration into an ethic of indiscriminate use, if not domination. If nature is not seen as intrinsically valuable, then it is difficult to resist those tendencies which encourage the definition of land as a commodity, the domain of net profit and loan rates. Its impact on human well-being, as expressed in the agrarian tradition, is similarly obscured. Land loses independent standing and value.

Theology itself has been an accomplice in this degeneration. The world of nature has been and is "simply not of central theological interest or importance"; theology pays attention to God's relationship to people, but "exhibits a relative disregard for nature or the world."[25] In short, the stewardship ethic is structured in such a way that it can easily degenerate into a justification for the careless use of nature so long as that usage serves human purposes. In practice this may become the functional equivalent of the efficiency tradition; certainly the two have operated in a complementary way.

There is an even more deeply rooted flaw in the stewardship ethic, however, which underlies its currently ineffectual character, and that is its fundamental assumption of the separation of nature and spirit. The stewardship model has operated with a deist notion of God at least in regard to nature. Deism posits that creation is a clockwork with God as the clockmaker. Alternately, in relation to the world of nature God is an absentee landlord who has taken a long trip and left human beings in charge of day-to-day operations. God is still involved in the lives of human beings, but curiously fails to be actively involved with the earth which, set in motion, operates mechanically like the escapement clock. God's ongoing care is directed solely to human beings. Thus the tradition has denied the intrinsic value of the land, animals, plants—the whole of the nonhuman world. This has also had the effect of obscuring the materiality of the human being, and has led as well to the denial of human physical nature.

Human beings were assumed to be superior to and apart from nature; if pressed, many religious thinkers identified the image of God (in which men and women were created) with the human spirit. The resultant lack of respect for nature meant that the stewardship ethic could dissociate human well-being from the health of the land. Thus, on this count as well, it offered little resistance to the instrumentally oriented efficiency tradition. Rather, it reinforced that tradition by associating stewardship with careful and industrious use of one's resources. The natural world *can,* in fact, almost be written out of the ethic which is the best that the Judeo-Christian heritage has to offer for its care. Nature has become at best a mechanical possession, at worse an alien machine.

The conclusion to which this leads is that the lack of respect for nature—our own physical natures and the earth—which is an essential premise of the efficiency tradition has been buttressed, often subterraneously, by the Judeo-Christian ethic. Echoing this interpretation is W. H. Auden's view that "the great vice of *Americans* is not materialism but a lack of respect for matter."[26] It follows from such an analysis that a recovery of the way in which human beings are natural, along with a subsequent increased respect for nature, would go far toward recovering respect for the land.[27]

Recovering Respect for Matter

The root problem that must be remedied if respect for land is to be recovered involves overcoming the nature-spirit split. There are resources in both the American and the Judeo-Christian heritages which can assist us in that undertaking. One way to overcome the nature-spirit split and refurbish the stewardship ethic is through creation-centered spirituality. That latter phrase connotes the emphasis articulated by many thinkers in the American and Christian past, which appreciates the fact that human beings are natural and the land is intrinsically valuable. A land ethic which respects matter has a wealth of resources to draw upon—the agrarian tradition itself, Native American thought, the feminist perspective, Hebrew Scripture, Christian theology, environmentalism, and the ecological perspective in many disciplines.

The agrarian tradition, an indigenous American mythology, has many streams. Among its diverse proponents are poets such as Walt

Whitman, politicians such as Thomas Jefferson, Benjamin Franklin, Thomas Paine, and William Jennings Bryan, the folklore of Johnny Appleseed and the American garden, and other expositors such as St. John de Crèvecoeur and Henry David Thoreau.[28] What holds these otherwise disparate thinkers together is an appreciation of how land contributes to and intersects with human character and well-being. In a compelling study of the American novel, *The Eternal Adam and the New World Garden*, David Noble goes so far as to argue that the dominating myth of American life involves the belief that the unique quality of the American experience lies in a national covenant with land and space, the experience of "spaciousness in space" leading to a new humanity.[29] That the new humanity to which the covenant with land was leading was a perfected one, free from sin, gives an early indication of the mixed nature of the tradition. That second emphasis, on unambiguous progress, prefigures the tension with the land which grew into its violation in the name of progress and issued in the view of land as unrestricted gift.

The primary point to be recognized, however, is that the agrarian tradition maintained—sometimes all too sentimentally—that the farmer's care of the land was tied to the success of democracy and of the economy, and to the virtue of the yeoman-farmer as undergirding national virtue. Another way of emphasizing the connection between land and humankind can be seen in political events: the Homestead Act (1862) which sought to disperse western lands widely so as to further democratic values or Shays's Rebellion (1780–81) which protested the young government's seizing farmers' lands.[30] In short, though the agrarian tradition carried within it the possibility of abuse, it did nevertheless affirm the relationship of nature and spirit. It recognized that nature has much to teach us.

Another resource upon which the nation can draw in overcoming the nature-spirit dichotomy is the Native American heritage in regard to land. Though there are numerous specific tribal emphases, a number of similar themes can be discerned within them. Two are particularly relevant.

First, the land cannot be owned, but belongs to all. This is graphically demonstrated by the fact that early immigrant settlers found no fences separating one Indian's property from another's. There was, moreover, not even a concept of buying or selling. In fact, Indian spirituality saw beyond mere ownership and reflected the belief that the Indian is an integral part of the land. As Lakota chief Luther Standing Bear puts it, people "once grew as naturally as the wild sunflower; [they] belong just as the buffalo belonged."[31] Mother Earth is seen as an undivided unity that cannot be disposed of or owned. All people are, after all, inescapably a part of the Great Spirit.

A second characteristic theme is that the land must be respected. The land is the immediate source of life and provides for the needs of human and nonhuman life. From this base is derived a sense of the interdependence of all life. To abuse the land is self-abuse; to respect the land is to respect one's self. Love of the land produces a sense of living in harmony with it.[32]

Another group that makes common cause with those already mentioned is that of feminist thinkers. Carol Merchant, Sherry Ortner, Susan Griffin, Mary Daly, and Carol Gilligan come to mind. These scholars are united by their sensitivity to the affinity between women and nature and the way both have been denigrated as inferior to men and culture. Rosemary Ruether, a feminist theologian, has been particularly prescient on this issue. Ruether refers back to Hebrew Scripture as *resisting* subsequent elements which have tied "class and sexist languages to a view of nature as a sphere of human domination": the view that consciousness is transcendent to visible nature while the bodily sphere is ontologically and morally inferior; and the reading of the spirit-nature split into classist and sexist relations, with women, slaves, and lower classes identified with the realm of inferior "bodily" nature.[33] Feminist thought tends also to oppose hierarchical and divisive schemes in favor of interactive and unitive patterns. Particularly responsible for this tendency is women's ability to accept their materiality and to recognize their connection with the natural world.

The Christian tradition also contains elements which can contribute to overcoming a desacralization of nature and thus lead to a recovery of the intrinsic value of land. William Temple provides a starting point in claiming that the Christian religion is "the most avowedly materialist of all the great religions" since its central belief is that "the Word was made flesh."[34] The Hebrew Scriptures similarly contain a holistic conception of human beings who were animated by the breath of Yahweh, which same breath animated the birds of the air and the fish of the sea. Moreover, the cosmic Christology of Paul asserts that all things find their home in Jesus Christ through whom they were redeemed. Jesus spoke of no sparrow falling without God's attending to it and of God's clothing the grasses and the lilies of the field. There are, furthermore, an array of Christian thinkers who are part of this "creation-centered spirituality." These sources have in common the claims that creation is ongoing in all nature, that God is not absent from her world, and that the earth is indeed the Lord's. The feminist imagery of God as mother continuously nurturing her human and nonhuman creatures is especially powerful in communicating this on-going creation and care. God cares for the land.

Three central Christian themes and one metaphor that gathers up those three suggest the course a creation-centered spirituality might more fully entail. The first is the theme of ongoing creation, "God is creating *now* and continuously in and through the . . . creativity that is itself God in the process of creating."[35] That quotation comes not from a theologian but from a biologist; not incidentally, many themes in contemporary science support this theological bent. The second theme is incarnation itself, the mediation of God in the en-fleshment of Jesus Christ. God is embedded in the world, active in natural processes which are also and simultaneously spiritual. The third theme is that of *shalom*—the cosmic unity of the world in God and, hence, human connectedness with all others and the world itself.

Catching up these three themes is the metaphor posed by Grace Jantzen in her recent book *God's World, God's Body*,[36] in which she suggests understanding the relationship between God and the world as that between a person and his or her body rather than seeing God and the world as being in essential contrast. God cannot be reduced to a body any more than a person can be reduced to his or her's; nor can God be reduced to mind. God's transcendence resides then in God's completely permeating or containing the world as His/Her body. What happens when this metaphor is employed? The world becomes God's deliberate and loving self-expression, a home where God is present and active. It also heightens human responsibility for the earth. If the world is God's body, and human beings are stewards of that body, then indeed ecological responsibility is central to Christian ethics. On the basis of the emphases recovered through attending to these creation-centered themes the stewardship ethic becomes capable once again of appreciating the land. The task of agriculture can be seen as a spiritual one—the land as a gift and a communication of God's presence. Unless this deeper conception of stewardship can be retrieved and its original thrust toward the care of the land restored, then it had best—for the sake of the land *and* human future—be forgotten.

It would be a mistake to correlate American agrarian, Native American, feminist, and Judeo-Christian themes in a facile manner; nevertheless, all four sources of wisdom counteract the efficiency tradition and suggest the interrelation of people and land. They restore to consciousness certain values that have been obscured, and they present the means to resurrect a tradition which preserves significant values—harmony, respect, justice—to be understood as environmental as well as social values. Then the land will be given its voice and we will be enriched by what it can teach. Finally, creation-centered traditions remind us that we are more than efficient machines and that we must learn to respect ourselves as members of one body, embodied in communion with the land.

NOTES

1. Henry A. Wallace, *New Frontiers* (New York: Reynal and Hitchcock, 1934), p. 188.

2. Gilbert C. Fite, *American Farmers: The New Minority* (Bloomington: Indiana University Press, 1981), pp. 60–62.

3. A study of the legislative history of U.S. agriculture reveals that subsidies have been pegged either to the amount of produce harvested or to the amount of land idled or commodity curtailed. In either case it has been the farmer with the most produce or the most land who has received the greatest subsidy. In Roosevelt's day, when farms were more homogeneous and almost all were small owner-operated units, this policy was basically egalitarian. The greater disparity in the size and capitalization of today's farm structure renders the same agricultural policy very different in impact. And yet, the 1985 Farm Bill seemed destined to incorporate many of the features of Roosevelt's policy.

4. Earl O. Heady, "Economic Policies and Variables: Potentials and Problems for the Future," in *Farms in Transition*, ed. David E. Brewster (Ames: Iowa State University Press, 1983), p. 30. Heady is an agricultural economist at Iowa State.

5. These traditions, of course, extend beyond simple application to agriculture and have to do with the foundations of political and economic life.

6. See Richard Kirkendall, "The Central Theme of American Agricultural History," *Agriculture and Human Values* 1:2 (Spring 1984): 6–8. Kirkendall associates these effects with the examples of Jeffersonian democracy, Theodore Roosevelt's Country Life Commission, and William Jennings Bryan's political stance.

7. Joe R. Motheral, "The Family Farm and the Three Traditions," *Journal of Farm Economics* 33 (Nov. 1951): 514. Motheral's article locates three rather than two traditions: the agrarian—emphasizing the goodness of the relationship between land and farmer; the democratic—emphasizing farming's contribution to developing responsible citizens; and the efficiency tradition. Frequently the first two are combined, as I will do here. Motheral's essay, however, is well worth reexcavation.

8. William Cronon, *Changes in the Land: Indians, Colonists, and the Ecology of New England* (New York: Hill and Wang, 1983), p. 165.

9. Ibid., p. 20. Interesting in another connection is John Winthrop's assessment of the ravages of imported smallpox and malaria on the native pop-

ulation as the means by which "God hath hereby cleared our title to this place" (as quoted in Cronon, *Changes*, p. 90)

10. Fite, *American Farmers*, p. 238.

11. See, for example, the preamble to the 1960 Family Farm Income Act in which Congress declares its intention to promote and perpetuate "the family system of agriculture against all forms of collectivization . . . in full recognition that the system of independent family farms was the beginning and foundation of free enterprise in America . . . that it holds for the future the greatest promise of security and abundance of food and fiber and that it is an ever-present source of strength for democratic processes and the American ideal." It is ironic that the present structure of agribusiness can be seen as simply a capitalist form of collectivization.

12. Fite, *American Farmers*, p. 112.

13. See my article "Commercialization and the Professions," *Business and Professional Ethics Journal* 2 (Winter 1983): 57–81, for evidence of this trend as it has affected the professions.

14. The term is of course Max Weber's; interestingly, Kirkendall talks not of an efficiency tradition but of the "modernization" tradition.

15. Wendell Berry, "From Agribusiness to Agriculture," *New Political Science* 13 (Winter 1984): 37.

16. See, inter alia, *Variations in Farm Incomes and Their Relations to Agricultural Policies* (Washington, D.C.: Agriculture Department, Chamber of Commerce of the United States, Mar. 1945), pp. 9, 20, 21; and *An Adaptive Program for Agriculture*, a statement on national policy by the Research and Policy Committee of the Committee for Economic Development (Washington, D.C.: GPO, July 1962), pp. 2, 3, 7, 19, 33–34, 59–60.

17. Walter Goldschmidt, *As You Sow: Three Studies in the Social Consequences of Agribusiness* (Montclair, N.J.: Allanheld, 1978).

18. See *Food for People Not for Profit*, ed. Catherine Lerza and Michael Jacobson (New York: Ballantine Books, 1975), p. 165. Recently nutrition has come into vogue; concern for the quality of the food one eats has expanded beyond fringe groups. With this development small-scale, careful horticulture is making something of a comeback. See J. Tevere MacFadyen, *Gaining Ground: The Renewal of America's Small Farms* (New York: Holt, Rinehart, and Winston, 1984). In America, of course, fads travel in and out with the speed of a revolving door; nevertheless, MacFadyen's book points to hopeful trends.

19. The USDA study is quoted by John Hart, "How Agribusiness Is Destroying Agriculture," *Christianity and Crisis* 45 (Apr. 15, 1985): 132. Bryon Dorgan, "America's Real Farm Problem: It Can Be Solved," *Washington Monthly*, Apr. 1983, p. 21, quotes a 1979 USDA study to the same effect. For a study of the slippery term *efficiency* and a discussion of the ways in which large and small farms are efficient, see Ingolf Vogeler, *The Myth of the Family Farm: Agribusiness Dominance of U.S. Agriculture* (Boulder, Colo.: Westview Press, 1981), esp. chap. 5.

20. See Erazim Kohak, *The Embers and the Stars: A Philosophical Inquiry into*

the Moral Sense of Nature (Chicago: University of Chicago Press, 1984), chaps. 1 and 2.

21. James E. Sellers, *Public Ethics: American Morals and Manners* (New York: Harper & Row, 1970), p. 101, but also pp. 45–107.

22. Margaret Mead, *And Keep Your Powder Dry: An Anthropologist Looks at America* (New York: William Morrow & Co., 1942), p. 21.

23. I simply cannot establish the analogous tenets of the two ethics here, much as I am tempted to. However, as my exposition of the stewardship ethics proceeds, it will not be difficult for the reader to see how the two traditions have led to many of the same consequences.

24. See the differing creation stories of Genesis 1:1–2:4a and 2:4b–3. The verbs are from 1:28 and 2:15.

25. Gordon D. Kaufman, "A Problem for Theology: The Concept of Nature," *Harvard Theological Review* 65 (July 1972): 350–51.

26. W. H. Auden, *The Dyer's Hand* (London: Faber and Faber, 1963), p. 336.

27. Toward this end, given the critique of stewardship, the question of whether we need a more radical alternative than stewardship arises. I think not if—and certainly this is open to dispute—the world can be understood on the basis of creation-centered spirituality. Any alternative model would, at least, have to include the basic strength of the stewardship model—namely, accountability to God or to what John Dewey, in *A Common Faith*, called "the community of life."

28. Much of the mythology and thought connected with this tradition is chronicled by Henry Nash Smith, *Virgin Land: The American West as Symbol and Myth* (Cambridge: Harvard University Press, 1950, 1970). See also the essays in Twelve Southerners, *I'll Take My Stand: The South and the Agrarian Tradition* (1930; Baton Rouge: Louisiana State University Press, 1962).

29. David Noble, *The Eternal Adam and the New World Garden: The Central Myth in the American Novel since 1830* (New York: Braziller, 1968).

30. John Hart, in his *Spirit of the Earth: A Theology of the Land* (Ramsey, N.J.: Paulist, 1984) indicates how Native American thought, American political thought, and Christian theology converge to support the value of land.

31. Luther Standing Bear, *Land of the Spotted Eagle* (Lincoln: University of Nebraska Press, 1978).

32. Amanda Porterfield (see article, this volume) asserts that the American Indian spirituality of nature is the result of a complex historical process in which Indians have defined themselves as nature's protectors in response to Western culture and the devastation of their own cultures. Whether these are ancient themes or represent more recent developments, the reverence toward land (and human beings!) they reflect is noteworthy. I appreciate Porterfield's careful work in this area.

33. Rosemary Radford Ruether, *New Woman/New Earth* (New York: Seabury Press, 1975), pp. 188–89.

34. William Temple, *Nature, Man, and God* (London: Macmillan and Co., 1935), p. 478.

35. A. R. Peacocke, "The New Biology and *Nature, Man, and God*," in *The Experiment of Life*, ed. F. Kenneth Hare (Toronto: University of Toronto Press, 1983), p. 46.

36. Grace Jantzen, *God's World, God's Body* (Philadelphia: Westminster Press, 1984).

JOEL CARPENTER

Youth for Christ and the New Evangelicals' Place in the Life of the Nation

On the evening of Memorial Day, 1945, 70,000 people gathered at the Soldier Field stadium in Chicago to witness an open-air pageant. Like other ceremonies on that day, this one remembered fallen servicemen and rededicated a nation still at war to a global mission. This rally had another major purpose, however. It celebrated the first anniversary of the Chicago-area chapter of "Youth for Christ," a rapidly growing evangelistic youth movement. By mid-1945, its leaders estimated that their Youth for Christ rallies thrived in three hundred to four hundred cities and towns, with nearly half a million attending, while soldiers and sailors held dozens of similar rallies in Europe and the Pacific.[1]

The Soldier Field rally reflected, in one spectacular event, the convergence of a renewed, exuberant evangelicalism and the war-inspired revival of the American civic faith. Its musical program praised God and country with a three-hundred-piece band, a choir of five thousand, and several well-known gospel singers, including George Beverly Shea. On the field, the religious and patriotic program began with a flag ceremony performed by high school cadets and four hundred marching nurses. Next followed a pageant featuring missionary volunteers in national costumes dramatizing the call to evangelize the world. Standing for America was a young evangelist named Billy Graham; he issued a summons for another great revival. On the platform, war heroes attested to their faith, as did intercollegiate boxing titlist Bob Finley. Track star Gil Dodds, the record-holder for the indoor mile, ran an exhibition lap before giving his testimony. The evening's preacher followed; he was Percy Crawford, director of the nationally broadcast "Young People's Church of the Air." At his gospel invitation, hundreds signed "decision cards." As the meeting drew to a close, a spotlight circled the darkened stadium, while a huge neon sign blazed "Jesus Saves" and the choir sang "We Shall Shine as Stars in the Morning."[2]

Indeed they did, for this extravaganza attracted major news coverage. The Chicago papers, the wire services, and *Newsweek* magazine carried stories of the rally, and, a few weeks later, William Randolph

Hearst editorially blessed the youth movement and ordered his twenty-two newspapers to feature the rallies. Not since the Scopes trial had evangelical Christianity received such coverage, and, this time, most of it was friendly.[3]

Youth for Christ was one of the most striking early signs of a rising new evangelical movement, which has remained a prominent factor in American life since then. By the late 1940s, rallies had grown to over one thousand in number, with an estimated weekly attendance of one million people: Youth for Christ evangelists had preached by then in forty-six countries. Too restless and visionary to settle down to the task of ministering to teenagers, many of the movement's early leaders, notably Billy Graham and Bob Pierce, founder of World Vision, infused a larger postwar evangelical coalition with their energy. These youthful evangelists created a variety of new organizations and communicated their message with popular broadcasts and publications. They merged their desire to be helpful contributors to the "American cause" with a renewed vision for world evangelization and revival in the United States.[4] Youth for Christ thus became the spearhead of a postwar evangelistic thrust and the first dramatic sign that American evangelicals were "coming in from the cold."[5]

The Youth for Christ sensation of 1944–47 has become a bit of trivia in American historical narrative, but it is worth recovering and examining. Historians are beginning to pay more attention to the World War II experience as a powerful shaper of contemporary America.[6] Likewise, they have devoted more interest recently to evangelical Christianity's role in American culture.[7] The Youth for Christ episode shows, moreover, that these two factors intersect, that the cultural and civic mood prompted by World War II and the early stages of the cold war encouraged the reinvigoration of evangelicalism.

Youth for Christ's public notoriety, then, helps illustrate evangelicals' ongoing struggle to find their place in modern American life. This episode shows very pointedly that the "new evangelicals" were re-visioning their mission to the nation. After years of alienation in the wake of the fundamentalists' defeats and public ridicule, a generation of postfundamentalist evangelical leaders was emerging, with the recovery of a "Christian America" as a prominent point on their agenda. This yearning to restore evangelicals' moral leadership continued as an important theme in the ensuing decades. Indeed, some conservative evangelicals, along with a newly politicized fundamentalist movement, have translated the "Christian America" myth into a political platform and have entered public affairs with considerable force. The surprising emergence of this "religious factor" in the

American public arena has sent social analysts scrambling to find out how, in what has been considered a secular society, it could happen.[8]

The Youth for Christ story can shed some light on this "intrusion" of religion in the public square, for as an early manifestation of contemporary evangelicalism it displays some of this persuasion's distinctive traits in a particularly striking and protean form. Youth for Christ's sensational showing in the late 1940s illustrates evangelicalism's symbiotic relationship with modernity and with American culture in particular. Since their early days, evangelicals have been adept at converting communications technology to sustain their internal needs and send forth their message.[9] In a democratic and free-market religious milieu, they have been very audience conscious, as Nathan Hatch puts it, shaping their message to address the desires and tastes of their hearers.[10] Evangelicals also find it easy to identify themselves and their message with the "mystic chords" of American collective memory and hope, since Puritan convenantal and evangelical revivalist and millennial motifs are mixed into the foundations of American cultural identity and mission.[11] Furthermore, evangelical values and the revival style became thickly embedded in national life during the nineteenth century.[12] These cultural strata now lie buried under much of twentieth-century American society but are still prominent in important parts of the landscape, such as the South, and often emerge elsewhere in the ideals and rhetoric of American politics.[13] In times when the terrain buckles, when newer ideological and institutional structures waver, the older values and myths may reemerge. The era of World War II was such a time, and Youth for Christ was a medium for the rebonding of evangelical religion and American civic faith. "In times like these, you need an anchor," sang the Youth for Christ rally crowds, one that "grips the Solid Rock."[14] They referred, of course, to Jesus, but accepting him, they assumed, meant taking on evangelical Christian piety and mores as well. These values, evangelicals believed, provided the best anchorage for their nation.

This essay will show, then, that Youth for Christ campaigners were given opportunities in wartime and early postwar America to move out of their religious ghettoes and into the national public arena. Their talent for grafting the tastes and techniques of popular communications onto evangelism and their efforts to leave behind some of the alienation of their sectarian background merged with three war-inspired trends: increased popular religiosity, revived faith in America's manifest destiny, and intensified concern for public morality—especially that of the emerging youth culture. As a result, Youth for Christ leaders found that their calls for the "spiritual revitalization of America" received a more congenial hearing than evangelicals had encountered for a generation. This success spurred on the postwar resurgence of evangelicalism, prompting the born-again to seek another Great Awakening with renewed confidence and anticipation. One simply cannot understand the new engagement of evangelicals in public discourse without seeing, first, the process by which they made their reentry a generation ago and, second, the triumphs and frustrations they have encountered since then. The aim of this essay is to recover the first half of that story, which is less well known, and to suggest that some of evangelicals' frustrations with public life in the ensuing years stemmed from the terms of admission they had accepted earlier.

In order to understand the full significance of Youth for Christ as a turning point for American evangelicals, it is important to know what was new about the rally movement. Most of the Youth for Christ pioneers were from fundamentalist backgrounds.[15] This may seem surprising, because only twenty years earlier fundamentalists were made the laughingstock of the cosmopolitan shapers of public opinion. Fundamentalists responded by nurturing feelings of alienation toward American culture and developing a network of religious institutions which allowed them to build a virtual subculture.

The same commitment and energy that insured fundamentalism's survival and growth as a grass-roots religious movement propelled it outward into increasing public exposure and activity, for like many sectarians fundamentalists felt compelled to make converts. The truth of their faith, they insisted, was validated as it transformed people. The institutional flourishing of fundamentalism in the 1930s meant not only the development of "shelter belts" from the winds of modern secularity but the provision of new tools for evangelization. Fundamentalists and other evangelicals developed radio broadcasting, journalism, and advertising techniques to retool mass evangelism and give it a contemporary idiom. Revived interest in evangelism and new organizational networks such as the National Association of Evangelicals and the Christian Business Men's Committees made the immense task of sustaining citywide campaigns possible once more. Radio preachers, mission and educational executives, evangelists, and publishers began to notice that their movement had created many thriving ministries and that they enjoyed a surprisingly receptive general audience. Perhaps, they surmised, the old, nearly forgotten dream of a nationwide revival could still come true.[16]

By the early 1940s, revival was becoming the fundamentalist watchword. Encouraged by their own success, fundamentalists were shifting from a separatistic, "pilgrim" stance toward a reformist, "puritan" pose, with revivalism as their major instrument for seeking national renewal. Under the leadership of the Moody Bible Institute president, Will H. Houghton, virtually every issue of the *Moody Monthly* carried an editorial or an article pleading for widespread repentance and conversion. Indeed, the theme of the Moody Bible Institute's annual Founder's Week Conference in 1942 was "America's God-given Opportunity for World-wide revival Today." [17] Editor Philip Howard's *Sunday School Times* conveyed the same expectancy, and in 1943 he helped launch the "Christ for America" evangelistic association to sponsor campaigns in major cities. [18] New hope for a revival was prominent in the messages of the first two conventions of the National Association of Evangelicals in 1942 and 1943. No doubt the wartime crisis summoned fundamentalists to recover these themes of covenant and revival. Said the NAE's first president Harold Ockenga in "Christ for America," his inaugural address, World War II had brought all of humanity to a crossroads. On one path lay "the rescue of western civilization by a . . . revival of evangelical Christianity," while the other led to "a return to the Dark Ages of heathendom." [19]

To sum up this brief excursion, then, a new generation of fundamentalist leaders and their allies among other evangelicals were ushering in a major shift in outlook and activity. They were moving from alienation to engagement, from separatist sectarianism to panevangelical cooperation, and from the pose of a prophetic faithful remnant to that of the nation's evangelists and chaplains. Youth for Christ rode the crest of this new wave, and helped it break into the larger public's attention.

Internal development accounts for only part of the story, however. These "new evangelicals" drew powerful encouragement and assistance from the changing cultural climate during World War II and shortly thereafter. From their perspective, the nation showed a greater spiritual need and a greater religious interest than they had seen in a generation. America was "ripe for revival," they believed. [20] These perceptions have something of a corresponding reality behind them, for World War II was in many respects a tonic for Americans' faith in their nation's commonly stated ideals. Indeed, suggested one historian, the nation lived on the "accumulated social and political capital" of this experience long into the postwar years. [21] While the Depression had discouraged many people about ever realizing the American dream, war mobilization brought unprecedented opportunity—if not prosperity—to even the poorest. The Depression had generated internal strife, but the war brought a renewed sense of common purpose. True, millions experienced disrupted lives, pain and grief, or frustration at injustice. Yet the experiences of wartime prosperity and mobility and of defending their nation against anti-democratic enemies regenerated Americans' civic faith. Their nation's social, political, and economic institutions, many now affirmed, offered the fullest and freest way of life on earth. Popular entertainment, to give an example, unabashedly celebrated the American dream in these years, with *Oklahoma!* and *Our Town* evoking the same nostalgic reaffirmation of traditional values that inspired Norman Rockwell's magazine art. While Kate Smith made a hit of Irving Berlin's "God Bless America," the black bass Paul Robeson, though a committed socialist, performed the "Ballad for Americans" with gusto.[22]

Religious faith appeared to many to be one of the values most worth remembering and conserving. The critical, condescending tone of much public discussion of religion since the 1920s was now muted by the renewed respect for faith that emerged at all levels. Many thought the war effort required all the spiritual reserves the country could muster. Religious trends among liberal intellectuals included heightened respect for Reinhold Niebuhr's neo-orthodoxy and the neo-Thomist Catholic philosophy of Jacques Maritain, while many Jewish intellectuals recognized that their identity as a people needed a religious focus.[23] At the same time, piety became more fashionable along the Potomac. A syndicated columnist in Washington, D.C., praised fundamentalist Charles E. Fuller's "Old-Fashioned Revival Hour" for "bringing the new-old story of religion" to war-weary people; and Peter Marshall, the unctuous young Scot who pastored the city's New York Avenue Presbyterian Church, preached to overflowing crowds of government workers, congressmen, and soldiers. On a popular level, church attendance and membership swung sharply upward, and wartime stories of heroic chaplains, foxhole epiphanies, and interfaith fellowship abounded. For three years in a row, a religious novel was the nation's best-seller in fiction, and *Going My Way,* a gently inspiring story which portrayed Bing Crosby and Barry Fitzgerald as priests in New York City, won several Academy Awards in 1944.[24]

One might expect conservative evangelicals to be cheered by evidence of popular religious interest, but several spokesmen thought that the pervading moral climate contradicted these positive signs. As the war progressed, people were singing "Praise the Lord and Pass the Ammunition" and "God Bless America," but one fundamentalist editor thought that "passing the Lord and praising the ammunition" better described the national mood, as Americans boasted that their production of weaponry would win the war.[25] Conservative religious critics noticed that the war, as one historian later put it, "was a spur to both religious sentiment and permissiveness." Church attendance increased but so did alcohol and cigarette consumption. While women's fashions were skimpier, Hollywood grew more brazen, and live entertainment became more vulgar. In the boomtowns created by military camps and war industries, divorce, vice, and violent crime abounded.[26] While evangelist Hyman Appleman thought that it was good and proper for President Roosevelt to call for special days of prayer, he asked how God could answer these petitions when drunkenness and debauchery polluted the land. The nation should remember, Appleman wrote, that "If I regard iniquity in my heart, the Lord will not hear me."[27] Revival, not a rebirth of religiosity, was the need of the day, but the great religious awakening Appleman and other old-fashioned evangelists sought seemed to be eluding them.

The Youth for Christ campaigners, however, found currents which propelled their efforts past those of the older evangelists. The wartime focus on the nation's young people was stimulating a new "youth culture," with its own fashions and celebrities, and a new "young people's evangelism" seemed to be the instinctive response of young preachers and laymen who had grown up with this mass-media-generated popular culture. They emulated the entertainment world's stars and restyled gospel music to the "swing" and "sweet" sounds then popular. And like the radio newsmen, their messages were fast-paced, filled with late-breaking bulletins, and breathlessly urgent. Examples of these kinds of emulation abound, but here are two of the most striking: *Newsweek* labeled Torrey Johnson the "religious counterpart to Frank Sinatra," and Billy Graham patterned his preaching after the clipped cadences of news commentator Walter Winchell. Much more than their predecessors, the youth evangelists strove to be "geared to the times."[28]

Rising teenage crime had become one of the most worrisome domestic effects of the war, and here, too, Youth for Christ responded to its audience. To many, the fundamentalists' thunderings about gambling, smoking, drinking, and divorce sounded tedious and dated, no doubt, but everyone from J. Edgar Hoover of the FBI to the liberal sociologist Robert S. Lynd agreed with the preachers that teenage violence and vice had become national scourges. Crime-prone street gangs emerged in most big cities, and bus and train stations were full of teenage "Victory girls" who offered sexual favors to servicemen in exchange for a good time.[29] Thus, when Youth for Christ leaders claimed they had a spiritual antidote for juvenile delinquency, many community leaders gave them a hearing.[30]

The Youth for Christ movement, then, should be seen as an evangelical response to these three wartime trends: a rising concern about youth and public morality, an increase of popular religiosity, and the renewal of American civic faith. The best way to see the movement's accommodation to popular tastes and widely felt needs is in the context of its rallies. Rally evangelists hammered at the sins of youthful desire while creating an atmosphere of wholesome entertainment, patriotic affirmation, and religious commitment. Their meetings featured carefully orchestrated visions of innocence, heroism, and loyalty to a global cause, all wrapped in a contemporary idiom borrowed from radio variety shows and patriotic musical revues. Cosmetic-free girl ushers greeted the crowds while girl choirs dressed in white serenaded them; and the fast-paced program featured testimonies by decorated war veterans and sports stars, swing-tempo gospel music, and rousing prayer bulletins on the armed forces, Youth for Christ, and the worldwide missionary offensive. Sermons were short, rapid-fire, and laced with examples drawn from current events.[31] Young people "want something that challenges the heroic," Torrey Johnson explained. "They want something that demands sacrifice, . . . that appeals to the highest and holiest . . . that is worth living for and dying for."[32] In response to these perceived yearnings, rally leaders merged celebrations of the war effort and American civic ideals with calls for spiritual commitment. Allied offensives and missionary expansion shared the spotlight.

The evangelists often singled out young people's morals in order to convict them of their need for salvation. Youth for Christ evangelists, who often had sown a few wild oats before their conversions, spoke knowingly about teenage temptations—more, perhaps, as older brothers than as threatened parents—and then stressed that evangelical commitment and chastity was the better way. Jack Wyrtzen, leader of the "Word of Life" rally in New York, was particularly expert at stirring youthful consciences. He translated the parable of the Prodigal Son into contemporary (and perhaps autobiographical) terms; the young runaway "got to hanging about beer joints," began "playing fast and loose with women," and was soon "eating out of the garbage pails of sin." A reporter remarked that the youngsters listened with rapt attention, and that "some had grown a shade pale."[33]

By contrast, the music, the personal testimonies, and the evangelists' invitation to potential converts stressed the joy and satisfaction of commitment to Christ. At one Word of Life meeting, the all-girl choir and soloist George Beverly Shea sang "Jesus Can Satisfy the Heart," "Now I Belong to Jesus," and "What a Friend We Have in Jesus." When Wyrtzen told the audience that by confessing their sins and committing themselves to Christ they would start "the joy bells ringing in their hearts," a reporter said he saw an "almost pathetic eagerness" on many faces.[34] Youth for Christ evangelists unabashedly invited hearers to make a "decision for Christ," and many came forward; at the larger rallies, the penitents sometimes numbered in the hundreds.[35] Among the converts at Youth for Christ meetings were a large number of servicemen. One sailor testified, "I was a sinner, but now, praise the Lord, I am clean, through Christ." Said another young seaman attending the Chicago rally, "Ever since I left the protection of my home, I have felt almost adrift, with no sense of security. I don't want to get caught in the current of vice. I needed something to stabilize me and in my new faith in Christ, I have found it."[36] For many young people who were restless and eager for challenges but also uprooted, morally confused, and perhaps guilt-laden, Youth for Christ's message and invitation was compelling.

The Youth for Christ rallies evoked considerable public comment, and much of it was favorable. Civic leaders repeatedly praised Youth for Christ for its community service. Walter Anderson, chief of police in Charlotte, North Carolina, became the city's rally director, claiming that "Youth for Christ is doing more than anything else I know to stop juvenile delinquency." Governor Arthur B. Lainglie of Washington said that his job would be easier if there were more such youth ministries. Their combination of wholesome fun and religious challenge, he thought, was the best cure for juvenile crime. After Chicagoland Youth for Christ's Soldier Field rally in 1945, Governor Dwight H. Green of Illinois wrote Torrey Johnson that "your Saturday night meetings are tremendous forces for alleviating juvenile delinquency," and he urged communities to support them. After viewing a Youth for Christ rally in the Washington state capitol, President Truman was said to have remarked that it was just what America needed.[37]

The rally leaders and publicists basked in this praise. At a time when the nation seemed to be pulling together as never before, they were encouraged that important people thought "born-again Christians" could render a valuable service to America. These young evangelists had wagered their reputations on the chance that their accommodation to worldly tastes and trends would bring positive results, and such praise as they received became ammunition for debate with their more sectarian opponents. Being despised in the world's eyes had been a badge of honor, but for many recruitment and conversion had higher priority. So the desire for evangelistic success was becoming a powerful acculturating force among evangelicals.

Youth for Christ rallies provoked critical responses as well. William Randolph Hearst's endorsement of the movement and its widespread support from conservative Protestant businessmen made some political and religious liberals suspicious. What was Youth for Christ really up to? The Department of Justice was at that time prosecuting a group of right-wing radicals who sympathized with the Nazis, and at least one of them, Gerald Winrod, was a fundamentalist. Many liberals believed that their conservative counterparts constituted a genuine threat to American security, and in this brief "Brown Scare," the liberal left hurled accusations at the fundamentalists in particular.[38] Rumors circulated that Youth for Christ was the stepchild of "fascist-minded" business interests, and gained some credence because of Hearst's favorable publicity. These allegations were quickly dispelled, however, by the liberal Protestant *Christian Century,* even though its editors were not sympathetic to Youth for Christ.[39]

Youth for Christ's spokesmen's answers to these allegations reveal a great deal about how the new evangelicals' strategy and motives were developing. The movement's leaders quickly denied any right-wing political connections or intentions. When a *Time* reporter asked about these charges, Torrey Johnson dissociated the movement from the fundamentalists of the far right, claiming that he did not know Winrod and disapproved of the demagogue's views. Johnson denied that Youth for Christ had any political motives. Its only goals, he claimed, were "the spiritual revitalization of America" and "the complete evangelization of the world in our generation."[40] He and other "new evangelicals" were spurred on by a revived sense of evangelicals' moral custodianship for America and new hope for the global expansion of their faith, but they avoided translating these themes into a political agenda. In a national climate which acknowledged religious needs, encouraged moderation and conformity, but punished extremism, Youth for Christ eagerly distanced itself from any tinge of radicalism. As part of the emerging "postfundamentalist" party, the youth evangelists sensed that evangelical politicization would dredge up memories of the fundamentalist political failures of the previous generation. Anxious to keep their welcome to the wider corridors of national life, the young evangelists eagerly assured the public that they would be civil. They had "no political axes to grind," Johnson said,[41] but wanted to contribute in a less controversial way to the well-being of their land. For the time being, the new evangelicals' politics remained latent or very general and spiritualized. A "Christian America" was still their goal, but their means would be revival.

After the war came to a close, Youth for Christ's leaders found yet another convergence between their concerns and those of national public leaders, which reinforced their belief that their revival campaigns were welcome. As the United States' interests clashed increasingly with those of the Soviet Union, concern for the nation's moral integrity took on a new element of urgency. Global intervention and victory had reawakened Americans' ideas of manifest destiny and directed them to see themselves as the free world's leaders in the struggle against totalitarianism. If America was to fulfill this role, her people must be rededicated to freedom and reformed in morals—or so went the postwar jeremiads.[42] The growth of juvenile delinquency and rising divorce rates, many thought, were part of a larger spiritual malady that might make it easier for subversive forces to capture the hearts and minds of the people. Youth for Christ leaders latched onto this spiritual crisis motif. "Let me tell you something," Torrey Johnson cautioned, "America cannot survive another twenty-five years like the last. . . . If we have another lost generation, . . . America is sunk." Did the nation have the moral backbone to keep the world safe and free? Johnson told rally leaders that "we are headed either for a definite turning to God or the greatest calamity ever to strike the human race."[43]

For the first time in a generation, fundamentalists and evangelicals found that political leaders echoed such warnings. As the nation faced new crises as a global power, the old themes of "covenant people" and "redeemer nation" gained new currency. Only a day after he had heard Winston Churchill's grim "Iron Curtain" speech in 1946, President Truman told the Federal Council of Churches convened in Columbus, Ohio, that without "a moral and spiritual awakening" America would be lost. Likewise, General Dwight D. Eisenhower told a meeting of Army chaplains that there was no hope for mankind "except through moral regeneration." Eagerly quoting the politicians' jeremiads, Youth for Christ leaders offered to do their part.[44] But while Truman and Eisenhower were careful to keep their admonitions general enough to encompass all "Judeo-Christian" faiths,[45] evangelicals heard them as calls for revival. Their hopes for a "Christian America" produced by widespread personal repentance and conversion had been restored.

World War II and the postwar tensions heightened the global dimension of evangelicals' sense of mission. Fundamentalist and other evangelical foreign missionary agencies had been growing steadily in the previous decades,[46] but now born-again Christians in the armed forces and at home saw new opportunities and means to proclaim their gospel around the globe. The result was an explosion of new mission agencies and recruits. Filled with what they called a new "world vision," hundreds of missionary volunteers swamped the evangelical colleges and Bible schools, and others contributed to mission funds as never before.[47] The Youth for Christ movement poured its energy and personnel into this task. Hundreds of missionary volunteers were secured through the movement's "world vision" rallies, and its young evangelists founded major postwar missionary agencies. The armed forces' pursuit of global victory with all the resources of modern communications and transportation was challenging evangelicals, said youth evangelist Merv Rosell, to dare "greater conquests for Christ."[48] Visions of *Pax Americana* thus provoked a new global triumphalism among American evangelical missionaries.

While these missions' foremost aims were to preach the gospel, make converts, and establish new churches, the specter of communism propelled them as well. After hearing the famed anti-Nazi pastor Martin Niemoeller lament that German youth were a lost generation, Torrey Johnson wired him, offering the services of Youth for Christ. "If Germany goes communistic," Johnson warned, "then you can write France, Italy, Spain, and Portugal off . . . , and you can shove England down the road of socialism." But Christian revival and conversion, he believed, provided a peaceful counterforce to this trend.[49] As Youth for Christ rallies spread through the American occupation forces, the movement's leaders followed with what they called "invasion teams." These evangelists toured Great Britain, Scandinavia, France, the Netherlands, Germany, Greece, and Italy; the Caribbean and South America; and India and China. Meanwhile, General Douglas MacArthur had invited Youth for Christ and other missionaries to Japan to "provide the surest foundation for the firm establishment of democracy."[50] Such invitations made fundamentalists and evangelicals feel more welcome than ever before in their memory to become responsible, respectable contributors to the American mission.

Thus, as World War II and the early postwar experience seemed to offer the nation another chance to fulfill its manifest destiny at home and abroad, a new generation of fundamentalist and evangelical leaders reshaped their outlook according to these trends and looked forward to a fresh start. Perhaps "revival in our time" was on its way. Perhaps the mythic Christian past could be restored if enough people came to Christ. Eagerly they quoted II Chronicles 7:14 and applied it to the American situation: "If my people, which are called by my name, shall humble themselves, and pray, and seek my face, and turn from their wicked ways; then will I hear from heaven, and will forgive their sin, and will heal their land."[51]

What the Youth for Christ movement started, the new evangelical coalition carried forward. While evangelicals were still a long way from the centers of intellectual and political power in the 1950s and early 1960s, and they enjoyed the notice of news media only occasionally, their status was changing. Billy Graham emerged as evangelist to the nation, and then counsellor to presidents. Civic "leadership prayer breakfasts," led by evangelicals, sprang up in Washington, D.C., and across the country. A small group of evangelical theologians with doctorates from the nation's finest universities invigorated the coalition's intellectual life and dreamed of launching a new Christian university. With Graham's help, they launched instead a new periodical in 1956, *Christianity Today*, which became their voice in national public discourse. Clearly, the new evangelicals were enjoying a honeymoon with American culture.[52]

At a time when religious faith was generally considered "a good thing" and popular religious interest was high, the new evangelicals' call for revival in America did not seem very threatening. Indeed, the extent to which evangelical Christians' desire to restore "Christian America" clashed with the pluralistic reality of American public life had been masked. Billy Graham, the movement's leading prophet, pointedly insisted that Americans had to be spiritually transformed if the nation was to be saved. And turning to God, in Graham's message, meant becoming a "born-again Christian." The apostle Paul warned that this message is an offense to the Jew and an absurdity to the Gentile, but Graham and his generation of evangelical leaders were often able to finesse the issue by sheer goodwill and their skillful evocation of the nation's evangelical legacy. While some pundits considered Graham's message scandalous, most found it eccentric, perhaps, but pretty much in line with the other, more generic calls for "moral and spiritual awakening" in a time of crisis. Martin Marty observed in 1959 that much as Graham tried to call the nation to repentance, his bearers seemed more charmed than convicted. This admirable, clean-cut young man seemed to many to embody American virtue, and his utterances comported well with the conventions of American folk piety.[53] And as Graham went, so went the movement. Sociologist James Hunter suggests that evangelicals' yearning for acceptance and respect has prompted many to adopt "no offense, but I'm an evangelical" as their public posture. Thus the Youth for Christ movement shows, in embryo, the new evangelicals' ability to mirror their audience's concerns, market their message with polish and civility, and affirm the "American Way of Life." These traits allowed them to avoid confrontation with American pluralism and secularity and to regain a place for themselves in national public life. That "place" has been a troubled one, however, for a variety of reasons, all derived from the character of the implicit bargains evangelicals made to gain it.

First, the new evangelicals' place on the public rostrum lacked substance. It seemed to be based not so much on a recognition that their distinctive religious perspective deserved a hearing, but because they were both effective communicators of the myth of American righteousness and die-hard supporters of a conservative strain of civic piety. Evangelicals' more particular message seemed to be selectively tuned out, or blandly tolerated, while presidential prayer breakfasts and "Honor America" rallies, rather, were the movement's admission tickets to the public arena.[54] For their part, the new evangelicals desired respect and admiration, so they blunted some of the jagged edges of their distinctiveness. These reformers of fundamentalism recovered a measure of civic responsibility, but at the same time they had become domesticated.[55] Fundamentalism's hairy-fisted, Bible-thumping condemnations of America's sins sounded impolitely shrill to the new evangelicals. Like the cosmopolitan German Jews in late nineteenth-century America, neo-evangelicals were often embarrassed by the tribalism of their less civil kinsmen.[56] Knowing that their own welcome was tenuous, they feared that the antics of the unreconstructed fundamentalists put their enterprise in jeopardy.

Evangelicals' role as civic chaplains made their place in public life particularly vulnerable to the powerful opposition to public piety that has mounted since the 1960s. A prominent cohort of government officials, political reform activists, jurists, journalists, and educators has generated this trend. This group's background has been the highly secular "culture of critical discourse" of the universities, the mass media, and the research-based industries. Their public service ideals are drawn more from a secular regard for humanity than traditional religious values. In the past two decades, this cultural group has succeeded remarkably in redirecting American public policy toward their position, which insists that religious conviction and expression have no legitimate public place. Dubbed the "New Class" by sociologists and "secular humanists" by conservative evangelicals, this group, evangelicals are convinced, threatens to privatize religion and smash evangelical hopes of restoring American righteousness.[57] By the late 1970s, with the rules of public civility seeming to tilt increasingly in favor of the secularists, conservative evangelicals seemed handcuffed in their attempts to reassert the legitimacy of their place.

The neo-evangelicals' country cousins, however, have come charging into the public arena. Militant fundamentalists and a host of pentecostal allies, newly politicized, have emerged out of the cultural hinterlands and have refused to go away. Just at the time when some evangelical leaders, in the wake of Vietnam and Watergate, began to abandon large parts of the "Christian America" myth and to insist that God's covenants are both more individual and more transnational,[58] politicized fundamentalists reasserted the older vision, without the polite veneer the neo-evangelicals had carefully devised.[59]

Yet even the fundamentalists want to be liked. Jerry Falwell, Tim LaHaye, and others have tried to calm the intense fear and hatred they have encountered with assurances that they are not antidemocratic theocrats. They want, states LaHaye's platform, to "restore traditional moral and spiritual values" to American life and to reinforce, not undermine, religious freedom and democracy. They want to throw out the new public rules that seem to exclude religious values, but, granted those changes, they promise to behave.[60] Recently, in a very candid conversation, Tim LaHaye was asked what he would do if he could have his way completely in American politics. With scarcely a pause, he said he would be satisfied with the full incorporation of President Reagan's platform.[61] So much for the alarmist nonsense about a fundamentalist-inspired Brown Shirt movement. And so much for the new fundamentalism's ability to sustain any prophetic independence. Perhaps, as Garrison Keillor recently suggested, fundamentalists' "mission in this country" is to "shake us up . . . with a very strong and very clear message."[62] But, having done some shaking, they are apparently very eager to beg pardon.

And so the assimilation process which domesticated much of sectarian evangelicalism in the 1940s is at work again. The terms are not quite the same; notably, the new fundamentalism is adamantly political, and the occasion is not a friendly invitation to participate but the forcible intrusion of resentful, uninvited guests. Yet the parallels are striking: an internally vigorous, culturally responsive, and powerfully communicative evangelical movement has again found the opportunity to emerge from political, cultural, and religious obscurity. As a variety of cultural critics have asserted, the nation's cultural and spiritual landscape has buckled,[63] and, as in the days of World War II and the cold war, many Americans have been prompted to receive older verities. Once again, evangelical Christianity, with fulsome grass-roots support, has been a powerful medium for this resurgence, and again it appears that evangelicals—in this case the new fundamentalists—are being absorbed and tamed.

This essay has three major points to contribute, then, to the larger discussion about the role religion has played in the life of the United States. First, the Youth for Christ episode supports those who argue against the notion that modernization produces irresistible and progressive secularization. Religious faith and practice, as Theodore Caplow's Middletown III project has recently underscored, is a vital component of contemporary American culture.[64] Despite the powerful influence of secular institutions and ideologies, these deeply inscribed and vigorously maintained religious interpretations of American common life have repeatedly come welling up to rebaptize the nation's civic hopes and values.

Second, Youth for Christ and the postwar evangelical resurgence point to the accommodationist character of evangelicalism in the United States. To be sure, there is a genuine and paradoxical tension in these movements between a sojourner's alienation from the present age and what Grant Wacker calls a "custodial ideal," a proprietary responsibility for American national morality.[65] Evangelicals still feel that "this world is not my home," but they also identify strongly with the American nation. Their convictions and American republican ideology have been too closely joined for them to easily sever the relationship. And being thus drawn to public engagement, evangelicals want to be liked, to be accepted. Evangelicals' very adaptability, then, has limited the range of their ministry. Successful as evangelists and as chaplains to the nation's civic soul, they have much more trouble sustaining a prophetic role.

And finally, this story illumines the cultural hegemony of the American civic faith. In many respects, the United States is a radically pluralistic nation, composed of widely divergent peoples and regions. Common rootedness in the soil and common racial memory have slight power to bind its people as a body public. Rather, somewhat like some African peoples—and not unlike evangelicalism—the Americans are an assimilative tribe.[66] Lacking the cohesion of a single ethnic source, they manufacture their identity and ideology out of the mythic past. Consequently, any attempt to "re-vision" America faces serious constraints. American public life encourages a facile tolerance, but tends to absorb, approve, and domesticate traditions and movements on previously established, safe cultural terms. Youth for Christ and the new evangelicalism's emergence into the public square shows this powerful homogenizing tendency at work. Evangelical Christianity has been and still seeks to be a resource for the American moral imagination, but the scope of its vision and those of other religious traditions is narrowed by the limits of that imagination. Things could be worse, though. One alternative, all too common among nations that lack a focal point for public discourse, is religious civil war.

NOTES

1. Accounts of Youth for Christ's rapid expansion in 1944–45 appear in Mel Larson, *Youth for Christ: Twentieth Century Wonder* (Grand Rapids: Zondervan, 1947), pp. 84–95; J. Elwin Wright, "Youth for Christ," *United Evangelical Action* 6 (Feb. 15, 1945): 8 (this periodical is cited hereinafter as *UEA*); James Hefley, *God Goes to High School* (Waco, Tex.: Word, 1970) pp. 38–49, 69. Youth for Christ was comprised of a variety of evangelical ministries to "young people." The formation of Youth for Christ International in the summer of 1945 did not by any means bring all of these into one organization. Other significant groups included Percy Crawford's Young People's Church of the Air, centered in Philadelphia; Jim Rayburn's Young Life Campaign, first headquartered in Dallas; Jack Wyrtzen's Word of Life organization in greater New York; and many smaller groups. Additional youth-related ministries participated in this evangelistic surge, including Dawson Trotman's Navigators ministry to servicemen and the North American branch of Inter Varsity Christian Fellowship, organized in 1938.

2. "Wanted: A Miracle of Good Weather and 'Youth for Christ' Rally Got It," *Newsweek*, June 11, 1945, p. 84; and Mel Larson, "70,000 Attend Chicago Youth for Christ Rally Held on Memorial Day," *UEA* 6 (June 15, 1945): 1, 8.

3. "Wanted: A Miracle"; "Youth's New Crusade," editorial reprinted from Hearst papers as "William Randolph Hearst's Editorial Endorsement of 'Youth for Christ'" *UEA* 6 (July 16, 1945): 13; "Hearst Papers Now Boost Youth for Christ," *UEA* 6 (July 2, 1945): 1; *Minutes of the First Annual Convention,* Youth for Christ International, July 22–29, 1945, pp. 6, 23–24, Youth for Christ Records, collection 48, box 13, folder 36, Billy Graham Center Archives. Other accounts of Youth for Christ in national publications during 1945–46 include William F. McDermott, "Bobby-Soxers Find the Sawdust Trail," *Colliers,* May 26, 1945, pp. 22–23; Frank S. Mead, "Apostle to Youth," *Christian Herald* 68 (Sept. 1945): 15–17; John Ray Evers, "'Youth for Christ' Meets Pittsburg," *Christian Century* 63 (Oct. 10, 1945): 1171–72; "Youth for Christ," *Time,* Feb. 4, 1946, pp. 46–47; Clarence Woodbury, "Bobby-Soxers Sing Hallelujah," *American Magazine* 141 (Mar. 1946): 26–27.

4. "Youth for Christ Expands in Continent," *UEA* 4 (Jan. 1, 1946): 9; "Five YFC Leaders Will Fly to Europe," *UEA* 5 (Mar. 1946): 10; "G.I. Missionaries to Manila," *Sunday* 7 (Feb. 1946): 26–29, 49–52; Larson, *Youth for Christ,* pp. 20–23, 60–63, 69–71, 80–81, 92–93; Hefley, *God Goes to High School,* pp. 29–30, 34–40, 55–65, 66–68. See also Joel A. Carpenter, "From Fundamentalism to the New Evangelical Coalition," in *Evangelicalism and Modern America,*

ed. George Marsden (Grand Rapids: Eerdmans, 1984), pp. 3–16. For a help-ful explanation of the distinction, assumed throughout this essay, between evangelical Christianity as a diverse family of movements which nonetheless share beliefs, influences, and tendencies and the more conscious coalition of "new evangelicals" being formed in the 1940s on the initiative of a "progres-sive" party in fundamentalism, see George Marsden "The Evangelical De-nomination," in ibid., pp. vii-xvi. These more consistently self-identified "evangelicals," who Marsden suggests "have attempted to speak or to set stan-dards for evangelicals generally," are the focus of this essay.

5. Richard John Neuhaus, *The Naked Public Square: Religion and Democracy in America* (Grand Rapids: Eerdmans, 1984), p. 260.

6. Charles C. Alexander, *Nationalism in American Thought, 1930–1945* (Chi-cago: Rand McNally, 1969); John Morton Blum, *V Was for Victory: Politics and American Culture during World War II* (New York: Harcourt Brace Jovanovich, 1976); and Geoffrey Perrett, *Days of Sadness, Years of Triumph: The American People, 1939–1945* (Baltimore: Penguin Books, 1974) remain the most in-sightful treatments of the war's impact on domestic cultural trends; while James Gilbert, *Another Chance: Postwar America, 1945–1968* (Philadelphia: Temple University Press, 1981) and Richard A. Pells, *The Liberal Mind in a Conservative Age: American Intellectuals in the 1940's and 1950's* (New York: Har-per and Row, 1984) provide interpretations of the war's effect on postwar culture.

7. Leonard I. Sweet's masterful bibliographical essay, "The Evangelical Tradition in America," in *The Evangelical Tradition in America*, ed. L. I. Sweet (Macon, Ga.: Mercer University Press, 1984), pp. 1–86, documents the recent flurry of scholarly interest in American evangelicals.

8. Works that assess the rise of the new religions right are legion already, and constantly growing. For a helpful guide to this literature through 1984, see Richard V. Pierard, "The New Religious Right in American Politics," in *Evangelicalism and Modern America*, pp. 161–74 and 206–12 (bibliography).

9. Harry S. Stout, "Religion, Communications, and the Ideological Origins of the American Revolution," *William and Mary Quarterly*, 3d ser., 34 (Oct. 1977): 419–544; Nathan O. Hatch, "The Christian Movement and the De-mand for a Theology of People," *Journal of American History* 67 (Dec. 1980): 545–67; Hatch, "Elias Smith and the Rise of Religious Journalism in the Early Republic," in *Printing and Society in Early America*, ed. William L. Joyce et al. (Worcester, Mass.: American Antiquarian Society, 1983), pp. 250–77; and Joan Jacobs Brumberg, *Mission for Life: The Story of the Family of Adoniram Judson* (New York: Free Press, 1980), pp. 44–78.

10. Nathan O. Hatch, "Evangelicalism as a Democratic Movement," in *Evangelism and Modern America*, pp. 71–82.

11. Ernest Lee Tuveson, *Redeemer Nation: The Idea of America's Millennial Role* (Chicago: University of Chicago Press, 1968); Nathan O. Hatch, *The Sa-cred Cause of Liberty: Republican Thought and the Millennium in Revolutionary New England* (New Haven: Yale University Press, 1977); Alan E. Heimert, *Religion*

and the American Mind: From the Great Awakening to the Revolution (Cambridge: Harvard University Press, 1966).

12. Perry Miller, *The Life of the Mind in America from the Revolution to the Civil War* (New York: Harcourt, Brace, & World, 1965), vol. 1, *The Evangelical Basis;* Gordon S. Wood, "Evangelical America and Early Mormonism," *New York History* 61 (Oct. 1980): 359–86; Martin E. Marty, *Righteous Empire: The Protestant Experience in America* (New York: Dial Press, 1970).

13. William Lee Miller, "The Seminarian Strain: Church and Statesmen in the Democratic Party," *New Republic,* July 9, 1984, pp. 18–21.

14. Ruth Caye Jones, "In Times like These," copyright 1944, assigned to Zondervan Publishing Company.

15. The notable exceptions were Charles Templeton, a Church of the Nazarene pastor in Toronto; Watson Argue, a pastor of an Assemblies of God congregation in Winnipeg; and Hubert Mitchell, of the International Church of the Foursquare Gospel in Los Angeles. Among those leaders who clearly were fundamentalist by training and affiliation were Torrey Johnson and Billy Graham of Chicago, Richard Harvey of St. Louis, Jack Wrytzen of New York, Percy Crawford and Walter Smyth of Philadelphia, John Huffman of Boston, George Wilson and Merv Rosell of Minneapolis, Roger Malsbary of Indianapolis, and Glenn Wagner of Washington, D.C. See Torrey Johnson and Robert Cook, *Reaching Youth for Christ* (Chicago: Moody Press, 1944), pp. 31–34; Larson, *Youth for Christ,* pp. 35, 45, 48–55, 59, 66–67, 86–87, 106–7, 112–13.

16. For more detailed exposition of these developments, see Carpenter, "From Fundamentalism to the New Evangelical Coalition," pp. 3–16; and Carpenter, "The Fundamentalist Leaven and the Rise of an Evangelical United Front," in *Evangelical Tradition in America,* pp. 257–88.

17. "Call to Founder's Week Conference," *Moody Monthly* (hereinafter *MM*) 42 (Dec. 1941): 188; John R. Riebe, "Founder's Week Conference Report," *MM* 42 (Mar. 1942): 407–10. On preoccupation with revival see G. Allen Fleece, "How Shall I Pray for Revival?" *MM* 42 (Mar. 1942): 406, 410; "Editorial Notes," *MM* 43 (Mar. 1943): 395; (June 1943): 560; (July 1943): 611; (Aug. 1943): 663; Armin R. Gesswein, "How Does a Revival Begin?" *MM* 44 (Oct. 1943): 61, 62, 86; "Editorial Notes," *MM* 44 (Nov. 1943): 115; (Dec. 1943): 184; (Feb. 1944): 315.

18. Horace F. Dean, "Christ for America," *Sunday School Times* (hereinafter *SST*) 85 (May 1, 1943): 351–52; Paul W. Rood, "A Statement to Fundamentalists," *SST* 84 (Apr. 25, 1942): 331; George T. B. Davis, "Nationwide Prayer for Revival and Victory," *SST* 84 (May 23, 1942): 412–13; Dan Gilbert, "The Fundamentals Convention in Boston," *SST* 84 (July 4, 1942): 539.

19. See addresses in the convention annuals *Evangelical Action! A Report of the Organization of the National Association of Evangelicals for United Action* (Boston: Fellowship Press, 1942); and *United We Stand, A Report of the Constitutional Convention of the National Association of Evangelicals,* Chicago, Ill., May 3–6, 1943. Ockenga's address quoted from ibid., p. 11.

20. J. Elwin Wright, "Observations of the President," *New England Fellowship Monthly* 43 (Apr. 1945): 8–9.

21. Perrett, *Days of Sadness,* p. 443.

22. Ibid., pp. 196–99, 325–42, 350–56, 407–9, 441–43 (quote on p. 443); Alexander, *Nationalism in American Thought,* pp. 190–201; Richard Pells, *Radical Visions and American Dreams: Culture and Social Thought in the Depression Years* (New York: Harper and Row, 1973), pp. 116–50, 358–64; Allan Nevins, "How We Felt about the War," in *While You Were Gone: A Report of Wartime Life in the United States,* ed. Jack Goodman (New York: Simon and Schuster, 1946), pp. 3–27; Philip Gleason, "Americans All: World War II and the Shaping of American Identity," *American Quarterly* 36 (Fall 1984): 342–58.

23. Pells, *Radical Visions,* pp. 141–50, 358–61; Alexander, *Nationalism,* pp. 155–56, 223–24, 229; Nathan Glazer, *American Judaism,* rev. ed. (Chicago: University of Chicago Press, 1972), p. 108.

24. Perrett, *Days of Sadness,* pp. 384–85; Lewis Gannett, "Books," and Bosley Crowther, "The Movies," in *While You Were Gone,* pp. 455, 516; Daniel P. Fuller, *Give the Winds a Mighty Voice: The Story of Charles E. Fuller* (Waco, Tex.: Word, 1972), pp. 140–41; Catherine Marshall, *A Man Called Peter* (New York: McGraw-Hill, 1951).

25. "Passing the Lord and Praising the Ammunition," *The Voice* 21 (Apr. 1943): 14; "'God Bless America,'" *Revelation* 12 (Sept. 1942): 396, 426–28; "V for What-Have-You," ibid. (Nov. 1942): 390, 490; "Prayer and Victory," *MM* 44 (June 1944): 543; William Ward Ayer, "The Pastor Says," *Calvary Pulpit* 3, no. 3 (1941): 2.

26. Perrett, *Days of Sadness,* pp. 384 (quote), 238–40, 385–87, 394–95.

27. Hyman J. Appleman, "America's First Line of Defense," *MM* 43 (July 1943): 615.

28. "Wanted: A Miracle," p. 84 (on Sinatra); Marshall Frady, *Billy Graham: A Parable of American Righteousness* (Boston: Little, Brown, 1979), p. 162; John Pollack, *Billy Graham: The Authorized Biography* (New York: McGraw-Hill, 1965), p. 85 (on Winchell); Johnson and Cook, *Reaching Youth for Christ,* p. 21.

29. Perrett, *Days of Sadness,* pp. 238–40, 347–50, 385–87, 394–95; Anna W. M. Wolf and Irene Simonton Black, "What Happened to the Younger People," in *While You Were Gone,* pp. 78–85; Agnes E. Meyer, *Journey through Chaos* (New York: Harcourt, Brace, and Co., 1944), pp. 6, 60–65, 209–13, 250.

30. Billy Graham, "Report of the Vice President at Large," *Minutes of the Second Annual Convention,* Youth for Christ International, Minneapolis, July 22–29, 1946, pp. 38–39, Youth for Christ Records, collection 48, box 13, folder 37, Billy Graham Center Archives; and Torrey M. Johnson to Herbert J. Taylor, Oct. 25, 1945, Herbert John Taylor Papers, collection 20, box 72, folder 2, Billy Graham Center Archives; both reveal that Youth for Christ evangelists actively courted the support of business and community leaders and were encouraged by the receptions they experienced.

31. "Youth for Christ," *Time,* pp. 46–47; "Wanted: A Miracle" p. 84; "Bobby-Sox Hit Sawdust Trail," *News-Views: The Chicago Daily News Pictorial Section,* Feb. 3, 1945, p. 2; Woodbury, "Bobby-Soxers Sing Hallelujah," pp. 26–27, 121; McDermott, "Bobby-Soxers Find the Sawdust Trail," pp. 22–23;

Mel Larson, "Youth for Christ Movements," *MM* 45 (Dec. 1944): 204–5; Evers, "'Youth for Christ' Meets Pittsburgh," pp. 1171–72; Mead, "Apostle to Youth," pp. 15–17.

32. Mel Larson, *Young Man on Fire: The Story of Torrey Johnson and Youth for Christ* (Chicago: Youth Publications, 1945), p. 112.

33. Woodbury, "Bobby-Soxers Sing Hallelujah," p. 121.

34. Ibid., pp. 27, 121.

35. Graham, "Report of the Vice President at Large."

36. Woodbury, "Bobby-Soxers Sing Hallelujah," p. 27; McDermott, "Bobby-Soxers Find the Sawdust Trail," p. 23.

37. Larson, *Youth for Christ*, p. 111; Willard M. Aldrich, "Young People Are a Crop," *MM* 45 (Nov. 1944): 138, 140; Larson, *Young Man*, p. 91; *Minutes of the First Annual Convention*, p. 16.

38. Leo P. Ribuffo, *The Old Christian Right: The Protestant Far Right from the Depression to the Cold War* (Philadelphia: Temple University Press, 1983), pp. 178–81.

39. "Has Youth for Christ Gone Fascist?" *Christian Century* 62 (Nov. 14, 1945): 1243–44.

40. "Anti-Semitism Is Denied," *New York Times*, Dec. 16, 1945, p. 31; "Lauds Youth for Christ," *New York Times*, Oct. 27, 1945, p. 44; Leslie Marston, "Youth for Christ or Moloch," *UEA* 4 (Dec. 15, 1945): 13; "Young Communists vs Youth for Christ," *UEA* 5 (Mar. 15, 1946): 14; "Youth for Christ," *Time*, pp. 46–47.

41. "Youth for Christ," *Time*, p. 47.

42. E. Stanley Jones, *The Christ of the American Road* (New York: Abingdon-Cokesbury, 1944); "Between War and Peace," *Catholic Action* 27 (Dec. 1945): 27–28; Charles Clayton Morrison, *Can Protestantism Win America?* (New York: Harper & Brothers, 1948); Willard L. Sperry, *Religion in America* (New York: Macmillan, 1946), pp. 258–63; Robert S. Alley, *So Help Me God: Religion and the Presidency, Wilson to Nixon* (Richmond: John Knox, 1972), pp. 69–81; John F. Wilson, *Public Religion in American Culture* (Philadelphia: Temple University Press, 1979), pp. 15, 50–51, 54–55; Robert T. Handy, *A Christian America: Protestant Hopes and Historical Realities*, 2d ed. (New York: Oxford University Press, 1984), pp. 186–87.

43. Torrey Johnson, "God Is in It!" in *Minutes of the First Annual Convention*, p. 30.

44. Harry S. Truman, "The Need for Moral Analyzing," *New York Times*, Mar. 6, 1946, p. 11; [Eisenhower], "Honoring Evangelical Chaplains of the Armed Forces," *New York Times*, Apr. 25, 1946, p. 5; Graham, "Report of the Vice President at Large," pp. 36, 41; Larson, *Youth for Christ*, p. 29; Hefley, *God Goes to High School*, p. 13.

45. Patrick Henry, "'And I Don't Care What It Is': The Tradition-History of a Civil Religion Proof-Text," *Journal of the American Academy of Religion* 49 (1981): 35–49; Mark Silk, "Notes on the Judeo-Christian Tradition in America," *American Quarterly* 36 (Spring 1984): 65–85.

46. Joel A. Carpenter, "Fundamentalist Institutions and the Rise of Evangelical Protestantism, 1929–1942," *Church History* 49 (Mar. 1980): 72–73.

47. R. Arthur Mathews, *Towers Pointing Upward* (Columbia, S.C.: Columbia Bible College, 1973), pp. 143–45; "Philadelphia Bible Institute Alumni Activities, Class of 1942 to 1953, Inclusive," paper in Alumni Office files, Philadelphia College of the Bible; Hefley, *God Goes to High School*, pp. 65–68; Ralph D. Winter, *The Twenty-Five Unbelievable Years, 1945 to 1969* (South Pasadena, Calif.: Institute of Church Growth, 1970), pp. 47–51.

48. Merv Rosell, "God's Global 'Go!'" *Winona Echoes* 51 (1945): 260–65; Torrey Johnson, "Almighty Challenge," ibid., pp. 157–65; F. D. Whitesell, "God's Purposes in World War No. 2," *The Voice* 23 (Sept. 1944): 8; Robert H. Glover, "Postwar Missions," *King's Business* 36 (Mar. 1945): 84, 117; Glover, "What Should Be Our Postwar Evangelical Missionary Strategy?" *UEA* 4 (Sept. 15, 1945): 6, 19; Roy Ostreicher, "Post War Plans," *Brown Gold* 3 (June 1945): 4; Johnson, "Pressing on in Youth for Christ," pp. 6–7.

49. Torrey Johnson, "Accepting the Challenge!" *Minutes of the First Annual Convention,* p. 18.

50. Larson, *Youth for Christ,* pp. 22–23, 79–81, 91–94; Hefley, *God Goes to High School,* pp. 13 (quote), 3–40.

51. J. Elwin Wright, "Post-War Opportunity Requires Action Now," *New England Fellowship Monthly* 43 (Mar. 1945): 8–9; James DeForest Murch, "The Church's Post-War Program," *UEA* 4 (Sept. 1, 1945): 12; "The Trouble Lies Deep," *UEA* 4 (Sept. 15, 1945): 12–13; Billy Graham, "We Need Revival" (sermon preached in 1949 Los Angeles meetings), in *Revival in Our Time: The Story of the Billy Graham Evangelistic Campaigns* (Wheaton, Ill.: Van Kampen, 1950), pp. 69–80; Harold John Ockenga, "Is America's Revival Breaking?" *Evangelical Beacon,* July 18, 1950, pp. 5–6.

52. Rudolph L. Nelson, "Fundamentalism at Harvard: The Case of Edward John Carnell," *Quarterly Review* 2 (Summer 1982): 79–98; Edwin H. Rian, "The Plight of Protestantism in Education," *MM* 46 (Oct. 1945): 76, 110–11; "Planning Curriculum for New University," *UEA* 5 (May 1, 1946): 9; Wilbur M. Smith, *Before I Forget* (Chicago: Moody Press, 1971), pp. 175–82, 283–95; Joel Carpenter, "The Moody Monthly," in *The Conservative Press in America,* ed. William Longton and Ronald Lora (Westport, Conn.: Greenwood Press, forthcoming). See Donald G. Bloesch, *The Evangelical Renaissance* (Grand Rapids: Eerdmans, 1973).

53. This paragraph owes much to the evaluation of Billy Graham in Martin Marty's *New Shape of American Religion* (New York: Harper & Brothers, 1959), pp. 21–27. A. Roy Echardt, *The Surge of Piety in America: An Appraisal* (New York: Association Press, 1958), pp. 42–67, notes Graham's basic affinity to the common concerns of American popular religion. See also Frady, *Billy Graham,* for a windy yet often insightful treatment of these themes. Hatch, "Evangelicalism as a Democratic Movement," reveals these character traits in the larger movement.

54. Richard V. Pierard, *The Unequal Yoke: Evangelical Christianity and Political*

Conservatism (Philadelphia: Lippincott, 1970); Robert D. Linder and Richard V. Pierard, *Twilight of the Saints: Biblical Christianity and Civil Religion in America* (Downers Grove, Ill.: InterVarsity Press, 1978), pp. 97–111, 140–43. Robert Booth Fowler, *A New Engagement: Evangelical Political Thought, 1966–1976* (Grand Rapids: Eerdmans, 1982), perceptively surveys the conservative political loyalties of the "evangelical mainstream" in chapters 2 through 4.

55. James Davison Hunter, *American Evangelicalism: Conservative Religion and the Quandary of Modernity* (New Brunswick, N.J.: Rutgers University Press, 1983), chap. 6, "Accommodation: The Domestication of Belief."

56. Neo-evangelicals register their exasperation with fundamentalism in Harold J. Ockenga, "Can Fundamentalism Win America?" *Christian Life and Times* 2 (June 1947): 13–15; Edward John Carnell, "Post-Fundamentalist Faith," *Christian Century* 76 (Aug. 26, 1959): 971; Carnell, *The Case for Orthodox Theology* (Philadelphia: Westminster, 1959), pp. 113–25; Ockenga, "Resurgent Evangelical Leadership," *Christianity Today* 4 (Oct. 10, 1960): 11–15; Harold Lindsell, "Who Are the Evangelicals?" *Christianity Today* 9 (June 18, 1967): 3–6. On Jewish internal tensions, see John Higham, *Send These to Me: Jews and Other Immigrants in Urban America* (New York: Atheneum, 1975), pp. 138–73.

57. Hunter, *American Evangelicalism*, pp. 107–19; he cites a variety of sociological studies of the New Class phenomenon, and also evangelical and fundamentalist polemics against secular humanism.

58. Mark A. Noll, Nathan O. Hatch, George M. Marsden, *The Search for Christian America* (Westchester, Ill.: Crossway, 1983); John Warwick Montgomery, *The Shaping of America* (Minneapolis: Bethany Fellowship, 1976); Richard V. Pierard, "From Evangelical Exclusiveness to Ecumenical Openness: Billy Graham and Sociopolitical Issues," *Journal of Ecumenical Studies* 20 (Summer 1983): 425–46.

59. Jerry Falwell, ed., *Listen America!* (New York: Doubleday, 1980); Peter Marshall and David Manuel, *The Light and the Glory* (Old Tappan, N.J.: Revell, 1977); John W. Whitehead, *The Second American Revolution* (Elgin, Ill.: David C. Cook, 1982); Francis Schaeffer, *A Christian Manifesto* (Westchester, Ill.: Crossway, 1981).

60. Richard John Neuhaus, "What Fundamentalists Want," *Commentary* 79 (May 1985): 41–46 (quote), informs this and the previous paragraph; see also Richard Lovelace, "Future Shock and Christian Hope," *Christianity Today* 27 (Aug. 5, 1983): 16; and "An Interview with the Lone Ranger of American Fundamentalism," *Christianity Today* 25 (Sept. 4, 1981): 22–23.

61. Tim LaHaye, in a discussion at the Center on Religion and Society's consultation, "The Bible, Politics, and Democracy," Billy Graham Center, Wheaton College (Ill.), Nov. 8, 1985, audio tape.

62. "Door Interview: Garrison Keillor," *Wittenburg Door*, no. 84 (Apr.-May 1985): 18.

63. On the decline of moral and political coherence, see Neuhaus, *Naked Public Square;* Christopher Lasch, "The Cultural Civil War and the Crisis of Faith," *Katallagete* 8 (Summer 1982): 12–18; Lasch, *The Culture of Narcissism:*

American Life in an Age of Diminishing Expectations (New York: W. W. Norton, 1978); Robert A. Nisbet, *The Twilight of Authority* (New York: Oxford, 1975); Daniel Yankelovich, *New Rules: Searching for Self-Fulfillment in a World Turned Upside Down* (New York: Random House, 1981); and Robert N. Bellah, Richard Madsen, William M. Sullivan, Ann Swidler, and Steven M. Tipton, *Habits of the Heart: Individualism and Commitment in American Life* (Berkeley: University of California Press, 1985).

64. Theodore Caplow, Howard M. Bahr, Bruce A. Chadwick, *All Faithful People: Change and Continuity in Middletown's Religion* (Minneapolis: University of Minnesota Press, 1983).

65. Grant Wacker, "Uneasy in Zion: Evangelicalism in Postmodern Society," in *Evangelicalism and Modern America*, pp. 22–24. George Marsden, "Preachers of Paradox: The Religious New Right in Historical Perspective," in *Religion and America: Spiritual Life in a Secular Age*, ed. Mary Douglas and Steven Tipton (Boston: Beacon Press, 1983), pp. 150–68, explains this tension.

66. John Higham, "Hanging Together: Divergent Unities in American History," *Journal of American History* 61 (June 1974): 7–28; John Ngusha Orkar, "Patterns of Assimilation of the Tiv," paper presented to the Centre for African Studies, Dalhousie University, 1983, cited by Marsden, "Evangelicals, History, and Modernity," in *Evangelicalism and Modern America*, p. 97. Marsden ascribes this characteristic to American evangelicals.

JONATHAN D. SARNA

Is Judaism Compatible with American Civil Religion?
The Problem of Christmas and the "National Faith"

Christmas Eve of 1968 found the three astronauts of Apollo 8 in lunar orbit. Their mission, America's first manned attempt to encircle the moon, had been eagerly anticipated for months and captured international attention. Millions sat riveted to their television sets on the evening of December 24 as the astronauts, "coming to you live from the moon," presented an awesome picture of the small receding earth and then, with their cameras turned around, focused on the "vast, lonely, forbidding type expanse of nothing . . . up here on the moon." A few moments later, precisely at lunar sunrise, they announced a "message." In a year that had witnessed two tragic assassinations, bloody race riots, the capture of the *Pueblo,* and the Tet offensive almost any Christmas message would have been appropriate. The message of the astronauts, however, was not primarily one of Christmas cheer, and had nothing to do with the "Prince of Peace" or the "spirit of the season." Instead, it consisted of a dramatic reading of the first ten verses of the Book of Genesis, the story of the creation of the world.[1]

"We thought a long time about that," astronaut William Anders later revealed, "I first thought we should use something specifically Christian, something about Christmas. But when we thought about the vastness of our world, we decided to read a message that did not belong to any one religion but which belonged to all men on earth. . . . My mail has been predominantly in favor of what we did."[2]

What is surprising about Anders's statement, and was not noticed at the time, is his reference to Christmas as something "specifically Christian." More commonly, Americans assume Christmas to be a universal celebration of peace and goodwill, one in which all patriotic Americans, regardless of their faith, can and should participate. To W. Lloyd Warner, for example,

> The ceremonial calendar of American society, this yearly round of holidays and holy days . . . is a symbol system used by *all* Americans. Christ-

mas, Thanksgiving, Memorial Day, and the Fourth of July are days in our ceremonial calendar which allow Americans to express common sentiments . . . and share their feelings with others on set days preestablished by the society for that very purpose. This calendar functions to draw all people together, to emphasize their similarities and common heritage, to minimize their differences, and to contribute to their thinking, feeling and acting alike.[3]

Christmas, according to this view, is part of American "civil religion" and not "specifically Christian" at all. Indeed, if it were "specifically Christian," how could it possibly be a *national* holiday? And yet as astronaut Anders understood, Christmas obviously *is* "specifically Christian"—that is what the "Christ" in Christmas is all about. The problem admits of no easy solution, for whether Christmas is a broadly national or a narrowly Christian holiday has implications that go far beyond the confines of the day itself. The ramifications of the problem, in fact, lead to fundamental questions reaching to the very heart of the relationship between Christianity, the state, and American civil religion.

Christmas is the only national holiday that is both rooted in a specific religious tradition and suffused with symbolic affirmations of a faith that many Americans—more than one in twenty[4]—do not share. Annually on December 25 these Americans face a dilemma: should they ignore the holiday and at least by implication alienate themselves from the "Christmas spirit" that is supposed to promote feelings of fellowship among all Americans, or should they celebrate Christmas in some fashion and overlook its Christian character? American civil religion beckons alluringly, inviting all to participate in the "Christmas spirit" whether they are Christian or not. Yet having been welcomed, non-Christians quickly find that the rites of the season unmistakably reflect Christianity's central myths and tenets. On no other day during the year do non-Christians so deeply feel the clash between the country they love and the faith they cherish.

This paper examines the "Christmas problem" through the eyes of the nation's largest non-Christian religious body, the Jews. It first sets out the problem, and argues, based on evidence from the American celebration of Christmas, that American civil religion, at least on this one day of the year, is far more unabashedly Christian than generally conceded. It then moves on to trace the various ways that Jews as a minority religious group have responded to the position they find themselves in on Christmas, and explains why none of these responses have succeeded. Finally, it turns to recent legal clashes over public expressions of Christmas—expressions which some view as manifestations of American civil religion but which Jews see as overt Christianity—paying particular attention to the recent Supreme Court decision in *Lynch v. Donnelly,* where the justices attempted to resolve some of the unique dilemmas that Christmas poses.

Seen from the perspective to be established here, the "Christmas problem" of American Jews casts into bold relief concerns central to any proper understanding of American religion. First, it recovers for renewed consideration some of the dilemmas faced by minority faiths in a majority Christian culture. Second, it demands substantial re-thinking of what civil religion means and how inclusive it is of non-Christians. Finally, it raises in yet another setting three related, on-going, and irresolvable tensions woven into the fabric of American life: church versus state, national unity versus religious diversity, and majority rule versus minority rights.

Although the first Christmas in America was apparently celebrated by Columbus in 1492, the holiday in its modern form—with trees, stockings, Santa Claus, and gift-giving—only took shape in the nine-teenth century. In the colonial period, many New England Protestants rejected any observance of the day, both as part of their rebellion against Anglicanism and on the grounds that Christmas was one of the "devices of men" and not grounded in Scripture. In 1659, the General Court of Massachusetts actually enacted a law to punish those who kept the day sacred. Dutch Reformed, Roman Catholic, Episco-palian, and Lutheran immigrants took a more positive view of the holiday, and celebrated it according to their ancestral traditions. Under their influence, and with the rise of immigration following the Revolution, Christmas observances became increasingly common na-tionwide. Still, it was not until 1849 that New York and Virginia rec-ognized Christmas as a legal holiday, and fully forty-one years later before the holiday had gained legal recognition in all of the states and territories. By then, James H. Barnett writes, "the various elements of Christmas had coalesced into a festival of great popularity and of con-siderable social significance. It not only embodied the import of the Nativity but also affirmed a secular faith in the durability of family ties and the importance of human brotherhood. In addition, Christ-mas folk imagery had become linked to patriotism . . . [the] celebra-tion foreshadowed the commercial exploitation of the contemporary Christmas."[5]

From a modern perspective, the development of Christmas into an *American* holiday, linked in the public mind with such other national holidays as New Year's Day, the Fourth of July, and Thanksgiving, poses an obvious problem, given the widely accepted ideas about American religious pluralism and church-state separation. Unlike New Year's, Christmas still retains sacred and specifically Christian associations in both its hymns and its symbols. While some of its characteristics are those normally associated with celebrations of American civil religion—independent of church ties, socially integrative, and reflecting "deep-seated values and commitments"[6]—these are conspicuously fused with elements of traditional Christianity. It is on account of this dualism—this mixture of the broadly civil with the narrowly Christian[7]—that non-Christians, and Jews specifically, have never been able to sanctify Christmas religiously the way they can all other sacred days in the American national calendar, Thanksgiving in particular.[8] That the day has nevertheless been accepted as part of American "civil religion" suggests that the basis of America's national faith is actually far more narrowly sectarian[9] than students of the subject have been prepared to admit. Christmas may be an exception to general patterns of American religious life, a once-a-year deviation from the norm. But even if it is, it still calls some of the most fundamental assumptions of American civil religion into question.

To demonstrate this, one need look no further than the presidential messages relating to Christmas that have been delivered over the past six decades.[10] Recall that Robert Bellah, in sustaining his argument that civil religion although selectively derived from Christianity "is clearly not itself Christianity," pointed to the fact that no president "mentions Christ in his inaugural address . . . although not one of them fails to mention God."[11] No similar claim could be made for presidential messages at Christmastide. Calvin Coolidge, who in 1923 both lit the first national Christmas tree and delivered the first formal presidential Christmas message, urged Americans in 1927 to make Christmas "a state of mind . . . if we think on these things there will be born in us a Savior and over us will shine a star sending its gleam of hope to the world." In his 1944 Christmas Eve address to the nation, Franklin Roosevelt declared that "we will celebrate this Christmas Day in our traditional American way—because of its deep spiritual meaning to us; because the teachings of Christ are fundamental in our lives; and because we want our youngest generation to grow up knowing the significance of this tradition and the story of the coming of the immortal Prince of Peace and Good Will." Three years later, Harry Truman urged Americans to "put our trust in the unerring Star which guided the Wise Men to the Manger of Bethlehem." In 1960, Dwight Eisenhower used his last Christmas message to the nation to link "zeal for America's progress in fulfilling her own high purposes" with the thought that with it "our veneration of Christmas and its meaning will be better understood throughout the world and we shall be true to ourselves, to our Nation, and the Man whose birth 2,000 years ago, we now celebrate." In 1962 Eisenhower's successor, John F. Kennedy, made the truly astonishing (and in its own way deeply revealing) statement that "Moslems, Hindus, Buddhists, as well as Christians, pause from their labors on the 25th day of December to celebrate the birthday of the Prince of Peace. There could be no more striking proof that Christmas is truly the universal holiday of all men." Lyndon Johnson, far more subdued—as all subsequent presidents have been—simply urged Americans to "pray at this season that in all we do as individuals and as a nation, we may be motivated by that spirit of generosity and compassion which Christ taught us so long ago." [12]

Christmas messages, of course, have not ignored those well-known civil religion themes usually associated with presidential utterances on ritual occasions—quite the opposite. President Ford, in 1976, managed in a Christmas message of fewer than three hundred words to refer to such familiar American *sancta* as "family ties," "friendly reunions," "timeless values," "domestic harmony," "brotherhood among all peoples," "love," and "lasting peace." President Reagan, in 1982, spoke in his Christmas radio address of "love, hope, prayer, and patriotism." He called America "uniquely blessed, not only with the rich bounty of our land but by a bounty of the spirit—a kind of year-round Christmas spirit that still makes our country a beacon of hope in a troubled world." [13] What makes these statements different from the usual ceremonial utterances of our presidents, studied by Bellah and others, is simply that around Christmas they are so frequently coupled with words appealing specifically to Christians, leaving out non-Christian Americans. Whereas the national faith as otherwise expressed in symbols, ceremonies, and myths is expansive and broadly inclusive, seeking to embrace citizens of every creed, on Christmas the focus momentarily narrows: civil religion and Christianity converge.

II

"For Jewish children," the Yiddish poet Morris Rosenfeld once observed, "Christmas is a sad season." [14] Part of the sadness lies in the fact that they feel left out, "without lights in the front yard or decorations in the window." [15] Part lies in the fact that on this day more than any other they have to confront America's predominantly Christian culture, and their own minority status within it. Of course, American Jews are by no means unique in experiencing feelings of this sort:

Jehovah's Witnesses, who refuse to salute the flag, and other minority religious groups feel the tension between themselves and the majority culture far more regularly.[16] But American Jews have always had quite different central assumptions about their relationship to the American mainstream: the Bill of Rights, civil religion, and the theory of the "triple melting pot" (Protestant-Catholic-Jew) all posit an America where Jews and Christians stand on an equal footing. Christmas reminds Jews that, notwithstanding this, they nevertheless remain a small religious minority, subject to majority rule. What makes their minority position especially difficult is the fact that America's "Christmas spirit" symbolizes highly prized civic virtues—generosity, family togetherness, peace, goodwill, and sharing—that Jews, however they relate to Christmas, surely do *not* wish to be seen as opposing (particularly since that would cast them in the popular mind with that infamous villain, Ebenezer Scrooge). The challenge facing Jews, then, is how to forge an appropriate response to Christmas, one that keeps them within the American mainstream and associates them with its values and civic ceremonies, even as it distances them from the Christmas religious celebration that as non-Christians they cannot embrace.

No single Jewish answer has ever emerged. Instead, Jewish responses have covered a broad spectrum, everything from thoroughgoing assimilation to strident identification. Rabbi Kenneth White has traced these responses at length,[17] surveying the subject from the mid-nineteenth century down to the present. His findings, on which this section liberally draws, shed light on the whole question of how members of a religious minority react when confronted with two opposing pressures: one from the majority prodding them to conform to the nation's religious norms, the other from coreligionists summoning them to remain loyal to their ancestral faith. Yet, more than just a standard study in assimilation and identity maintenance is involved here, for American law and tradition embrace religious pluralism; any form of established religious conformity is constitutionally enjoined. The "Christmas problem" of American Jews is thus, at a deeper level, a struggle between two American values: the one, reflected in civil religion, recognizes the need for national unity; the other, reflected in the First Amendment, appreciates the value of religious diversity. While Christmas, the only major ritual of American civil religion rooted in Christianity, serves as a prime focus of this clash, the basic issues involved—the limits of unity, the limits of diversity—are as old as the Republic itself.

The spectrum of Jewish responses to Christmas divides into three broad spans that may roughly be labeled acceptance, rejection, and accommodation. The range of acceptance includes examples going back as early as 1848, when a family letter records that the young children of one of America's leading Jews, Mordecai M. Noah, were "making arrangements to hang up their stockings . . . for Christmas."[18] A generation later, in 1880, a correspondent named "Observer" from Philadelphia, writing in the *American Israelite,* revealed that "The festivities of the season celebrated among our Gentile neighbors are rarely forbidden in the Jewish home. There is a decided tendency to make Christmas as well as New Years a national observation upon the plea that many Christians do not take the cause of the holiday into consideration while participating in its enjoyment; presents are interchanged in Jewish homes, and even trees decorated to please the children who would otherwise be deprived of that which their neighbors enjoy."[19] By 1940, according to *Time,* "perhaps half" of American Jews "gave their friends Christmas presents, told their children about Santa Claus; some even put trees in their living rooms and wreaths in their windows."[20]

But if many American Jews seemed outwardly to accept Christmas, they did not all do so for the same reasons. Some, leaders and intellectuals, rationalized their actions as based on religious tolerance, respect for Christianity, and the quest for national religious unity. Mordecai Noah thus reinterpreted Christmas as the birthday of that religion which spread monotheism throughout the world—"a great event worthy of being commemorated among civilized communities."[21] Daniel De Leon, shortly to become a leading Socialist, believed that Jews and Gentiles could agree "upon the sublimity of the character of Jesus of Nazareth" and that by joining together in Christmas celebrations all contributed "toward ushering in that longed for era when hostility between race and race shall cease, and the amalgamation between them shall be accomplished." In 1891, one unnamed but notable Cincinnati Jew justified his Christmas celebrations on the grounds that they "show our Christian neighbors that we Jews have become liberal enough to rejoice with them in the birth of their Savior, and magnanimous enough to forgive them for the years of persecution we have suffered through them." Rabbi Louis Witt, whose "Thank God for Christmas" created a furor in 1940, argued that the spectacle of "a Jew celebrating Christmas" might be "neither treason of Jew nor triumph of Christian but partnership of Jew and Christian in the making of a better world."[22]

For other Jews, however, Christmas celebrations held no Christological significance whatsoever. They celebrated Christmas as, in Rabbi Emil G. Hirsch's words, a "universal holiday . . . neither Christian nor Jewish,"[23] and consequently observed only those rituals, like the tree and the exchange of gifts, that seemed to them thoroughly secular (or pagan) in origin and purpose. Charles Dickens's *A Christmas Carol,* "a literary sermon against selfishness and panegyric on brotherhood and benevolence, particularly at Christmas," gave secular observers of Christmas a sacred text. The Jewish poet Emma Lazarus's homage to "The mystic glories of the wondrous tree" helped to universalize Christmas's leading symbol.[24] For the rest, Jews could exercise their own imaginations. The wealthy Haas family of San Francisco customarily put on an annual family Christmas extravaganza, devoid of serious religious sentiment but filled with excitement and enthusiasm: "One Christmas, the guests were magically transplanted to Mexico. Santa Claus pinatas dangled from glass fixtures, while colorful sombreros, Indian baskets, papier-mâché chickens and horses, and full-blown paper poppies decorated the long dining tables. In a scramble of merriment, gleeful children whacked noisily at the Santa pinatas and were showered with small gifts and candies."[25] Anne Roiphe described a more austere but no less secular Christmas celebration in a controversial *New York Times* article in 1978.[26]

The importance of these efforts to distinguish Christian from non-Christian aspects of Christmas and to accept only the latter can scarcely be underestimated,[27] especially in light of the analysis offered above and the recent endorsement of this line of argument by the Supreme Court. If the Christmas of civil religion really could be separated from the Christmas of Christianity, then the tension between rites of national unity and Jewish identity maintenance would be resolved, and the problem of explaining how Christmas could be a national holiday without America being a Christian country would disappear. For most Americans, however, Christmas is *not* divided into secular and religious components but is a unified whole. And that whole is inextricably bound up with Jesus of Nazareth.

Some Jews, taking an opposite approach to this problem, have rejected Christmas entirely, national holiday or not. Typically, Jewish opponents of Christmas have recalled the day's long and sad history for Jews, the fact that "in olden times many of our people were murdered on that day."[28] Had not Jews traditionally spent "Nittel night" (Judeo-German for Christmas) far removed from Christians and in anything but a Christmas frame of mind? "To celebrate a day which has cost us so much pain, so much blood, so much sorrowful experiences with joy and merriment," Felix Adler once cried, "is this not a bitter and cruel mockery?" Rev. Jacob Voorsanger likewise wondered, in 1883, why Jews should "pay respect to a day that . . . holds up the presumed truth of Christianity and the falsity of all other creeds." [29]

More than just history and polemics, however, were involved here. The deeper problem, as Rabbi Julius Eckman expressed it as far back as 1866, was one of some Jews "aping Christians." He looked upon "the Christmas tree or the Christmas present in the house of the Jew as an act of denial of identity—an attempt [by the American Jew] to appear to be what he is not." [30] Already Christmas had assumed, at least for rejectionists, a larger symbolic meaning: it gauged assimilationist trends in general. By opposing Jewish celebrations of Christmas, Jewish leaders sought to stem the assimilationist tide, keeping Jews firmly within the fold. As "Close Observor" explained in 1888, "the 'Christmas tree' is [called] but an innocent amusement but these little innocent amusements unfortunately recoil and become almost the vengeance of Providence upon the perpetrators. Hence the present increase of intermarriages . . . disrespect of parents . . . disregard for religion." [31] Similar arguments relating Jewish observance of Christmas to assimilation and ultimate apostasy have been repeated down to the present day; they form one of the mainstays of rejectionist ideology.

In spurning Christmas, rejectionists have also consistently protested the idea that Christmas could ever be a *secular* American holiday. As forcefully as others might insist that "the essence of Christmas [is] peace on earth, goodwill toward men, the carols, the presents," they have insisted, as the American Jewish Congress put it in 1946, that "the observance of the day which marks the birth of the Savior is nothing and can be nothing but a Christian religious holiday." [32] Indeed, when Catholic and Protestant leaders in the 1960s mounted a campaign to "put Christ back into Christmas," Jewish leaders, led by Rabbi Julius Mark of Temple Emanu-El in New York, offered them warm support: "I sympathize wholeheartedly with my colleagues of the Christian faith—both Catholics and Protestants—who have been protesting against the commercialization and the paganization of Christmas. . . . It's a religious holiday, a solemn occasion." [33] An open letter "from a Christian to one of my best friends—a Jew," frequently reprinted in Jewish publications, drove the point home:

> You showed me the Christmas tree you placed in our home. You thought I would be flattered and pleased. It is a beautiful tree carefully set up and painstakingly decorated, but I am neither flattered nor pleased. I am somewhat resentful, a little ashamed, and deeply sorry.
>
> To me, a Christian, the tree is a symbol of my most sacred religious holiday. During the Christmas season it is a constant reminder of the birth of our Lord and Savior. It has become, in our home, the mark of

our Christianity during the season of the year when we celebrate the birth of our Christ.

I ask myself what meaning the tree has for you? It cannot be a Christian religious symbol, since you have told me often that as a Jew you do not accept Christ. For you, it must then be no more than a pretty decoration. How can I help feeling resentful when you take my sacred religious symbol and make it a mere "decoration"?[34]

In stressing the thoroughly Christian character of Christmas, even that of its seemingly most neutral symbols, Jewish rejectionists were, at least by implication, admitting to their minority status. They rejected any thought of concessions to "secular" aspects of the national holiday, and made Jews who observed Christmas rituals, however they justified them, feel guilty by telling them that they were either following the sacred tenets of another religion (and not just some "popular folk rituals") or unwittingly insulting their Christian friends by impiously treating their sacred symbols in a profane manner. The only problem with all of this was that it made no effort to explain to Jews, who after all denied that America was a Christian country, how the Christian holiday of Christmas ever came to be observed on a national basis. How could sacred Christian symbols be allowed to adorn government property? By denying that there was any broadly civil or exclusively secular quality to the holiday, rejectionists undermined the most commonly offered explanation for why Christmas did not violate church-state separation in America. At the same time, although nobody realized it, they also undermined their own arguments against allowing overtly Christian symbols like the crèche on public property: if the tree was a Christian religious symbol and permitted why should a crèche be any different?[35]

Jews, in short, faced an agonizing dilemma. For them to reject the national holiday of Christmas by declaring it a thoroughly Christian religious day promoted Jewish identity, but at the cost of admitting that America was a Christian society from which Jews necessarily stood apart. For them to embrace a secular Christmas as an American holiday strengthened the hands of those who insisted that America, while religious, was *not* a Christian society, but at the cost of promoting manifest assimilation. Both alternatives were fraught with conspicuous difficulties.

Walter M. Gerson, in his pioneering study of Jewish "strain-reducing mechanisms" at Christmas time,[36] listed various ways in which American Jews have sought to overcome some of these difficulties: peer support, social insulation, psychological compartmentalization, redefinition of rituals in secular terms, and patterned evasion. Yet, more important than all of these has been the effort by Jews to create functional alternatives to Christmas celebrations, alternatives at once similar enough to substitute for those of Christmas and still distinctive enough for their own Jewish character to shine through unmistakably. Throughout American Jewish history Jews have responded to Christian challenges in this way, in the process creating numerous and in many cases highly beneficial communal innovations.[37] The most widely accepted of these by far has been the late nineteenth-century revitalization of the half-forgotten festival of Chanukah.

Chanukah, the festival of lights, commemorates the successful revolt by Jewish forces, led by Mattathias, the son of Hasmoneus, and his sons, known as the Maccabees, against the Syrian-Greek persecutions and demands for Jewish subservience to Hellenism. The holiday recalls the Temple's rededication on the twenty-fifth day of the Jewish month of Kislev, 165 B.C.E It also reminds the faithful of the "miracle of Chanukah"—that the single undefiled cruse of oil found in the Temple, an amount sufficient to light the Temple lamp (menorah) for only one day, burned fully for eight days, until additional oil could be obtained. Yet while observed annually by practicing Jews through the lighting of Chanukah candles and various other rituals and folkways, Chanukah never historically achieved the status of a major Jewish holiday: gifts were not traditionally exchanged, families did not traditionally gather. Indeed in America prior to the Civil War, many Jews do not seem to have celebrated Chanukah at all.[38]

With the burgeoning spread of Christmas, concerned Jews in various quarters moved to "revive" Chanukah so as to counteract those who "ignore[d] their holy days and celebrate[d] those of Christians." By 1870, "Chanukah festivals" emphasizing candle lighting, food, plays, and singing had been instituted in Jewish Sunday schools—an obvious response to Protestant Sunday school Christmas festivals.[39] In 1879, when young Jews connected with the Young Men's Hebrew Association looked to Chanukah as part of their effort to revitalize American Judaism, the holiday really took off. The *American Hebrew* spoke that year of a "Chanukah tidal wave" that had "swept the country." Chanukah pageants, advertised as the "Grand Revival of the Jewish National Holiday of Chanucka," won widespread publicity and attracted crowds beyond the wildest expectations of even the youthful organizers. "Every worker in the cause of a revived Judaism," one of them wrote, "must have felt the inspiration exuded from the enthusiastic interest evinced by such a mass of Israel's people." Rabbi Max Lilienthal of Cincinnati urged Jews everywhere to "imitate such festivals . . . We need no Christmas trees in our Jewish houses: our Chanukah can be celebrated to the delight of old and young." Speaking to the famed Pittsburgh rabbinical conference in 1885, Rabbi Kaufmann Kohler brought the point home to Jewish leaders: "Chanukah ought to appear in a more festive garb of light and joy in order to be a strong competitor of the Christmas festivity."[40]

The subsequent magnification of Chanukah into a Jewish holiday, celebrated according to a recent survey by more Jews than attend synagogue services on the Day of Atonement,[41] has been amply described elsewhere.[42] Chanukah succeeded somewhat in placating Jewish children who longed for the gifts and pageantry that their Christmas-observing Christian friends enjoyed and is partly responsible for the great decline in the number of Jewish homes that sport Christmas trees.[43] But Chanukah could do nothing to solve the fundamental problem connected with Christmas—that it is a *national* holiday. The many different failed attempts over the years to bring Chanukah and Christmas ever more closely into line bear emphatic testimony to this basic reality.[44]

The only activities that have temporarily succeeded in overcoming Jews' "Christmas problem" (winning in the process widespread Jewish approbation) are those involving charity and goodwill, such as efforts to aid the needy on Christmas Day and programs that see Jews volunteering to work in public institutions for Christian employees to enjoy the day off with their families.[45] These programs place Jews where they can at once be both part of the larger community and apart from it, and thus provide a way for Jews to display their civic-mindedness, to practice the kind of traditional values that Christmas represents, and to do so without requiring them in any way actually to observe Christmas rituals or to otherwise assimilate. Momentarily, they succeed in achieving for Jews a magic synthesis of national unity and religious diversity which allows them to associate with other Americans in the "Christmas spirit" without directly participating in Christmas rituals—but only momentarily, for these are but short-term, makeshift solutions to Jews' anomalous situation on Christmas. The fundamental dilemma produced by Christmas's unique status in the American national calendar remains unresolved.

III

"It is indeed [as] unwise to make noise, as it is vulgar," a writer in the *American Israelite* warned in 1907. "If your convictions tell you that Christmas thoughts must not enter into the life of your little ones, if you fear the contamination of young souls by the tinsel of foreign symbols, keep them away from places where such danger is lurking. . . . By injudicious protests we make ourselves obnoxious. We must cultivate a spirit of amity with those amongst whom we live, and we must respect the traditions of the majority, when our conscience can be sa[l]ved by means less vigorous than official protest. In the newer language of the day, we must know ourselves as a minority."[46]

This attitude, a mixture of civility, vigilance, pragmatism, and resignation, found widespread acceptance in American Jewish circles for many decades. As members of a historically persecuted minority faith, eager to gain acceptance as full participants in the life of the nation, understandably fearful of religious controversy, and wary of being considered unpatriotic, Jews for the most part hesitated to alienate their Christian neighbors by taking their complaints about the national observance of Christmas into the public arena. However much they discussed the problem among themselves, they considered it impolitic, if not downright dangerous, to contest the issue openly.

Immigrant Jews, especially those associated with radical movements, might have been expected to take a firmer stance in opposition to Christmas, but so long as they remained huddled together in areas of first settlement they were largely isolated from the holiday's major manifestations. In an exceptional 1906 case, Eastern European Jews in New York did encourage a boycott of the city's public schools to protest Christmas exercises taking place there, but the majority of students in the schools concerned were Jewish, and the boycott was in good part directed against an insensitive school principal who at the previous year's assembly had urged Jewish students "to be more like Christ."[47] Where Christmas pageantry was outside areas of Jewish concentration, not overtly evangelistic, and mostly "secular," these Jews too usually kept their complaints to themselves.

Substantial Jewish opposition to public celebrations of Christmas arose only in more recent decades. The Holocaust, the creation of the State of Israel, the rise of a native-born generation of Jews, and growing minority group consciousness throughout the United States help account for this development—part of a larger trend toward American Jewish communal assertiveness that cannot be traced here. What does merit notice is the fact that Jews now do not hesitate to challenge the majority's most sacred practices in courts of law. To some extent this reflects a greater sense of Jewish security in America—a security so great that it permits Jews to worry less about "a spirit of amity" than about minority rights. But to at least an equal extent this also reflects a change in America itself. Postwar decades have seen the American judiciary assume a new activist stance, one that encourages disadvantaged groups of all sorts to seek redress even in the face of long-standing American traditions. Segregation and school prayer have been found repugnant to the Constitution, why not state-sanctioned observances of Christmas as well? Furthermore, as Phillip Hammond has shown, the judiciary has increasingly taken on a "theological function" in America—"the erstwhile religious task of articulating a moral architecture."[48] In the absence of a religious consensus, courts have had to decide between conflicting claims, maintaining the delicate balance between "no establishment" and "free exercise," national unity and religious diversity, majority rule and minority rights. As a result, it has been in the courtroom that the most recent battles over Christmas have been waged.

The specific issue of Christmas displays on public property has received the lion's share of judicial attention.[49] These displays seem to many Christians to be perfectly acceptable holiday pageants—*as American as Christmas itself.* Jews, by contrast, see the same displays as thoroughly Christian and, hence, inappropriate for the public square. Resulting clashes have frequently been ugly. In Indianapolis, for example, Jewish community and American Civil Liberties Union opposition to a Nativity scene erected in University Park led in 1976 to what one observer has called "an antisemitic firestorm." Many could not understand why Jews advocated removal of the Christian symbols when they were invited (and declined) to erect their own Chanukah display in the same park.[50] Angry letters to the city's newspapers pointed to majority rule, to America's Christian heritage, and to the constitutional guarantee of "free exercise" in firmly opposing the Jewish community's stance. In the end, a projected court challenge was dropped, and the Nativity scene remained where it was.[51]

What proved to be a more far-reaching dispute over the legality of a Nativity scene took place in Pawtucket, Rhode Island, where a Christmas display erected by the city in a park owned by a nonprofit organization and located in the heart of the shopping district was challenged. The display, which had been erected annually for more than forty years and "was essentially like those to be found in hundreds of towns or cities across the nation," included such objects as a Santa Claus house, a Christmas tree, a banner reading "Season's Greetings," and most significantly a Nativity scene (crèche) complete with "the infant Jesus, Mary, Joseph, angels, shepherds, kings and animals, all ranging in height from five inches to five feet." As far as Pawtucket's mayor was concerned, the display was diverse enough to appeal to all citizens, and was one that the city as a whole could take pride in. The American Civil Liberties Union and many Jews disagreed, alleging that the Nativity scene had the effect of "affiliating the City with the Christian beliefs that the crèche represents," in violation of the First Amendment to the Constitution. The case, known as *Lynch v. Donnelly,* proceeded through the courts until it reached the Supreme Court. There, in a 5–4 decision, the mayor's position was sustained.[52]

In a sense, *Lynch v. Donnelly* merely played out on a new stage a dispute over national values and the meaning of Christmas that has raged elsewhere for more than a century. Yet analysis of the Court's split decision reveals that on two critical issues—Christmas as a national holiday and the compartmentalization of Christmas into secular and religious components—there was no dispute at all: the nine justices of the Court seemed united. Chief Justice Burger argued for the majority that in erecting a Christmas crèche, Pawtucket "has principally taken note of a significant historical religious event long celebrated in the Western World," and "long recognized" in the United States "as a National Holiday." "We are satisfied," he continued, that Pawtucket "has a secular purpose for including the crèche, that the City has not impermissibly advanced religion, and that including the crèche does not create excessive entanglement between religion and government."[53] Justice Brennan, speaking for the minority, dissented from the Court's secular interpretation of the crèche itself but agreed that "Christmas as a public holiday is constitutionally acceptable" (although his justification—government "accommodation" to the activities of "many Americans"—is thoroughly unconvincing) and likewise agreed "that the celebration of Christmas has both secular and sectarian elements."[54]

None of the justices really came to grips with the fact that Christmas alone of all national holidays celebrates a religious event that many Americans do not recognize. Justice O'Connor came close, in her concurring opinion, when she admitted that government endorsement of religion is unconstitutional because it "sends a message to nonadherents that they are outsiders, not full members of the political community." But then in seeming disregard of her own logic, she concluded that Pawtucket's crèche "does not communicate a message that the government intends to endorse the Christian beliefs represented by the crèche. . . . The display celebrates a public holiday, and no one contends that declaration of that holiday is understood to be an endorsement of religion."[55]

The minority opinion of Justice Brennan made more evident concessions to the sensitivities of non-Christians, but it too avoided the essential point. Brennan hinted that a public Christmas display might have to include a Jewish symbol ("a Menorah") if such a request were made. He also stressed the fact that for non-Christians and especially for Jews "the symbolic re-enactment of the birth of a divine being who has been miraculously incarnated as a man stands as a dramatic reminder of their differences with Christian faith." A supporting footnote cited Martin Buber as calling this difference "the ultimate division between Judaism and Christianity."[56] The divergent majority view, enunciated by the Chief Justice, that the crèche is thoroughly secular but, like a Sunday closing law, "happens to coincide or harmonize with the tenets of some . . . religions," seems, by contrast, weak and unpersuasive.[57] Still, the difference between the majority and the minority position proves in the final analysis to be one of degree rather than of kind. All agreed that Christmas is a secular national holiday. Where they disagreed is on the question of whether the crèche is an acceptable symbol of *that* holiday or only a symbol of the related *religious* holiday that occurs on the same day and carries the same name.

In the end then, the justices of the Supreme Court, like most recent presidents and presumably most other Americans, pronounced Christmas a holiday for everyone. Without denying the Christian origins of Christmas, they nevertheless argued that Christmas is a secular holiday—part of American civil religion—a day in which people of goodwill everywhere can faithfully join. Some justices showed more sensitivity than others to the stark dilemma that Christmas poses to the non-Christian. But the only possible solution, calling Christmas "specifically Christian," as astronaut William Anders did, and divorcing it from the state altogether, is not one that any of them were prepared to accept. As a result, Christmas seems destined to remain an anomaly in American religion: a Christian holiday recognized as a holiday for all Americans, with Jews and other non-Christian Americans left out.

NOTES

I am grateful to Ms. Chai Feldblum, Dr. Hugo Freund, Prof. Samuel Z. Klausner, Prof. Benny Kraut, Rabbi Clifford E. Librach, Prof. Rowland A. Sherrill, Dr. Lester I. Vogel, and Prof. Stephen J. Whitfield for assistance and helpful suggestions in the preparation and revision of this paper—even if they do not necessarily agree with all of its findings and interpretations.

1. *New York Times,* Dec. 25, 1968, p. 36.

2. *Life* 16 (Jan. 17, 1969): p. 31; cf. Charles Reagan Wilson, "American

Heavens: Apollo and the Civil Religion," *Journal of Church and State* 26 (Spring 1984): 220–21.

3. W. Lloyd Warner, *Structure of American Life* (Edinburgh, 1952), p. 2, as quoted in Russell E. Richey and Donald G. Jones, *American Civil Religion* (New York, 1974), pp. 81–82 (emphasis added). See Catherine L. Albanese, "Dominant and Public Center: Reflections on the 'One' Religion of the United States," *South Atlantic Quarterly* 81 (Winter 1982): 24.

4. This rough estimate includes Jews, Muslims, and adherents of Eastern religions; see *Year Book of American and Canadian Churches* (Nashville, 1984), p. 244. George Gallup estimates that about 6 percent of Americans adhere to non-Christian religions, with an equal number identifying with no religion at all; see Jackson W. Carroll, Douglas W. Johnson, and Martin E. Marty, *Religion in America: 1950 to the Present* (New York, 1979), p. 9. Note that many Eastern Orthodox Christian churches do not recognize Christmas but celebrate Epiphany on Jan. 6, and several Western Christian churches either do not celebrate Christmas as a holiday because it is not found in the Bible or celebrate the day (as Adventists do) without any of its modern trappings.

5. James H. Barnett, *The American Christmas* (New York, 1954), p. 21. Besides Barnett's excellent volume, see on the history of Christmas in America, Ruth C. Kainen, *America's Christmas Heritage* (New York, 1969), and Katherine L. Richards, *How Christmas Came to the Sunday Schools* (New York, 1934). For additional bibliography, see Sue Samuelson, *Christmas: An Annotated Bibliography* (New York: 1982).

6. Robert Bellah, "Civil Religion in America," in *American Civil Religion,* ed. Russell E. Richey and Donald G. Jones (New York, 1974), p. 23.

7. Emil G. Hirsch, "How the Jew Regards Christmas," *Ladies' Home Journal* 24 (Dec. 1906): 10, pointed out that "to the theological associations of the festival the Jew must take exception," even though Christmas had become "the symbol and expression of the tenderest sympathies to which the heart of man may throb in responsive rhythms." Cf. Emil G. Hirsch, *My Religion* (New York, 1925), pp. 150–67.

8. Indeed, Jews consistently fought efforts to "Christianize" Thanksgiving, precisely because they sought inclusion in America's "public religion." See Morris U. Schappes, *A Documentary History of the Jews in the United States 1654– 1875* (New York, 1971), pp. 235–46; Hyman P. Grinstein, *The Rise of the Jewish Community of New York* (Philadelphia, 1945), pp. 269–70; *American Hebrew* 56 (Nov. 23, 1894): 86; and John F. Wilson, *Public Religion in American Culture* (Philadelphia, 1979), pp. 56–60. Easter and Good Friday, of course, are not national holidays and therefore pose no similar problems.

9. This tradition goes back at least as far as the so-called Maryland Toleration Act of 1649 which ruled that "noe person . . . professing to beleive in Jesus Christ shall from henceforth bee any waies troubled"; cf. Sidney E. Mead, *The Nation with the Soul of a Church* (New York, 1975), p. 25.

10. I am indebted to Congressman Bill Gradison and to Dr. Lester I. Vogel of the Library of Congress for their assistance in locating this material. According to Vogel, quoting Albert J. Menendez, "the first Christmas tree was

erected in the White House by Franklin Pierce. Benjamin Harrison was the first to publicly discuss his Christmas observance during an interview in 1889 with a popular woman's magazine. The first crèche didn't appear until the Eisenhower Administration" (Vogel to Sarna, Feb. 25, 1985); cf. Albert J. Menendez, *Christmas in the White House* (Philadelphia, 1983).

11. Bellah, "Civil Religion in America," p. 28; cf. Wilson, *Public Religion*, pp. 45–66; Cynthia Toolin, "American Civil Religion from 1789 to 1981: A Content Analysis of Presidential Inaugural Addresses," *Review of Religious Research* 25 (Sept. 1983): 39–48.

12. Menendez, *Christmas in the White House*, p. 113; *The Public Papers and Addresses of Franklin D. Roosevelt: 1944–45 Volume* (New York, 1950), p. 444; *Public Papers of the Presidents of the United States: Harry S. Truman . . . 1947* (Washington, D.C., 1963), p. 530; *Public Papers of the Presidents of the United States: Dwight D. Eisenhower, 1960–61* (Washington, D.C., 1968), p. 885; *Public Papers of the Presidents of the United States: John F. Kennedy . . . 1962* (Washington, D.C., 1962), p. 888; *Public Papers of the Presidents of the United States: Lyndon B. Johnson . . . July 1 to December 31, 1964* (Washington, D.C., 1965), p. 1666. President Jimmy Carter seems to have been unique in directing his brief Christmas messages specifically "to those of our fellow citizens who join us in the joyous celebration of Christmas" (*Public Papers of the Presidents of the United States: Jimmy Carter . . . September 29, 1980 to January 20, 1981* [Washington, D.C., 1982], p. 2764).

13. *Public Papers of the Presidents of the United States: Gerald R. Ford . . . July 10, 1976 to January 20, 1977* (Washington, D.C., 1979), p. 2872; *Public Papers of the Presidents of the United States: Ronald Reagan . . . July 3 to December 31, 1982* (Washington, D.C., 1983), pp. 1643–44.

14. *Jewish Daily Forward*, Dec. 14, 1910, quoted in Irving Howe and Kenneth Libo, *How We Lived* (New York, 1979), p. 200. For a remarkably similar contemporary statement, see the comments of Rabbi Gary E. Zola, quoted in Robert Webb, "Jewish Feelings at Christmas," *Cincinnati Enquirer*, Jan. 24, 1985, p. A–14.

15. Eli N. Evans, *The Provincials* (New York, 1973), p. 140.

16. See on this point *God's New Israel*, ed. Conrad Cherry (Englewood Cliffs, N.J., 1971), p. 16.

17. Kenneth N. White, "American Jewish Responses to Christmas" (unpublished Ordination thesis, Hebrew Union College-Jewish Institute of Religion, 1982); see also Walter M. Gerson, "Jews at Christmas Time: Role Strain and Strain-Reducing Mechanisms," in *Social Problems in a Changing World*, ed. Walter M. Gerson (New York, 1969), pp. 65–76.

18. Jonathan D. Sarna, *Jacksonian Jew: The Two Worlds of Mordecai Noah* (New York, 1981), p. 142.

19. *American Israelite*, Jan. 16, 1880, quoted in White, "American Jewish Responses to Christmas," p. 19.

20. *Time*, Jan. 1, 1940, p. 32, reprinted in White, "American Jewish Responses to Christmas," p. 298.

21. Sarna, *Jacksonian Jew*, p. 142.

22. *New York Reformer and Jewish Times,* Feb. 14, 1879, p. 5; *American Israelite,* Dec. 24, 1891, p. 5; *Time,* Jan. 1, 1940, p. 32; all found in White, "American Jewish Responses to Christmas," pp. 28, 276, 289, 298. De Leon was responding to Felix Adler's attack on the Christmas tree, cited below (n. 29).

23. *American Israelite,* Jan. 7, 1897, p. 5, reprinted in White, "American Jewish Responses to Christmas," p. 295.

24. Barnett, *American Christmas,* pp. 14–18; cf. White, "American Jewish Responses to Christmas," pp. 25, 37; Emma Lazarus, "The Christmas Tree," *Lippincott's* 19 (Feb. 1877): 229–30.

25. Frances B. Rothman, *The Haas Sisters of Franklin Street* (Berkeley, 1979), p. 8.

26. Anne Roiphe, "Christmas Comes to a Jewish Home," *New York Times,* Dec. 21, 1978, p. C6; Anne Roiphe, *Generation without Memory* (New York, 1981), p. 126.

27. Irving Canter found that about half of the Jewish youths whom he interviewed in 1960 "distinguished between religious and non-religious elements [of Christmas]. The crèche, pictures of Jesus, religious songs, sermons on the life and teachings of Jesus and prayers were not considered valid for public schools. However, the tree, the winter carols, and the ornaments were put in the non-religious category and therefore considered acceptable." See "Uncle Sam, the Hanukkah Man: Assimilation or Contra-Culturation?" *Reconstructionist* 27 (Dec. 1, 1961): 8.

28. *American Israelite,* Jan. 16, 1880, p. 3, quoted in White, "American Jewish Responses to Christmas," p. 94.

29. Felix Adler, "The Christmas Tree," *Jewish Times,* Dec. 31, 1869, quoted in Benny Kraut, *From Reform Judaism to Ethical Culture: The Religious Evolution of Felix Adler* (Cincinnati, 1979), p. 31, but note that Adler later changed his mind on this issue, ibid., p. 176; *Sabbath Visitor* 11 (Dec. 21, 1883): 393, quoted in White, "American Jewish Responses to Christmas," p. 97.

30. *Occident* 24 (Feb. 1867): 510, reprinted in White, "American Jewish Responses to Christmas," p. 270.

31. *American Israelite,* Jan. 10, 1888, p. 5, quoted in White, "American Jewish Responses to Christmas," p. 100. For other examples, see Canter, "Uncle Sam, the Hanukkah Man."

32. Leonard Gross, "The Jew and Christmas," *Look,* Dec. 28, 1965, p. 24; *Congress Weekly,* Dec. 20, 1946, pp. 3–4, as quoted in White, "American Jewish Responses to Christmas," p. 116. Gross notes the case of one Orthodox Jewish day school that resolutely continued to hold classes on Dec. 25 on the argument that "Just as Our Lady of Mercy is open on Yom Kippur, so is Yeshiva of Forest Hills open on Christmas" (p. 23). Many Orthodox synagogues continue to schedule daily morning prayers at the regular weekday hour on Christmas, rather than at the later Sunday or holiday hour.

33. *New York Times,* Dec. 11, 1961, p. 38, quoted in White, "American Jewish Responses to Christmas," pp. 125–26.

34. The full letter first appeared in Abraham J. Karp, *Our December Dilemma* (New York, 1958), p. 8.

35. Avraham Weiss, "The Menorah-Crèche Controversy" *New York Law Journal,* Dec. 26, 1984, understands this problem, but argues that the tree, although it has "significant religious meaning," is still a "far more general symbol than the crèche." He attempts to distinguish symbols that have both universal and religious meaning (the tree and the menorah), from those that are religious alone (the crèche and the Torah scroll). Unfortunately, Rabbi Weiss offers no clear test for distinguishing one class of religious symbols from the other (why isn't a Torah scroll as "universal" as a menorah?). Still, it is easy to sympathize with his conclusion: "to permit the display of Christmas trees on public land while denying the right of placement of the *chanukiah* [menorah] would be discriminatory." I am grateful to Professor Jeffrey Gurock for bringing this item to my attention.

36. Gerson, "Jews at Christmas Time," pp. 69–73.

37. See Jonathan D. Sarna, "The Impact of Nineteenth Century Christian Missions on American Jews," in *Jewish Apostasy in the Modern World,* ed. Todd Endelman (New York: Holmes and Meier, 1987), pp. 232–54.

38. "There are some who seem to evince no pride in the exploits of the Maccabees, how sad we feel that they should be so forgotten" (*Jewish Messenger,* Nov. 26, 1858, p. 113, as quoted in White, "American Jewish Responses to Christmas," p. 183). For Rabbi Isaac M. Wise's opposition to the kindling of Chanukah lights, see James G. Heller, *Isaac M. Wise: His Life, Work and Thought* (New York, 1965), p. 564. Lafcadio Hearn, in his 1873 discussion of the holidays celebrated by Cincinnati Jews, made no mention of Chanukah ("The Hebrews of Cincinnati," *Cincinnati Enquirer,* Nov. 9, 1873). To this day, Chanukah is a comparatively minor holiday in Israel.

39. Julius Eckman, "Hannucah and Christmas," *Occident* 24 (Feb. 1867): 510; *American Israelite,* Dec. 30, 1870, p. 9, both in White, "American Jewish Responses to Christmas," pp. 270, 186; see pp. 183–94 for Chanukah activities reflected in Jewish newspapers.

40. *American Hebrew,* Dec. 26, 1879, p. 61, as quoted in Yehezkel Wyszowski, "'The American Hebrew' Views the Jewish Community in the United States, 1879–1884, 1894–1898, and 1903–1908," (Ph.D. diss., Yeshiva University, 1979), p. 386; "Grand Revival," 1879 handbill in Solomon Solis-Cohen Archives, Philadelphia; 1879 newspaper clippings, YMHA scrapbook, YMHA Archives, 92nd Street Y, New York; Max Cohen to Solomon Solis-Cohen, Dec. 22, 1879, Solomon Solis-Cohen Archives; *Sabbath Visitor* 6 (Jan. 17, 1879): 20; *Proceedings of the Pittsburgh Rabbinical Conference, November 16, 17, 18, 1885* (New York, 1923), p. 18.

41. Steven M. Cohen, "The 1981 National Survey of American Jews" (typescript), p. 4.

42. Jakob J. Petuchowski, "The Magnification of Chanukah," *Commentary* 29 (Jan. 1960): 38. It is difficult to date precisely when Chanukah replaced Purim as the holiday on which Jews exchanged gifts. When Mordecai Kaplan made the suggestion in 1934 in his highly influential *Judaism as a Civilization* ([1934; New York, 1967], p. 451) the transfer had obviously not yet completely taken hold.

43. Twelve percent of Kansas City Jews had Christmas trees in their homes in 1962; more recent national data suggest figures ranging from 5 to 12 percent. See *Mid-America's Promise: A Profile of Kansas City Jewry,* ed. Joseph P. Schultz (Kansas City, 1982), p. 365; Steven M. Cohen, *The 1984 National Survey of American Jews* (New York, 1984), p. 51; Egon Mayer (personal communication). On the decline of the "Chanukah Bush" and the Jewish Christmas tree, see Milton Matz, "The Meaning of the Christmas Tree to the American Jew," *Jewish Journal of Sociology* 3 (June 1961): 129–37; Marden D. Paru, "Tannenbaum and the Jewish Problem," *Jewish Social Studies* 35 (1973): 283–89.

44. As early as 1878, Henrietta Szold suggested that Chanukah be reinterpreted: "Christmas truly fulfills its mission of bringing peace and good will to men. All this and more Chanukah should be to us" (*Jewish Messenger,* Jan. 10, 1879, p. 5, quoted in White, "American Jewish Responses to Christmas," p. 192). Cf. Alice Ginott, "The Annual Dilemma: Should a Jewish Child Celebrate Christmas," *Ladies' Home Journal* 95 (Dec. 1978): 201. For other suggested reinterpretations of Chanukah, see Petuchowski, "Magnification of Chanukah," pp. 38–43. More radical suggestions for bringing the two holidays into line are discussed in Benny Kraut, "A Unitarian Rabbi? The Case of Solomon H. Sonneschein" (forthcoming); Alvin J. Reines, *A Concise Guide to the Celebration and Understanding of Chanukah the Festival of Affirmation* (Cincinnati, 1980); and White, "American Jewish Responses to Christmas," pp. 41–54, 227–28; see also Irvin Canter, "Uncle Sam, the Hanukkah Man," p. 5; Daniel Bloom, "A Bloom by Any Other Name," *Moment* 10 (Dec. 1984): 63–64.

45. White, "American Jewish Responses to Christmas," pp. 229–36, traces examples of Jewish expressions of goodwill at Christmas time dating back to the nineteenth century; see also Barnett, *American Christmas,* p. 54.

46. *American Israelite,* Jan. 3, 1907, reprinted in Robert T. Gan, "A Documentary Source Book for Jewish-Christian Relations in the United States, 1865–1914" (unpublished Ordination thesis, Hebrew Union College-Jewish Institute of Religion, Cincinnati, 1967), p. 114.

47. Leonard Bloom, "A Successful Jewish Boycott of the New York City Public Schools—Christmas 1906," *American Jewish History* 70 (Dec. 1980): 180–88; Deborah Dash Moore, *At Home in America: Second Generation New York Jews* (New York, 1981), pp. 116–17; for other cases, see White, "American Jewish Responses to Christmas," pp. 144–46, 151–54.

48. Phillip E. Hammond, "The Rudimentary Forms of Civil Religion," in *Varieties of Civil Religion,* ed. Robert N. Bellah and Phillip E. Hammond (New York, 1980), pp. 154–55; cf. William A. Cole and Phillip E. Hammond, "Religious Pluralism, Legal Development and Societal Complexity: Rudimentary Forms of Civil Religion," *Journal for the Scientific Study of Religion* 13 (1974): 177–89.

49. Earlier court cases dealt with the issue of Christmas in the public schools, but the substantive legal issues involved here receded under the weight of Supreme Court rulings on the general questions of religion in the public schools. General guidelines permit Christmas assemblies and cultural

events so long as schools present them "in a prudent and objective manner and as a traditional part of the culture and religious heritage of the particular holiday." See *Florey v. Sioux Falls School District,* 464 F. Supp. 911, 918 (D.S.D. 1979), *aff'd,* 619 F.2d 1311, 1317, 1319 (8th Cir.), *cert. denied,* 449 U.S. 987 (1980); and David Silverberg, "Santa and the First Amendment," *Baltimore Jewish Times,* Dec. 19, 1980, pp. 56–59. For earlier disputes see Anson Phelps Stokes and Leo Pfeffer, *Church and State in the United States* (New York, 1964), pp. 382–84; Albert I. Gordon, *Jews in Suburbia* (Boston, 1959), pp. 188–94; White, "American Jewish Responses to Christmas," pp. 154–65. A particularly ugly dispute on this issue wracked the community of Westfield, New Jersey. A compromise reached in 1972 allowed a high school Christmas passion play to continue to be held, but only after school hours with attendance voluntary; see Evelyn Averick, *A Historic Narrative: The Story of Emanu-El* (New York, 1981), pp. 53–55.

50. "In East Orange, New Jersey, for example, the problem created by a Nativity scene . . . was resolved by erecting a huge Chanukah Menorah across from it" (Gordon, *Jews in Suburbia,* p. 190).

51. Gerald L. Houseman, "Antisemitism in City Politics: The Separation Clause and the Indianapolis Nativity Scene Controversy," *Jewish Social Studies* 42 (Winter 1980): 21–36; Judith E. Endelman, *The Jewish Community of Indianapolis* (Bloomington, 1984), pp. 250–51.

52. *Lynch v. Donnelly,* 465 U.S. 668, 104 S. Ct. 1335 (1984). On this case, see 98 Harvard Law Review 174 (1984); Nathan Z. Dershowitz, "Did the Crèche Case Set a Dangerous Precedent?" *Jewish Monthly,* May 1984, pp. 26–30; Ruti G. Teitel, "Memorandum: *Lynch v. Donnelly*" (typescript, Anti-Defamation League, Apr. 4, 1984).

53. *Lynch v. Donnelly,* at 1363, 1365. This follows the language of *Lemon v. Kurtzman,* 403 U.S. 602, 614 (1971).

54. *Lynch v. Donnelly,* at 1378. Brennan's argument follows the logic first set forth in *McCollum v. Board of Education,* 333 U.S. 203 (1948); cf. 98 Harvard Law Rev. 174 (1984) at 179.

55. *Lynch v. Donnelly,* at 1361, 1369.

56. *Id.,* at 1374, 1377 n. 14.

57. *Id.,* at 1364, quoting *Marsh v. Chambers,* 463 U.S. 783, 103 S. Ct. 3330, 3336 (1983).

JOHN K. ROTH

American Ground:
Recovering Individualism in the Spiritual Life of the Nation

"This land is your land, this land is my land. . . . This land was made for you and me."
                                            —Woody Guthrie

In 1962, the American novelist John Steinbeck published *Travels with Charley: In Search of America.* For decades he had lived in and written about the United States, but late in life Steinbeck felt out of touch with his own country. So, after packing "Rocinante," a customized van named after Don Quixote's horse, he and his dog, Charley, set off on a journey of recovery through what Steinbeck called "this monster land." [1]

The voyage involved much more than geography. Steinbeck wanted to renew his feeling for the country, yearning to revitalize contact with the multiple dimensions of American ground. The "human-scape" of the nation, as well as its landscape, was his to restore. Within both he looked for common ground, for beliefs, attitudes, and hopes that Americans could be thought to share. He sought, too, for what might be called "evidentiary ground"—foundations and experiences that provide good reasons to think that Americans possess a future worth having. In his own American style, Steinbeck polished his findings only to have a puzzle remain:

> Americans as I saw them and talked to them were indeed individuals, each one different from the others, but gradually I began to feel that the Americans exist, that they really do have generalized characteristics regardless of their states, their social and financial status, their education, their religions, and their political convictions. But if there is indeed an American image built of truth rather than reflecting either hostility or wishful thinking, what is this image? What does it look like? What does it do? [2]

Steinbeck's quandary has been shared by other Americans before and since his *Travels with Charley*. It exists not only because Americans are individuals but also because they have been deeply touched by the

concept of *individualism*. Typically that concept stresses the separateness of one human being from another and the responsibility and
initiative that each person must take on his or her own behalf. Where
such convictions lead from one generation to the next is problematical. Individually or collectively, however, it is unlikely that Americans
will set their individualism aside. Thus, a perennial issue for the corporate possibilities of the nation is to determine critically what individualism at its best does and does not mean. Fortunately, that task is
not entirely one of new discoveries, for some Americans have
thoughtfully explored the paths of individualism before. The continuous recovery of their American ground—the "human-scape" as
well as the landscape, the evidentiary ground that clears common
ground—affords the opportunity for Americans to civilize "this monster land" anew in each generation.

Alexis de Tocqueville and American Habits of the Heart

Outside observers often understand Americans better than the citizenry does itself. As that astute French explorer, Alexis de Tocqueville, surveyed American ground in the 1830s, he reckoned that
"Among the lucky circumstances that favored the establishment and
assured the maintenance of democratic republic in the United States,
the most important was the choice of the land itself in which the
Americans live." A "limitless continent," Tocqueville believed, promised the opportunity and general prosperity that could blend with the
Americans' love of equality and liberty to yield favorable outcomes for
the pursuit of happiness. Tocqueville envisioned Americans "preparing the triumphal progress of civilization across the wilderness," but
on other occasions he had second thoughts.[3] They often focused on
individualism.

Among the first to use the concept, Tocqueville understood individualism to be of "democratic origin," and early on he questioned a
basic American belief—namely, that individualism is a virtue. Democracy fosters equality, Tocqueville believed, and in so doing "disposes
each citizen to isolate himself from the mass of his fellows and with-
draw into the circle of family and friends." Damming "the spring of
public virtues," leaving "the greater society to look after itself," individualism does not have far to go before it results in "egoism" or narcissism—"a passionate and exaggerated love of self which leads a man
to think of all things in terms of himself and to prefer himself to all"
(pp. 506–7).

Tocqueville's worries about individualism centered on the negative implications it had for a healthy society. He knew, of course, that individualism did include many assets—self-reliance and personal initiative to name but two. He even believed that Americans had succeeded in mitigating the worst effects of individualism by using their liberty to cultivate political institutions and voluntary associations "so that there should be an infinite number of occasions for the citizens to act together and so that every day they should feel that they depended on one another" (p. 511). But Tocqueville never completely stilled his uneasiness that individualism might eventually prove to be an ironic asset that would turn American ground into wasteland.

The second half of *Democracy in America* began with a chapter entitled "Concerning the Philosophical Approach of the Americans." "Less attention," Tocqueville there observed, "is paid to philosophy in the United States than in any other country of the civilized world." Prizing individualism so much, he explained, Americans are Cartesians in their propensity to display "a general distaste for accepting any man's word as proof of anything." Instead they rely on "individual effort and judgment" to determine what they believe (pp. 429–30).

As with most of the American qualities he discussed, Tocqueville found "the philosophical approach of the Americans" to possess both strengths and weaknesses. Skepticism might nurture a praiseworthy critical attitude; self-reliance could produce desirable innovation. But another consequence of those assets was the undermining of authority and tradition. That result, in turn, could lead to other mischief. For where reliance on authority and tradition are severely undermined people still seek confirmation of their views in the judgments of others. The despotism of unthinking conformity, which stands at a far remove from the public spirit that ensures real freedom, is not far behind.

Tocqueville's uneasiness about American individualism was justified, and the consequences for the national well-being have been enormous. In sum, while American individualism honed ingenuity and industry that brought the country to a position of economic and political world leadership, the same spirit drew men and women further apart even as they lived closer together in conformity. Now giving self-fulfillment precedence over civic virtue and a publicly responsible patriotism, Americans care more for individual wealth than for the commonwealth.

Abundant evidence for the accuracy of Tocqueville's fears can be found in the sociological survey of American ground conducted recently by Robert N. Bellah and his associates. Borrowing one of Tocqueville's phrases to title the study, they assayed "habits of the heart" in the powerful American middle class of the 1980s. There, Bellah found, "individualism may have grown cancerous—that it may be destroying those social integuments that Tocqueville saw as moderating its more destructive potentialities, that it may be threatening the survival of freedom itself."[4] In short, many Americans tend to be so obsessed with personal self-fulfillment that the capacity for commitment to the basic institutions of marriage, family, politics, and religion is dangerously impaired. Tocqueville, of course, would have found none of this surprising. His ambivalence toward democracy was considerable, precisely because he feared it would unleash a sense of self-interest so badly understood as to starve any sense of civic obligation and wither any concern to seek first what is best for the community as a whole.

Sensing that "radical" is more apt than "rugged" to describe America's contemporary individualism, Bellah is skeptical that an adequate social ethic can be built on its foundations. Nor is he very optimistic that altogether different foundations can be secured on American ground. Once more following Tocqueville, however, Bellah and his colleagues think that "biblical religion" might provide a cause for hope. Biblical religion, of course, is not one thing. Thus, it often has had divisive effects in America. What Bellah banks on, however, is the power of religion to make people concerned for persons and causes beyond the confines of individualistic self-fulfillment. Religion can have this effect, at least in part, because it points to a moral order that stands beyond the vicissitudes of historical relativity and thereby can inspire individuals to pursue what is good for the community.

Bellah's hopes include some ironic twists. While religious leaders and churchfolk are increasingly drawn to the social and psychological sciences for solutions to problems of religious life, Bellah and his colleagues are social scientists who think that religion contains vital solutions for social and psychological maladies in our culture. They do not suppose, however, that religion provides a sufficient resource to accomplish all that is needed if American ground is to support the public beliefs and institutions that sustain democracy and freedom. The requirement is to locate and create a variety of resources to drive home the importance of pursuing the common good. Fortunately, the land still contains such possibilities. To identify some of them is to preserve among our national treasures some notable American philosophers and theologians who in turn can help us to understand both how a healthy democracy requires obligations that transcend individual interests and how religion has a special part to play in fostering that understanding.

The Recovery of American Reflection

Tocqueville wrote that "the Americans have no school of philosophy peculiar to themselves, and they pay very little attention to the rival European schools. Indeed they hardly know their names" (p. 429). Like many of his judgments, that one was not infallible then and is even less accurate now. For American thinkers have developed a variety of distinctive philosophical perspectives, and, in one way or another, issues about individualism and community have often been their focal point.

Celebrant of democracy, the poet-philosopher Walt Whitman tells us in *Democratic Vistas* (1871) that he liked to think of "the words America and democracy as convertible terms." That same work, however, displays Whitman's philosophical concern about the validity of his hopes. Specifically, he worried that there were too few persons with "some definite instinct why and for what [America] has arisen." Lacking that instinct, he added, the United States might "prove to be the most tremendous failure of time." In any case, he contended, America would have to count "for her justification and success . . . almost entirely on the future."[5] While Whitman himself did not state all that the requisite instinct involved, he linked it to his version of individualism, which he called "personalism."[6] Democracy American-style, thought Whitman, insists on an equality of individuals. That equality means nothing, however, unless it entails a twofold recognition: first, whatever the differences, people are one in being persons, and, second, being persons entitles all to dignity and enjoins each to respect others. In short, if America and democracy deserve to be convertible terms, one fundamental reason for America's existence is to encourage an individualism that esteems persons.

Whitman saw another crucial element—everything depends on how to answer "What is a person?" He, however, was not the one who best spelled out an American philosophical response to that question. That honor might be shared by Josiah Royce, America's great philosopher of community, and by thinkers such as George Santayana, John Dewey, and Reinhold Niebuhr, who were influenced by him. Royce understood a person to be relational, stretched out into a past and a future as well as existing in the present. He argued that a community exists just to the degree that persons share memories and hopes, which include ethical commitments and collective loyalties. He held further that "my idea of myself is an interpretation of my past,— linked also with an interpretation of my hopes and intentions as to my future." [7] His point was that a coherent individualism requires caring relations that reach far and wide.

Such relations found an American expression on 20 May 1927. Opening the throttle on the *Spirit of St. Louis* at 7:52 that Friday morning, Charles A. Lindbergh taxied down a Long Island runway to begin his solo flight across the Atlantic. Nearly thirty-four hours later—it was 10:24 P.M., Paris time, on Saturday—"Lucky Lindy" and his plane emerged from the darkness to touch ground again. A world had journeyed with the "Lone Eagle," and his flight's significance was not lost on American ministers who preached to their Christian congregations the next day. A typical example of that Sunday's rhetoric was the sermon given by the Reverend Dr. Russell Bowie of Grace Episcopal Church in New York City. In "The Lure of the 'Impossible,'" Bowie remarked that Lindbergh "manifested that indomitable heroism which, whether . . . in victory or defeat, has made possible the progress of the human race toward the mastery of its world. . . . There is a fund of moral heroism as well as a fund of physical heroism among men, which thrills to the challenge of the impossible." [8]

That same Sunday morning, far to the west of Paris and New York, another Christian pastor preached to his congregation. The record does not show what Reinhold Niebuhr told those predominantly blue-collar workers in Detroit, but it is doubtful that his sermon was as effusive and glowing as Russell Bowie's. For during this period one of the entries in Niebuhr's diary included these words: "I wish that some of our romanticists and sentimentalists could sit through a series of meetings where the real social problems of a city are discussed. They would be cured of their optimism. A city which is built around a productive process and which gives only casual thought and incidental attention to human problems is really a kind of hell. Thousands in this town are really living in torment while the rest of us eat, drink and make merry. What a civilization!" [9]

The world Reinhold Niebuhr saw was certainly "this side of paradise," to borrow the title of one of F. Scott Fitzgerald's early novels. Moreover, Niebuhr struggled within it quite differently from Fitzgerald's Amory Blaine, an American who honestly admitted that "I detest poor people." [10] As a young pastor in Detroit, and later as one of the most perceptive thinkers America has yet produced, Niebuhr worked to develop a religious perspective relevant to the broad social and political questions that faced the United States and the world in the twentieth century. During the period from 1930 to 1960, he was to theology in America what John Dewey was to philosophy. Together with George Santayana, another observer of American life who addresses the concerns of this essay, they can still contribute greatly to a much-needed public philosophy that recovers insight about "why and for what" America exists.

George Santayana and American Character

Inside the former Nazi concentration camp at Dachau, the following words have been inscribed: "Those who cannot remember the past are condemned to repeat it." That often-quoted warning comes from *The Life of Reason,* a beautifully written book by George Santayana. Born in Madrid, he remained a Spanish citizen throughout his life. His university training, however, was at Harvard, where his teachers included William James and Josiah Royce. Between 1889 and 1912, he taught philosophy there and wrote many books, but upon his resignation, Santayana left the United States, never to return. England was home for a while, then Rome where he died, leaving behind a long list of literary credits. Describing himself as an American only "by long association," Santayana nevertheless acknowledged the influence of American thought, culture, and friends. Indeed, he affirmed, "it is as an American writer that I must be counted, if I am counted at all."[11]

In 1920, Santayana published a series of essays entitled *Character and Opinion in the United States.* For its motto, he might have taken one of F. Scott Fitzgerald's comments in *This Side of Paradise,* which was published in the same year. Describing his character Amory Blaine, Fitzgerald wrote, "It was always the becoming he dreamed of, never the being." Santayana would have thought that such a trait was not only "quite characteristic of Amory" but of Americans in general.[12]

In *Character and Opinion in the United States,* Santayana warned that his way of speaking would be "mythical." For he reflected on "the American in the singular, as if there were not millions of them, north and south, east and west, of both sexes, of all ages, and of various races, professions, and religions."[13] At the same time, he argued, his assessment of the American in the singular would be "largely adequate to the facts" (p. 168). As Santayana proceeded, then, he found, first of all, that every American is an exile—either voluntary or involuntary. Pilgrim voyages, pioneer treks, the violence of forced relocations, or just changed jobs—these things make up a nation of people who live together in being pulled apart. But exile status is more complicated than that. American uprootedness, combined with a spirit of youth which Santayana underscored repeatedly, leads Americans to think very little about the past. Ignoring or forgetting it—putting things behind them; out of sight, out of mind—is a quality matched only by romantic nostalgia when Americans do choose to recollect.

As a people, Santayana believed, the Americans are fascinated by the future. He also detected overwhelming optimism about what lies ahead, often supported by religion or by industrious trust in nature's bounty. Blend and clash of idealism and materialism though it may be, Americans have a tendency to think that all things do and shall work together for good—at least in the United States.

According to Santayana, these attitudes supported a rough-and-ready individualism. He emphasized, for example, that Americans expect "every man to stand on his own legs." The possible harshness in that outlook he found tempered by the feeling that there is also a responsibility to help each other. But, Santayana observed, when an American "has given his neighbor a chance he thinks he has done enough for him"—humanitarian concern, yes; "coddling socialism," no (p. 171).

American character revealed still other qualities as Santayana described it in 1920. It was imaginative and inventive, conservative generally but quick to act in emergencies. Santayana held, moreover, that these qualities are linked to another peculiar trait. It includes but is not exhausted by open space; the Americans' perpetual motion as a people is involved as well. Together, said Santayana, they produce "the moral emptiness of a settlement where men and even houses are easily moved about, and no one, almost, lives where he was born or believes what he has been taught" (p. 172). As a result, experimentation and novelty are American bywords. To compensate for instability, there is a driving spirit to get down to business: "For the American the urgency of his novel attack upon matter, his zeal in gathering its fruits, precludes meanderings in primrose paths; devices must be short cuts, and symbols must be mere symbols" (p. 174). Americans look to the future, but it is also a very *immediate* future because they may not be here tomorrow. Gone west . . . or just gone . . . is the destination set by the pace of American life as Santayana mapped it.

All the while, though, Americans sense fulfillment close at hand. Indeed, Santayana contended that the American "is not a revolutionist; he believes he is already on the right track and moving towards an excellent destiny" (p. 176). Americans have youthful enthusiasm. Others may not have the gumption or the spirit to succeed, but that will not be America's fate. Thus, even if Santayana thought that

Americans take too lightly the long record of human failure and self-delusion, he could assert that "the American is wonderfully alive" (p. 178).

Not so differently from Whitman, however, Santayana also wondered how the epic of America would continue. For, he noted, the American "has never yet had to face the trials of Job." Neither the Civil War nor World War I, he believed, had seriously undermined an optimistic and "apparently complete absorption in material enterprise and prosperity." If Santayana saw this materialism less as love of wealth and more as "preoccupation with quantity," he also recognized how complex an American fate might be because our materialistic values existed side by side with expansive moral and spiritual ideals: Liberty and opportunity for all . . . Equal justice under the law . . . One nation, under God, indivisible . . . America the beautiful (pp. 185–88).

Santayana called the American "an idealist working on matter" (p. 175). That provocative description made Santayana pause: if "serious and irremediable tribulation" ever overtook the land, would the American's concern for the material or for the ideal be more at the heart of our national character? For at least two reasons, Santayana could not be sure. First, he took the ideal and the material to be inseparable in American life. Americans' ideals depend on the existence of places and things; the relationship works the other way as well. Second, he understood that the becoming would do much to determine the being. He therefore concluded with Whitman that to think of the being without placing a premium on the ideal would incline America toward becoming one of the most tragic wrecks of time.

More than six decades later, perhaps not all of Santayana's observations provide an accurate American profile. One feature that remains valid, however, is the expectation for people "to stand on [their] own legs and to be helpful in [their] turn" (p. 171). However divided over what the nature of the help should be, Americans are not mean-spirited and the reason is that they have a fundamentally shared commitment to the individual's pursuit of happiness. Probably more than anything else, that commitment accounts for American suspicion of Marxist analysis and antipathy toward Communism. Though promising liberation and happiness together, their appeal to the nation is muted because the meanings they give those words are not "American."

Such disagreement, however, is not confined to ideological conflict on an international scale. It exists domestically as well. For as Abraham Lincoln once stated, Americans "all declare for liberty, but in using the same *word* we do not all mean the same *thing*."¹⁴ That American fact may preclude there being any single answer to Whitman's question about "why and for what" America exists. But if irreducible differences of opinion about fundamentals are in some sense a feature of American character, that reality enjoins further reflection about the *individualism* that Santayana saw as foundational to America's way of life.

John Dewey and Individualism's Discontents

Born in Vermont, that bastion of Yankee individualism, John Dewey spent most of his life in the collective hustle of Chicago and New York. His experiences led him to *Individualism Old and New* (1929–30). Writing during the Depression, Dewey saw that the long-standing American emphasis on "individualism" provided a pivotal issue for the nation and the world. In the United States, argued Dewey, individualism has a natural history. If the outcome of that history has been problematic, the ideal neither can nor should be excised. American identity depends on it. Therefore, Dewey's effort was to "revision" individualism so it would not be a hindrance but a help.

Always somewhat mythological, old-style American individualism, contended Dewey, had been modeled after the image of self-reliant, self-made pioneers. They saw opportunities for personal fortunes and set out to win them on their own. Dewey believed that circumstances were threatening that ideal, and that a basic reason for this was that America was increasingly organized in huge corporations. Ironically, that had occurred because the old individualism had succeeded so mightily. By spurring people to build amazing businesses and industrial plants, this very success had burst the bubble. Though individuals remained, more and more their lives were becoming cogs in wheels that turned out products collectively. People were becoming incorporated; most lacked the opportunity needed to "make it" on their own.

According to Dewey, a dangerous exception to his analysis did exist. Old individualism could still take the form of measuring success in terms of money. Even within the corporate structure, such individualism could yet find expression in grabs for all-that-one-can-get. Dewey believed, too, that Americans had learned new ways to clutch collectively so that management and labor, even government and people, seated themselves repeatedly at a table of hard bargains. In most cases, though, Dewey sensed that the individual remained the loser. As the old individualism persisted, alienation and frustration rose. Even if the old ideal dissolved in one person, its presence in others took a toll as the rounds of competition spiraled on—right into a crash.

Dewey advocated no return to a preindustrial, precorporate America. Assuming such a reversal had been possible, he would not have favored it. Even in the midst of an economic slump, he saw vast increases in knowledge and technological power as vindicating the potential for good that use of scientific method can bring to life. His point was rather that human intelligence must be used more extensively and rigorously than ever to harness that potential and to channel it toward humanizing benefits. Instead of encouraging the practical rationality of "cost-effectiveness" to become the tail that wags the dog, Dewey thought that Americans must rally ingenuity to discern a revised and renewed understanding of what the initiatives of individualism ought to entail.

The individualism advocated by Dewey supplements Santayana's profile of American character. For example, Dewey's "new" individual would be scientifically oriented, at least in terms of an education that would equip him or her with critical methods for tackling life's problems. In addition, this individual's concern would focus on the social utility of action and planning, on the broad range of effects that policies have on national and international life. While recognizing that Americans must build upon and beyond—rather than tear down—their existing industrial, scientific, and technological base, Dewey's individual would have an awareness tempered by understanding that economic concerns are appropriate only to the extent that they serve civic quality. That concern, Dewey believed, argued in favor of a strong role for government in guiding social and economic development. It also suggested that the individual's pursuit of happiness would best find its fulfillment in working for the well-being of society. If those efforts sometimes required persons to oppose established policies, Dewey hoped their attitudes would nonetheless seek to overcome alienation between individuals and society, labor and management, government and people.

Viewing this sketch today, Americans would not be likely to agree about its contents. But they might concur with Dewey when he argued that "the problem of constructing a new individuality consonant with the objective conditions under which we live is the deepest problem of our times."[15] The reason for that concurrence, moreover, would not be simply that "the United States has steadily moved from an earlier pioneer individualism to a condition of dominant corporateness" (p. 36). In the 1980s, an era when there have been more small businesses started than at any comparable period in American history, the fact remains that Americans also live in the shadows of multinational corporations and of unprecedented economic competition from other countries, most notably those of Asia. National destiny, and thus the American's sense of individualism, is influenced and threatened by a web of economic and political forces that move beyond American control.

John Dewey thought "the publicity agent is perhaps the most significant symbol of our present life" (p. 43). That observation remains keen. The only change is that the publicity may be controlled by Arab oil or Japanese productivity. Far from being a nation of the self-employed, Americans find it increasingly difficult to know their real employers face to face. Companies own companies as much as individuals do. Too many Americans live "in a situation which is so incomplete that it cannot be admitted into the affections and yet is so pervasive that it cannot be escaped: a situation which defines an individual divided within himself" (p. 50). That part of Dewey's appraisal still fits.

The basic problem facing Americans, Dewey contended, was that "of forming a new psychological and moral type" (p. 83). If that order seems more than can be accomplished, it may also be true, fortunately, that such an order is unnecessary to recover and act upon the purposes for which America has arisen. For what Dewey talked about was essentially something quite close to the core of an already-existing American sensitivity which is alive, if muted, even now.

Robert Bellah observed, for example, that contemporary Americans do not always practice the radical individualism they preach. Functionally, their lives are given meaning by familial, communal, public ties that transcend the individualistic calculus of self-fulfillment and cost-benefit analysis at which the culture has become so verbally adept. If they need experiences of social commitments that sustain, nevertheless Americans do sense that those relationships of memory and hope are the substance of essential life—which must be embraced not only as means to personal self-satisfaction but as substantive elements of personhood.[16]

Reinhold Niebuhr and the Irony of American Individualism

Anticipating what Bellah has confirmed, Reinhold Niebuhr shared Dewey's ethical and pragmatic concerns, but his sense of tragedy in human life was more profound, thus giving him affinities with Santayana as well as a perspective for criticizing some of the excesses to

which national life, including that of the United States, is prone. The
difference between Santayana and Niebuhr was also significant, however, for Santayana saw religion mainly as an aesthetic phenomenon,
while Niebuhr was fundamentally committed to the notion that history is not simply a drama involving men and women but also one
that includes God. Yet the focus of Niebuhr's theology was not so
much on God as on history itself, as expressed in one of his most
influential books, *The Nature and Destiny of Man.*

Niebuhr's previously mentioned diary ended in 1928, as he was
about to begin his career as a professor and a writer. But it contains
many of the notes that Niebuhr would sound repeatedly in the decades ahead as he explored the relations among love, power, and justice. In one of its last entries, for example, he wrote:

> I persevere in the effort to combine the ethic of Jesus with what might
> be called Greek caution because I see no great gain in ascetic experi-
> ments. I might claim for such a strategy the full authority of the gospel
> except that it seems to me more likely to avoid dishonesty if one admits
> that the principle of love is not qualified in the gospel and that it must
> be qualified in other than the most intimate human associations. When
> one deals with the affairs of a civilization, one is trying to make the
> principle of love effective as far as possible, but one cannot escape the
> conclusion that society as such is brutal, and that the Christian principle
> may never be more than a leaven in it.[17]

Following up on those observations, *Moral Man and Immoral Society*
(1932) remains one of Niebuhr's most significant books. The study
owes that status to its investigation of the hypothesis that individuals
can be—and even are likely to be—far more moral than human
groups, especially as those groups are organized today into modern
political states. Thus, if F. Scott Fitzgerald correctly called Amory
Blaine a "romantic egotist," Niebuhr argued that the dangers of such
individualism were pale by contrast with what emerged when *collective
egoism* came to the fore.[18] It could consume the individual, bring good
intentions to naught, and unleash global power struggles that endan-
ger every person. Standing beside such might, the contributions of
morally or religiously motivated men and women seemed fragile and
weak, and yet Niebuhr also believed they can work like leaven and
make all the difference. "Realities are always defeating ideals," Niebuhr had written as early as 1919, "but ideals have a way of taking
vengeance upon the facts which momentarily imprison them."[19] Perhaps "vengeance" was overly strong, however, for later in the same
book Niebuhr noted that all too often moral and religious ideals "can
be victorious only by snatching victory out of defeat."[20]

As well as any American ever has, Niebuhr understood the nature of human power and aspiration. He discerned the cunning within reason and the irony within history. Undergirding his interpretation of American experience in particular were at least two premises that are especially important. First, he believed, human beings are infected by *original sin*. Niebuhr's understanding of that admittedly unpopular notion, however, was very down-to-earth, even commonsensical, for in *The Irony of American History* he located its significance in "the obvious fact that all men are persistently inclined to regard themselves more highly and are more assiduously concerned with their own interests than any 'objective' view of their importance would warrant."[21] Second, he found the American version of this original sin to be located in the nation's presumption that its ways not only represent a clean break from a corrupted past but also remain so fundamentally innocent and virtuous that they could rightly be identified with God's will for the world. As Niebuhr saw them, the facts suggested an alternative view. "The irony of our situation," he argued, "lies in the fact that we could not be virtuous (in the sense of practicing the virtues which are implicit in meeting our vast world responsibilities) if we were really as innocent as we pretend to be" (p. 23).

American ground spawns power. Such might, Niebuhr affirmed, is never won, used, or even lost innocently. The land, however, is riddled with irony when people persuade themselves differently. To make his case, Niebuhr distinguished irony from pathos and tragedy. Pathos resides in unmerited suffering that results from events in which none of the agents involved can rightly be held responsible or guilty. Its clearest examples are found in the pain and grief brought on by nature's fury in earthquakes or tornados. Tragedy arises from conflict of another kind. The many claims life makes are not always harmonious. One good must sometimes be sacrificed for another, but even more unfortunate is the fact that life so often involves what Niebuhr called "conscious choices of evil for the sake of good" (p. vii). Such choices are the essence of tragedy. By contrast with both pathos and tragedy, irony dwells in the gaps between intention and consequence that yawn neither by accident nor by conscious design alone.

Niebuhr's point was not that American life lacks pathos, tragedy, or even an abundance of blatant wrongdoing. But neither did he think that the United States was the most corrupt nation on earth. Just the opposite struck Niebuhr as closer to the truth, and therefore he anguished over the peculiar degree to which Americans wreak havoc in the world and upon each other because they know themselves insufficiently. Niebuhr tried to show Americans that their virtues contain hidden defects, that the nation's strength is weak to the extent that it is vain, that its yearnings for security will breed insecurity if they go too far, that America's considerable wisdom may be reduced to folly unless limits are better recognized.

Pretension, grandiose pride, and unwarranted self-righteousness—these perennial idols were the objects of Niebuhr's criticism. He wanted Americans to learn, not to their sorrow but before it became too late, that their reach may exceed their grasp. Yet he recognized one irony more, namely, that such disillusionment has no foregone conclusion. It "either must lead," he warned in *The Irony of American History,* "to an abatement of the pretention, which means contrition; or it leads to a desperate accentuation of the vanities to the point where irony turns into pure evil" (p. viii). In a nuclear age, Niebuhr's ultimate "either/or" is especially harsh, for it portends apocalypse if Americans fail to act wisely. But even if they do, Niebuhr would be the first to admit, such action may not be enough. For the United States is not the only responsible party or even necessarily the one most likely to bring about the end. America cannot save the world or even itself singlehandedly. That was one of Niebuhr's fundamental points. Yet his revisioning critique was offered with a hopeful expectation that looked for Americans to do their best.

Recognizing that love untempered by justice becomes sentimental and impotent, Niebuhr believed that justice without mercy retains a harsh edge that will leave people unreconciled in hatred. He was, as Santayana thought "the American" to be, an idealist working on matter—the matter of history, power politics, bureaucracy, and a modernized, industrial, economic order. His realism about human beings was somber enough to suit the most dour of Puritans, but if he was correct in saying that there is "enough original sin in human nature to create opposition" to the substance of the gospel, Niebuhr also found that "there is enough natural grace in the human heart" to respond to that message as well.[22] As Fitzgerald described Amory Blaine, there was "no God in his heart, . . . his ideas were still in riot."[23] That description might fit many Americans, then and now, but not Niebuhr. He kept confidence in "a Divine Power, whose resources are greater than those of men, and whose suffering love can overcome the corruptions of man's achievements, without negating the significance of our striving."[24]

Niebuhr never counted on religion to be the unifying element in American life. Not only did he recognize that the varieties of our religious and nonreligious experience were too extensive for that outcome to occur, he also harbored skepticism about so-called civil religion, suspecting that it typically legitimated established ways undeserving of the favor. In that respect, Niebuhr had learned from Karl Marx. But he also drew the line where Marx's influence was concerned. Though Niebuhr agreed that religion could be the opium of the people, he stressed that its role could and must be very different. Religion, he believed, was properly a critic of culture. Within America, he affirmed, one of religion's tasks was to keep attention focused on the personalism that lies at the core of democratic individualism.[25]

The best insights of Western religious and democratic political theory, attested Niebuhr, converge to affirm the sanctity of individual personhood. The religious sensitivity of Americans could provide much-needed energy, he added, to make that belief a "resource for the highest forms of social realization."[26] For to the extent that any individual or group takes seriously the individual personhood of others, the recognition that respect is owed them receives a boost. Thus, Niebuhr insisted that religion, though it cannot unify the country, remains a vital ingredient in any sound understanding of "why and for what" America exists.

Niebuhr's instinct about America suggested to him a creed that combined competition and cooperation. The energy encouraged by individual freedom, he thought, could result in common purposes. Quarrelsome differences among American brothers and sisters might keep driving home the fact that they are one people, if not a family. By communally ensuring each other basic rights to go personal ways, they could stay together on the same way. Still seeking the covenant so rarely found, America needs to use the irony within its history as a prod to discover the twists of biblical paradox that Niebuhr also loved to employ: the ones who try to secure their own ways alone are far more likely to lose themselves than those who do their best individually in order to take on the risks of giving their lives for others. A coherent individualism requires caring to understand that interdependence makes independence possible. Personal initiative that does not serve others impoverishes the communal spirit that gives it birth and vitality.

Dwelling in Possibility

Each in his own way, Santayana, Dewey, and Niebuhr urged that, through ability and effort, individual Americans could achieve success and thereby reveal the depth of the potential for creating and sharing a true commonwealth, one that would extend well beyond the borders of American ground. Yet, hopeful though they were about a recovery of American individualism and its future, their optimism also remained rightly guarded by critical—even skeptical—questions. Santayana wondered what the mix of idealism and materialism in American life would be. Dewey pondered whether Americans would use their vast scientific and technological skill for rational moral ends. Niebuhr tried to find the needed ways to make relevant the messages contained in the ancient traditions of Passover and Easter. They all might have affirmed, not only for themselves but also for the nation, what Walt Whitman, Josiah Royce, and F. Scott Fitzgerald would also have found convincing in the words of their nineteenth-century American sister, the poet Emily Dickinson, when she wrote:

> I dwell in Possibility—
> A fairer House than Prose—
> More numerous of Windows—
> Superior—for Doors—
>
> Of Chambers as the Cedars—
> Impregnable of Eye—
> And for an Everlasting Roof
> The Gambrels of the Sky—
>
> Of Visitors—the fairest—
> For Occupation—This—
> The spreading wide my narrow Hands
> To gather Paradise—[27]

Emily Dickinson knew possibility to be a fickle friend. It guarantees no fortunes; it may spell disaster. If possibility permits glimpses of paradise, only rarely does it tend that way. Yet to dwell in possibility is the ambiguous legacy handed from one American generation to the next. If this complex fate means, as Walt Whitman said, "that the fruition of democracy . . . resides altogether in the future,"[28] then contemporary Americans need to follow some earlier thinkers in recovering "why and for what America exists." If this land is truly made for you *and* me, that prospect requires public recovery of insight that understands how the highest forms of social realization depend not only on *the sanctity of the individual person's life* but also on *cooperative dependence*. Such a process entails that more than the becoming should occupy American ground. The being, the substance of what America has been and is, must grip the people equally. For the being informs and even determines what a becoming individualism can possibly be.

NOTES

1. John Steinbeck, *Travels with Charley: In Search of America* (New York: Penguin Books, 1984), p. 5.

2. Ibid., pp. 241–42. I am indebted to Professor Rowland A. Sherrill for assistance in elaborating the nuances of the concept "American Ground."

3. Alexis de Tocqueville, *Democracy in America,* ed. J. P. Mayer and trans. George Lawrence (Garden City, N.Y.: Doubleday Anchor, 1969), pp. 279–80. Subsequent references to this work are cited in the text.

4. Robert N. Bellah, Richard Madsen, William M. Sullivan, Ann Swidler, and Steven M. Tipton, *Habits of the Heart* (Berkeley: University of California Press, 1985), p. viii.

5. Walt Whitman, *Democratic Vistas* (New York: Liberal Arts Press, 1949), p. 2.

6. Ibid., p. 32.

7. Josiah Royce, *The Problem of Christianity,* 2 vols. (Chicago: Henry Regnery Company), vol. 2, p. 42. Where the theme of community is concerned, this work by Royce—originally published in 1913—remains one of the definitive statements by any American thinker. See also Royce's *The Philosophy of Loyalty* (New York: Macmillan Company, 1908).

8. Quoted from Kenneth S. Davis, *The Hero: Charles A. Lindbergh and the American Dream* (Garden City, N.Y.: Doubleday & Company, 1959), pp. 213–14.

9. Reinhold Niebuhr, *Leaves from the Notebook of a Tamed Cynic* (San Francisco: Harper & Row, 1980), p. 143.

10. F. Scott Fitzgerald, *This Side of Paradise* (New York: Charles Scribner's Sons, 1970), p. 256.

11. Quoted from Santayana's "Apologia Pro Mente Sua" (1940). See *The Philosophy of George Santayana,* ed. Paul Arthur Schilpp (New York: Tudor Publishing Company, 1951), p. 603.

12. Fitzgerald, *This Side of Paradise,* pp. 17–18.

13. George Santayana, *Character and Opinion in the United States* (New York: W. W. Norton, 1967), p. 167. Subsequent references to this work are cited in the text.

14. Quoted from an address given at Baltimore, Maryland, dated 18 Apr. 1864, in *The Political Thought of Abraham Lincoln,* ed. Richard N. Current (Indianapolis: Bobbs-Merrill, 1967), p. 329. Lincoln's italics.

15. John Dewey, *Individualism Old and New* (New York: Capricorn Books, 1962), p. 32.

16. On these points, see Bellah, *Habits of the Heart,* esp. pp. 20–22, 50–51, 81–84, 138–41, 150–55, 246–57, 277, 281–96, and 307.

17. Niebuhr, *Leaves,* pp. 196–97.

18. See Fitzgerald, *This Side of Paradise,* p. 1. See also Reinhold Niebuhr, *Moral Man and Immoral Society* (New York: Charles Scribner's Sons, 1960), p. xii.

19. Niebuhr, *Leaves,* p. 23.

20. Ibid., p. 39.

21. Reinhold Niebuhr, *The Irony of American History* (New York: Charles Scribner's Sons, 1962), p. 17. Subsequent references to this work are cited in the text.

22. Niebuhr, *Leaves*, p. 41.

23. Fitzgerald, *This Side of Paradise*, p. 282.

24. Reinhold Niebuhr, *The Children of Light and the Children of Darkness* (New York: Charles Scribner's Sons, 1972), p. 190.

25. Reinhold Niebuhr's writings were filled with references to Karl Marx's philosophy and its subsequent Soviet interpretations. He found merit in Marx's critical insights about the development of capitalism in the nineteenth century, but there was little sympathy for the versions of Marx's theory and practice that Soviet policy from Lenin onward has carried out.

It is worth noting, too, that in 1963 Niebuhr wrote the introduction for a standard collection of Marx's writings on religion. Acknowledging an "original humanistic passion" in Marx's critiques of nineteenth-century religion, Niebuhr nevertheless concluded that "it was from the very beginning too indiscriminate, too lacking in empirical precision, too much the weapon of the 'class struggle' and the instrument of the revolutionary prophet who had transmuted atheism into a new religion. The priests of this religion are now the priest-kings of an empire based on utopian illusions, of a culture in which materialism has become the canonized philosophy. The vaunted affinity between empiricism and materialism has been transmuted into a new dogma." (See Reinhold Niebuhr, "Introduction" to *On Religion* by Karl Marx and Friedrich Engels [New York: Schocken Books, 1971], p. xiv.) Niebuhr spent much of his life disputing Marxist dogma, but doing so, he urged, required continuous self-critical analysis of American democracy as well.

26. Niebuhr, *Children of Light*, p. 81.

27. Written c. 1862, this poem (#657) was originally published in 1929. See *The Complete Poems of Emily Dickinson*, ed. Thomas H. Johnson (Boston: Little, Brown, and Company, 1960), p. 327.

28. Whitman, *Democratic Vistas*, p. 30.

RICHARD T. HUGHES

Recovering First Times:
The Logic of Primitivism in American Life

When J. Hector St. John de Crèvecoeur observed that "the American is a new man, who acts upon new principles; he must therefore entertain new ideas, and form new opinions," he was only offering a realistic assessment of American life, labor, and social structures as he perceived them.[1] There were others, however, in Crèvecoeur's generation and the next, who infused the image of American newness with a mythic dimension. For these interpreters, Americans were new in that they had been cut loose from the constraints of history and time and stood on the threshold of a radically new age which was wholly discontinuous with all previous epochs. Thus, Charles Pinckney argued in 1787 that the American situation was simply "unexampled" in the past,[2] and Gulian Verplanck told students at Union College in 1836 that America was "without a parallel in past history."[3] Three years later, a writer in the *Democratic Review* contended that America had little connection with the histories of modern nations "and still less with all antiquity, its glories, or its crimes. On the contrary, our national birth was the beginning of a new history, . . . which separates us from the past and connects us with the future only."[4] Poetically, Walt Whitman captured the essence of this sentiment in *Pioneers! O Pioneers!:* "All the past we leave behind, / We debouch upon a newer, mightier world, varied world." And graphically, the Great Seal of the United States captured this sentiment of radical American newness when it pictured all human history prior to America as a barren and arid wilderness from which emerged the American *novus ordo seclorum* (new order of the ages) in 1776.

That millennial visions are implicit in this understanding is obvious, and, indeed, anyone even casually acquainted with American religion in this period knows that millennialism of various kinds flourished in America between the Revolution and the Civil War. Intrigued by the various visions of millennial newness and the way those visions related to American purpose and identity during the period, scholars have explored the meaning of nineteenth-century American millennialism in painstaking and minute detail.[5] Most of those writing on this subject, however, have failed to recognize that generally implicit in the rhetoric of American newness and millennialism was the fundamental theme of recovery—recovery of something primal, ancient, and old. To be sure, most Americans were not concerned to recover their recent past, or even an ancient past which was merely history, fully as corrupt and degenerate as the recent past from which they had sprung. But they were concerned to recover the primordial past that stood behind the historical past. The objective of their recovery was, to use the language of Mircea Eliade, sacred time, not profane time—the time of the gods, not the time of humankind.[6]

Implicit in this conception is the notion of a fall from primal purity and rightness, and it was history—the long duration of human time— which embodied the disastrous aftermath of that fall. Understood in this way, millennialism was itself a kind of recovery of sacred time. Far from depicting a vacuous, contentless vision of the last age, most millennial visions elaborated a very specific content drawn from a first age whose perfections had been lost or obscured in a fall, but which now might be recovered, or restored, in the millennial dawn.

Crucial to this understanding is the fact that any given historical moment could function for any given believer as mythic, sacred time, "the time of the gods." For some Christians sacred time was the time of the apostles and the primitive church. For Mormons, primal time embraced a constellation of sacred times, ranging from the age of the patriarchs to the primitive church, all defined by direct communication of gods and angels with humankind. For the American Founding Fathers, sacred time was the creation itself, and nature was the bearer of the perfections of the first age. And as Eliade observes, Homer belonged to the primordium so far as Walt Whitman was concerned.[7] Regardless of the particular age a believer construed as sacred time, however, all millennialists of the nineteenth century might well have agreed with Alexander Campbell that "just in so far as the ancient order of things . . . is restored, just so far has the Millennium commenced."[8]

Yet, the obvious and frequent connections between recovery (primitivism) and millennialism have been lost on many scholars. Further, among those who have perceived those connections, few have taken with fundamental seriousness the importance of this theme of recovery for understanding American identity. Ernest Tuveson is a case in point. While recognizing that the "real point" of millennialism is that things will finally "be restored to the state in which God created them,"[9] he never really develops this theme and finally roots America's redemptive consciousness in its millennial aspirations. In fact, he sometimes misses the connections between recovery and millennialism as when, for example, he argues that the theme of manifest destiny could be inspired by two "widely divergent" conceptions: the recovery of an ancient civilization like Rome, on the one hand, or the erection of a millennial kingdom which necessarily implies "a separateness and unique quality in the new country," on the other.[10] In failing to take with fundamental seriousness the theme of recovery for understanding American identity, Tuveson has been more or less typical of most American scholarship.

At the same time, a few scholars have sensed the importance of the notion of recovery and have written cogently and suggestively regarding this theme. Thus, Fred Somkin in his *Unquiet Eagle* finds it notable that delegates to the Constitutional Convention looked for instruction to the classic world rather than to the England of the Commonwealth. What this meant, Somkin argues, was that the delegates sought to identify "with a universalism that transcended the mere homeland." Then Somkin makes the crucial point: "In the classic, archetypal forms of political life were to be found the rights of man, as distinguished from the rights of Englishmen. Such a point of view argued an American alienation from the grasp of an organic, efficacious past, as though America were itself a kind of rebuke to time. An appeal to the nature of man, rather than to his history, evidenced a faith in something that had emerged unscathed from the gauntlet of historical time."[11] Unlike Tuveson, therefore, Somkin sees that an appeal to ancient Rome could indeed be an appeal to a primordium that lay outside the bounds of profane and ordinary time.

Further, Somkin clearly recognizes that America's newness was predicated precisely upon her oldness, that is, upon her identification with primordial norms. Thus, while writing of America's "unprecedentedness" and of her "utterly new beginning" (p. 57), Somkin can also write that "America . . . , by cleaving to the primitively old, to that which had not grown old through the agency of time, gained the possibility of continuing to be always new" (p. 61). With this sort of description, Somkin comes close to suggesting the image of the American nation as straddling the stream of history with one foot planted squarely in the primordium and the other in the millennial dawn. In this way, America became "a providential conspiracy against time, . . . an attempt to outwit time by an evasion of the exigencies of temporal causality" (p. 60).

None of this means, of course, that Americans were ahistorical or unhistorical or failed either to know or to appreciate the past. Quite to the contrary. "As record, as deposit, the past undoubtedly existed," Somkin observes, "but Americans contested the extent of its jurisdiction" (p. 57).

Contesting the extent of the jurisdiction of the past is precisely what Sidney Mead had in mind when he wrote of the sense of "historylessness" that shaped the perspective of American denominations in the nineteenth century.[12] Contending with one another in the new free market of souls, created and sustained by religious freedom and pluralism in the new nation, both right-wing denominations and left-wing sects sought legitimacy by claiming to duplicate primitive Christianity more closely than the others. In so doing, Mead observes, both sects and denominations in America became at one and the same time both radically new and radically old so that all, to one degree or another, embraced "the idea of building anew in the American wilderness on the true and ancient foundations."[13]

In addition to the work of Mead and Somkin, a few scholars have explored the theme of recovery in American life in highly specialized contexts. One thinks, for example, of works like R. W. B. Lewis's *American Adam*, Henry Nash Smith's *Virgin Land,* Catherine Albanese's *Sons of the Fathers,* and Charles L. Sanford's *The Quest for Paradise.* No one, however, has yet undertaken the arduous task of exploring in a comprehensive and systematic way this particular theme of recovery in relation to American identity and to the life of the American nation.[14]

This essay is a modest and preliminary step in that direction. It will first briefly summarize the history of the recovery theme from its Renaissance and Reformation roots to its American budding and flowering in the early nineteenth century. It then will seek to probe the dilemmas and paradoxes of that motif by assessing its dynamics in the lives of two popular religious movements born on American soil—in many ways microcosms of the larger nation—the Mormons and the "Christians." Finally, this essay will suggest that the dilemmas that plagued Mormons and Christians as they embraced the recovery theme are the same dilemmas that have plagued the larger nation and for precisely the same reason: an innocent, primordial people, convinced of its calling to redeem, unify, or liberate the nations cannot escape, in the final analysis, its finite location in the stream of human history made most evident by the nagging and persistent fact of cultural, political, and religious pluralism in an ever-shrinking world.

II

When the recovery or restorationist ideal appeared at the end of the Middle Ages, it was not a cosmic ideology, poised to revolutionize the world. It was rather a tool in the hands of intellectuals, first the Italian Humanists and later the Christian Humanists north of the Alps. The explicit objective of the Christian Humanists was to retrieve both the letters and morals of Christian antiquity from the decay of the ages: a modest enough objective. But soon enough the rhythm of decay and return, fall and restoration, loss and recovery became a central theme in the agenda of Reformed theologians especially in Zurich and Strassburg, most of whom had been schooled in the assumptions of Christian Humanism.[15]

The very notion of fall and recovery presupposed an agent by whose complicity the fall had occurred, and Protestants generally agreed in identifying that agent as the Roman Catholic church. Further, since the fall involved the kingdom of God, it stood to reason that any agency which would subvert that kingdom from its original purity would be an enemy to God and therefore fundamentally demonic. Thus was the stage prepared for a cosmic struggle between Protestants and Catholics, now depicted as a battle between light and darkness, good and evil, the lamb and the beast, God and Satan. And significantly, the central focus of this struggle would be the recovery of the primitive church.

Nowhere was this struggle painted with bolder strokes, and nowhere did the ideal of primitive Christianity take on more urgency, than in England. After all, according to medieval legend, Joseph of Arimathea established the primitive church in England early on, only to have it subverted by Augustine of Canterbury who brought the "Romish service" which trod "the souls, bodies and estates of Englishmen . . . by the foul feet of the Roman Antichrist."[16] In addition, William Tyndale's enormously influential deuteronomic theology which portrayed England as a New Israel, covenanted to God as His chosen people, embraced inherently the rhythms of decay and recovery. What was covenant-keeping, after all, if not allegiance to a mythic beginning when God had revealed his will to his people? But what was implicit became explicit when, during the reign of Edward VI, the Reformed theologians from the Continent—especially Bullinger and Bucer—taught the English that covenant-keeping meant recovering the primitive church.

When Mary succeeded young Edward VI on the English throne and sought to bind England back to Rome, it was apparent to the embryonic Puritans who exiled themselves to the Continent that England had faulted its covenant with God and that Mary was the agent of his wrath. And why? Because England had reformed the church but had not restored her to her native, pristine purity? This deuteronomic perspective was wonderfully buttressed by John Foxe's *Actes and Monuments*. These early Puritans, therefore, pledged themselves to overthrow all traditions and inventions of men and to recover the pure, apostolic patterns.[17] They knew the cost would be high, for their struggle, they believed, was not with flesh and blood but with the principalities and powers of Hell. Thus, for example, the Geneva Bible identified the locusts that poured from the bottomless pit (Rev. 9:3) as "Prelates, with Monkes, Freres, Cardinals, Patriarkes, Archebishops, Bishops, Doctors, Baschelers & masters which forsake Christ to mainteine the false doctrine," and the king of the locusts (Rev. 9:11) as "Antichrist the Pope, king of hypocrites and Satans ambassadour." Clearly, the Puritans' sense of recovery provided both content and model for their developing apocalypticism.

Nor did Anglicans escape the Puritans' censure. Early on, the central issue between Anglicans and Puritans was the role of history and tradition in the Christian faith,[18] and this debate would be significant for the future messianic consciousness of the American people. Anglicans argued that there were timeless truths of primitive Christianity which should be restored and preserved but also that efforts to recover the form and structure of primitive Christianity in minute detail were bound to fail. After all, the primitive church lived in a particular time and culture which could not be replicated. The force of history and tradition, therefore, was unavoidable. To be human was to live under the constraints and limitations of history. But the Puritans disagreed. It might be difficult to escape the bounds of history and to replicate the pure beginnings of the faith, but, as God's chosen people, they really had no choice. Thus, when accused of innovation, Thomas Cartwright defended his model of Presbyterian churchmanship by arguing that "thys is no innovation but a renovation and the doctrine not newe but renued no straunger but borne in Sion whereunto it . . . ought now of right to be restored."[19] And John Robinson, the Separatist-Congregationalist pastor of the Leiden Pilgrims, proclaimed the genius of the recovery motif among Puritans when he declared that "the things we teach are not new, but old truths renewed; so are we not less persuaded, that the church constitution in which we are set, is cast in the apostolical and primitive mould, and not one day nor hour younger in the nature and form of it, than the first church of the New Testament."[20] And in Massachusetts, John Cotton was therefore typical when he argued that the New England way was as close as could be to what "the Lord Jesus (would erect) were he here himself in person."[21]

Thus armed with the innocence of pure beginnings, and fired by a deuteronomic theology that demanded virtue's preservation, the colonists embarked in the eighteenth century on a fifty-year apocalyptic struggle that began with the Great Awakening, continued through the French and Indian War, and finally culminated in the American Revolution. In the course of this struggle, the elusive and wily serpent first donned the disguise of impiety, then of Roman Catholicism, and finally of tyranny. But when the Revolution was won, the Americans discovered that to counter Satan's snares they had gradually but dramatically transformed their perspective regarding precisely what should be recovered. The concern now was not so much to recover the truths of primitive Christianity as it was to restore a state of liberty that was thought to have existed at the time of the creation itself.[22] Thus, the nation that was "a new order of the ages" was, at one and the same time, a recovery of the beginning of time, untrammeled by tradition or civilization. For all the disapprobation he received, Thomas Paine nonetheless spoke for many when he argued that the rights of man were grounded in the creation itself and that the birth of the American Republic was a virtual restoration of the birth of the world: "The case and circumstance of America present themselves as in the beginning of a world," he argued. When we view the American Republic, "We are brought at once to the point of seeing government begin, as if we had lived in the beginning of time."[23]

Americans, indeed, had bypassed history in their quest for national identification. Other nations may belong to time and tradition, but America belonged to the perfections of beginnings. Inescapably implicit in this assumption was the notion of American innocence. Other nations may bear the scars and stains that finitude inevitably brings, but, like a newborn babe, America was pure and undefiled. Further, since America had inherited William Tyndale's now-familiar deuteronomic theology, it was imperative that America's purity and innocence be maintained. There was therefore no room for flaws or imperfections in the fabric of the American Republic.

It was precisely this sense of having recovered the perfections of the first age that made it seem reasonable to many Americans that the Republic might now inaugurate the perfections of the millennial dawn. Timothy Dwight doubtless spoke for many when he proclaimed, "Here Empire's last, and brightest throne shall rise; / And Peace and Right, and Freedom, greet the skies." And he made the restoration underpinnings of his vision abundantly clear when he wrote, "To nature's bounds, reviving Freedom reign, / And truth, and Virtue, light the world again"[24] or again, "And Man once more, self-ruin'd Phoenix, rise, / On wings of Eden, to his native skies."[25] As

Tuveson observes, America had become for Dwight—and he might have added, for numerous other Americans as well—both "Eden *redivivus* and the prototype of the millennium."[26]

III

The clues are legion that innumerable Americans felt suspended between primordium and millennium and alienated from both history and tradition during the opening years of the nineteenth century. This is seen especially in the common rejection of traditional churches with their historic creeds and the appeal instead to primitive Christianity. Numerous factors prompted this development. In one sense, it was merely a continuation of the traditional Puritan quest for the primitive church. But, even more, it was a response to a nation that had planted one foot squarely in the primordium and stepped boldly with the other toward the millennial dawn. It simply made no sense to tolerate the traditions and creeds of history in one's church when history had been eclipsed by one's nation.

In such a vision, the common appeal to the first age was often an ideological premise for assertions of religious liberty. As Byron Cecil Lambert has shown, those who took refuge in the primitive church made themselves immune to the power plays of the New England standing order following disestablishment by the simple expedient of rejecting Christian history with its creeds, clerics, and traditions, and dismissing all as the "inventions of men."[27] Anxious to escape bondage to Calvinism, for example, one Kentucky primitivist declared that "we are not personally acquainted with the writings of John Calvan [*sic*], nor are we certain how nearly we agree with his views of divine truth; neither do we care."[28] And finally, the recovery motif was a handy way of dealing with the pesky problem of religious pluralism. While other sects and denominations were born of particular times and places in the long history of the Christian faith, one could claim that one's own communion was born of the first age and was therefore primal and true while all other faiths were historical and therefore false.

In all these senses, the various primitive gospel movements of the early nineteenth century were microcosms of the larger Republic. If the nation had transcended history and time, so did they. If the nation rooted its liberties and identity in Nature's primordium, the primitive gospel movements rooted their liberties in the Christian primordium. In both instances, the appeal was to pure beginnings. Further, if the nation could relegate European nations to the ash heap of history and claim ultimate legitimacy for itself alone by virtue of its primal identity, the primitive gospel movements could likewise dismiss religious pluralism as a grotesque aberration from the primal norm. But there was still a further sense in which the nation and the primitive gospel movements shared much in common and that was their mutual claim to an innocence uncontaminated by history or time. Each, so each thought, had sprung fresh from the hands of God. And each, therefore—nation and sect alike—thought itself God's agent to redeem, unify, or liberate the world, depending on the community's perspective.

Rejection of the historic churches, therefore, appeared on every hand in the first three decades of the nineteenth century. One thinks, for example, of Elias Smith and Abner Jones, of James O'Kelley and Barton Stone, of Sidney Rigdon and Parley Pratt, or even of Anne Lee's Shakers. Lucy Mack Smith, mother of the Mormon Prophet, was typical when she lamented that "there was not then upon the earth the religion which I sought. I therefore determined to examine my Bible, and, taking Jesus and His disciples for my guide, I endeavored to obtain from God that which man could neither give nor take away." [29] Periodicals, books, and tracts dedicated to the recovery theme proliferated during this period, with such titles as *The Evangelical Restorationist, The Gospel Restored,* and *Priestcraft Exposed and Primitive Christianity Defended.* [30] Indeed, John Nevin, writing in the *Mercersburg Review,* observed that "the principle of primitive judgment [was] the hobby of all the sects." [31]

The two most significant manifestations of the recovery motif during this period, however, were two primitive gospel movements destined to rank among the largest of all religious movements in America: the Christians/Disciples of Christ, led by Alexander Campbell and Barton W. Stone, and the Church of Jesus Christ of Latter-day Saints, led by the Mormon Prophet, Joseph Smith. Indeed, the very names of these movements suggested their American origins and thus, paradoxically, their sense of recovering the first age. Far from adopting names that reflected historical leaders or forms of church organization, these groups appropriated names that were primitive and therefore universal: Christians/Disciples of Christ and Church of Jesus Christ. And like the larger Republic which gave them birth, both of these groups embodied all the tensions, paradoxes, and dilemmas that inevitably came from standing squarely in the stream of history while at the same time deriving fundamental identity from the innocence of the first age.

Significantly, the Christian movement, like the Republic which was its womb, was born in a passion for liberty. The American Revolution had made Americans free politically, but clerics and creeds still tyrannized the consciences of the faithful. The Christians therefore simply sidestepped the traditional churches by moving outside of history to a realm of pure beginnings where arguments drawn from history did not matter. Thus, an anonymous Kentuckian argued that "the primitive christian never heard of the five points of Dort, nor of Calvinism."[32] His point was clear: eighteen centuries of Christian history and theology were now, in these latter days, irrelevant. Christians therefore should be *Christians only*, unqualified by theology and the inventions of men.

Not surprisingly, then, these Christians argued that one of the principal characteristics of the primitive church was freedom. Further, they claimed that the church fell from its original purity, not when it spawned false doctrine but rather when it enforced creedal uniformity under Constantine. Perhaps most significant, they judged creeds and confessions of faith, as products of finite history, to be fundamentally un-American and "anti-republican in soul, body, and spirit."[33]

Ironically, a second theme in the Christians' agenda grew from a profound discomfort with religious pluralism in the new Republic. Thus they argued passionately for Christian unity. But the unity for which they pled would not be contrived or legislated; rather, it would occur quite naturally through the compelling attraction of the recovered primitive church. Alexander Campbell, for example, fully expected all humanity to abandon the creeds and traditions of men— whether Jewish, Moslem, or Christian—and to march into the primitive ark of ecumenism. Further—and here is the third theme in their agenda—the introduction of a united, recovered primitive church, untrammeled by the footsteps of history, would inaugurate the millennial dawn. As Walter Scott, a colleague of both Campbell and Stone, proclaimed, "The ancient Gospel and ancient order of the Church must prevail" and then "the Millenium . . . will doubtless be a wonder, a terrible wonder, to ALL."[34]

The fundamental dilemma of the Christians revolved around the issue of pluralism. Indeed, so long as the Christians lived in their transhistorical possibilities, standing with one foot in primitive Christianity and the other in the millennial dawn, they had no need to take seriously the historical expressions of the Christian faith incarnate in the denominations. In fact, the Christians claimed that they were not a denomination at all and that, when the millennium arrived, all denominational structures would fall. All that would be left would be the true, New Testament Christians who, having once inhabited the denominational temples of history, would now be united and free in a primitive, apostolic church.

But the millennium did not dawn and Christian unity failed to transpire. And when these failures became apparent, the Christians were left to eat the husks of history and to grapple with their identity respecting both themselves and others. Indeed, a fine line separated two important concepts—the primitive church as the millennial ark of liberty and ecumenism, on the one hand, and the primitive church as the true church in a sea of false churches, on the other. As the millennial vision faded and the denominational structures failed to fall, and, as the Christians became increasingly conscious of their own identity as one group among others, many of them crossed that line. The cosmic vision of liberty and unity now became, for some at least, a provincial vision of sectarian exclusivism, though ironically rooted and grounded in the well-worn primitivist ideology. The goal of restoring the primitive church was thereby transformed into a *fait accompli* and the plea to be Christians only, unqualified by history and tradition, into a claim to be the only Christians. The lack of tradition now constituted a tradition in its own right, the rejection of theology now became a fundamental theological maxim, and the commitment to transcend history became the substance of the particular history of this particular people. Thus, it is no surprise that some among the Christians now regarded themselves as true and therefore innocent and others as false,[35] since others belonged to history while the Christians belonged to the first age.

The dynamics and dilemmas of Mormonism were similar, though rooted in a much more explicit rejection of pluralism than characterized even the Christians. Like the Christians, however, Mormons also responded to religious pluralism with claims to primitivism and innocence.

Anxiety over pluralism was implicit in the very beginning of the Mormon experience when young Joseph Smith, perplexed by the competing claims of the various Christian sects, retired to the woods in 1820 to put a simple question to the Lord: which of all the churches is the true church? Significantly, the Lord responded that "I must join none of them, for they were all wrong" and that "all their creeds were an abomination in His sight."[36] Seven years later, Smith's restoration of primitive Christianity commenced with the recovery of the golden plates, the basis for the Book of Mormon. Indeed, the Book of Mormon was, in and of itself, a recovery of ancient Christianity once delivered to the Americas but lost by the Nephites because of wickedness and unbelief. With the establishment of the Church of Christ in 1830, the restoration of the gospel and of the church was complete.

What now remained was extension of the Mormon "gathering" throughout the earth, a "gathering" that would inaugurate religious unity on Mormon terms[37] and, as a direct result, the millennial age. In holding to this familiar recovery-unity-millennium progression, Mormons resembled the Christians. But there were at least two fundamental differences. First, restoration for the earliest Christians was a metaphysical expectation; for Mormons it was an accomplished fact, predicated on the recovery of a tangible and visible book. To be sure, empirical reality was central to Mormonism at every significant point. But, second, while the Christians aimed at a recovery of New Testament Christianity alone, Mormons aimed at a kind of "cosmic regeneration," blending multiple sacred times—Eden, the age of the patriarchs, the theocracy of ancient Israel, and the teachings and practices of the primitive church. What defined a sacred time in the Mormon imagination was direct communication between God and humankind, and each of those epochs manifested that dimension in rich detail.[38]

Of all the sacred times which Mormons sought to recover, however, the one which dominated in the Mormon imagination was that of ancient Israel.[39] For this reason, the Church of Jesus Christ of Latter-day Saints was far more than a church. It was a kingdom—a new Israel. As God's kingdom, now restored to its ancient purity, it was destined to swallow all other kingdoms and churches until, at last, the Saints would literally rule with Christ upon the earth. One can hardly imagine a more effective antidote to American religious pluralism.

Implicit in this Mormon version of recovery was the innocence of the Saints and the degeneracy of the Gentile religions. There was, in this case, no subtlety of ideological development as had been the case with the Christians. Rather, it was all very straightforward. The apostles of the church perhaps put it best in an 1845 proclamation to "All the Kings of the World, to the President of the United States of America, to the Governors of the Several States, and to the Rulers and Peoples of all Nations." That proclamation announced that "the kingdom of God has come, as has been predicted by the ancient prophets . . . even that Kingdom which shall fill the whole earth and stand forever." The apostles then warned the world leaders that these events "are calculated, in their very nature, to reduce all nations and creeds to *one* political and religious standard, and thus put an end to Babel forms and names and to strife and war."[40]

Indeed, Mormon primitivism sometimes asserted Mormon innocence and Gentile depravity so thoroughly that visions of violence were by no means out of the question. Thus, Martin Harris, for example, was reported to have issued the following prediction in 1832:

> Within four years there will not be one wicked person left in the United States; . . . the righteous will be gathered to Zion, . . . and there will be no President over these United States, after that time.
>
> I do hereby assert and declare that in four years from the date thereof [September 1832] every sectarian and religious denomination in the United States will be broken down, and every Christian shall be gathered unto the Mormonites, and the rest of the human race shall perish.[41]

And Parley Pratt proclaimed that all who refused the message of the Saints "shall alike feel the hand of the almighty, by pestilence, famine, earthquake, and the sword: yea, ye shall be drunken with your own blood . . . until your cities are desolate . . . until all lyings, priestcrafts, and all manner of abominations, shall be done away."[42] Even in the midst of such visions, however, the Saints were confident of their innocence. They were, after all, not only God's saints in a world of Gentiles; they also stood removed from the finite sphere of history. Having replicated the primordium and now providing the locus for the millennium, they found their identity not in profane time but in sacred time.

In the early years, this meant that the Saints, themselves, were not responsible for violent retribution. Thus, Sidney Rigdon assured the Missourians that any guilt for violence would be the Missourians' alone: "We will never be the aggressors," Rigdon warned. Nonetheless, he went on, any "mob that comes on to us to disturb us; it shall be between us and them a war of extermination, for we will follow them, till the last drop of their blood is spilled, or else they will have to exterminate us."[43]

In 1838, when war finally erupted between the Gentiles and the Saints, Mormons preserved their innocence by identifying their cause with the cause of God. "I care not how many come against us," Joseph proclaimed. "God will send us angels to our deliverance and we can conquer 10,000 as easily as ten!"[44] But their innocence ultimately was rooted not in an abstract identification with God but in a concrete identification with the sacred times: the times of Adam, of the patriarchs, of ancient Israel, and of the primitive church. Thus, the armies of the Saints were not, as they appeared, mere nineteenth-century mortals engaged in another war in the long stream of military history. They rather were "the armies of Israel . . . established by Revelation from God," who soon would "take the kingdom" according to the prophecy of Daniel.[45] The innocent or primordial but violent saints would be a recurring theme in the life of the American Republic.

IV

These two American traditions—Christian and Mormon—provide highly instructive paradigms for understanding both the myth of primitive, redemptive innocence in American history and the dilemmas that myth has wrought in American society. Indeed, the experience of Mormons and Christians parallels the larger American experience at several significant points.

In the first place, America's founders from the beginning imagined this Republic a primordial nation, conceived in the womb of the creation itself. No one made this point more clearly than Tom Paine, who argued that the liberties and rights of humankind, now incarnate in the United States of America, did not derive from historical precedent but from the very hands of the Creator. He criticized those who fashion society on "precedents drawn from antiquity" because "they do not go the whole way" and stop instead "in some of the intermediate stages of an hundred or a thousand years." Paine rejected such homage to mere history as producing "no authority at all": "But if we proceed on, we shall at last come out right; we shall come to the time when man came from the hand of his Maker. . . . We are now got at the origin of man, and at the origin of his rights."[46] Thomas Jefferson plowed this very perspective into the Declaration of Independence when he claimed for himself and for "all men . . . certain inalienable rights" and then predicated these rights not on history or on historical precedent but rather on "Nature and Nature's God."

Behind these appeals to "creation," to "the Maker," and to "Nature and Nature's God" was the intent to ground the rights of humankind not in a historically particularized vision, meaningful only to one cultural or one religious perspective, but, rather, in a universal perspective, accessible and potentially meaningful to all, of whatever nation, culture, or religion. Even Mormons, who sometimes despaired of their treatment at the hands of the United States government, nonetheless readily proclaimed their faith in the primal and therefore eternal and universal validity of basic American institutions. Thus, Parley Pratt, one of the original Twelve Apostles of the Latter-day Saints, unequivocally affirmed: "In the principles of the Constitution formed by our fathers . . . there is no difficulty, that is, in the laws and instruments themselves. They embrace eternal truths, principles of eternal liberty, not the principles of one peculiar country, or the sectional interest of any particular people, but the great, fundamental, eternal principles of liberty to rational beings."[47] America's Founding Fathers sought, by invoking precisely this vision, first in the Declaration of Independence and then in the First Amendment, to provide for cultural and religious pluralism in the new nation, and it is this faith—this vision—that Sidney Mead has called "the theology of the Republic." Indeed, Mead hopes that this very theology might one day become the perspective of the nations: "May we not dream with generations of Americans that our commonwealth is the bearer in history of a political cosmopolitanism which may someday be incarnated in world institutions that will compel the now absolutistic nations also to live together in overt peace under recognized law until the necessity is metamorphosed into an ideal, and its practice in a virtue?"[48]

Mead's profound hope that the political cosmopolitanism of America might someday become incarnate in the world at large has indeed been shared by millions of Americans since the birth of the Republic. And Americans seem in general to have agreed that this global incarnation should be accomplished through the power of example rather than through coercion or force. In this sense, the hopes of most Americans have not been unlike the aspirations of participants in the early Christian movement. In both instances, the faithful believed that their community was true, right, and natural because it stood as a virtual recovery of the truths of the first age. Its power and rectitude should therefore be obvious to any reasonable observer. And as the Christians fully expected denominational absolutism to melt away under the bright rays of the primitive church now restored in their midst, so many Americans in the nineteenth century fully expected the birth of their primordial nation, newly sprung from the hand of God Himself, to inspire millions of oppressed peoples to break the yoke of tyranny.

This was precisely the vision of Lyman Beecher, who argued in 1827 that the American Revolution would spark "revolutions and overturnings, until the world is free." To Beecher's mind, this was the inevitable conclusion to history. Tyrants may renew their efforts to drive again "the bolt of every chain," but they could not possibly extinguish "the rising flame" of freedom: "Still it burns, and still the mountain heaves and murmers. And soon it will explode with voices and thunderings and great earth quakes. Then will the trumpet of Jubilee sound, and earth's debased millions will leap from the dust, and shake off their chains, and cry, 'Hosanna to the Son of David.'"[49] Beecher could project such millennial visions because to him America was the recovery of the first age and was not of profane or historical origin.

"Our republic," he said, "in its constitution borrows from the Bible its elements, proportions, and power. It was God that gave these elementary principles to our forefathers."[50] In expressing this sentiment, Beecher spoke for multitudes of Americans of his age.

Yet, Beecher's vision contained a profound ambiguity that subtly undercut the premises expressed by Jefferson, by Tom Paine, or even by Parley Pratt. For if for Jefferson, Paine, or Pratt, America was primordial because born of *natural* principles, rooted in the creation itself, for Beecher America was primordial because born of *biblical* principles, and, he might well have added, biblical principles shaped to a Protestant standard.

Sidney Mead has argued that the orthodox Christian mind of the early nineteenth century, uncomfortable with the cosmopolitan Enlightenment premises of the new nation, castigated those premises as "infidelity" which was "drowned in the great tidal wave of [Christian] revivalism."[51] But that, in fact, is only half the story. For when the orthodox realized that the "infidel" sentiments of universality had been plowed deep into the American experience and were there to stay, they invoked the old saw "if you can't whip them, join them." In this way, they now portrayed "Nature's God" as fundamentally Christian and their tribal deities as essentially universal. This process of particularizing "Nature's God" began, in fact, as early as the Revolution, a development Catherine Albanese suggests when she writes of Nature's God donning the armor of Jehovah, God of Battles.[52] In this way, the primordium of nature and the primordium of the Christian story became so amalgamated as to be almost interchangeable in the popular imagination, and the American identity grew increasingly particularized in many American minds. Thus could Beecher write of a constitution that had borrowed "from the Bible its elements, proportions, and power." Because this perspective was so pervasive, America became in the minds of many what it has continued to be for millions of Americans ever since—a fundamentally Christian nation.

It was at this point that America's "sense of historylessness" betrayed her, for what Mead observes regarding the denominations was equally true of the Republic: "the very freedom which they felt and acted upon, a freedom without historical perspective, served many times to bind them to the obvious tendencies of the moment. In all innocence they built into the life of the denominations what time and tide happened to bring to their shores."[53] Or, as Henry Bowden has written of nineteenth-century Protestantism, their "narrow search, looking down through centuries of Catholic darkness, produced only the reflection of a Protestant face at the bottom of a deep well."[54] But what Protestants saw at the bottom of the well was not only a Protestant face, but also a white face and a male face and, typically, an Anglo-Saxon face, for all of this had time and tide brought to their shores.

Lest the tale told here be wholly one-sided, however, it must be added that many of those Founders who searched their very souls in an honest attempt to provide cosmopolitan, universal foundations for the Republic were likewise seduced by the illusion of historylessness. Thus, while proclaiming inalienable rights for all men, it was clear in most instances, at least, that "all men" meant all white men, and did not include women, slaves, or Native Americans.

Finally, now, it is clear that the recovery theme working in the life of the Republic was structurally similar in fundamental respects to the recovery theme working in the life of the movement designated "Christian." For, like the Christians, the nation early on found itself plunged back into the very vortex of history it had thought to escape. And if the Christians had thought themselves a primordial/millennial ark of liberty and ecumenism, only to emerge for some as the true church in a sea of false churches, so the nation, conceived as a bastion of freedom for the world, found itself proscribing the freedom of many within its borders. Thus, what has already been said of the Christians may now be said of the new nation in the early nineteenth century: "the cosmic vision of liberty and unity now became, for some at least, a provincial vision of sectarian exclusivism, though ironically rooted and grounded in the well-worn primitivist ideology."

This leads to the third point of analogy between Christians and Mormons, on the one hand, and the nation, on the other. If Christians and Mormons thought themselves primordial and thus universal people, so did the nation. And if many Christians, finally confronted with the terrors of history, responded with affirmations of sectarian exclusivism and cloaked their particularities in primordial illusions, so did the nation. But the paradigm for understanding the nation's third and final step was furnished by the early Mormons: as nineteenth-century America increasingly particularized and even absolutized its primordial identity, redemption through persuasive example gave way to redemption through coercion. This development was fully consistent with the logic of primitivism in American life. For after all, how could a nation which had sidestepped history and which had become, in Somkin's words, a "rebuke to time," coexist with nations and peoples whose allegiance to their own histories and their own traditions remained unabated and unabashed? This question became especially acute as Americans increasingly committed themselves to highly particularized Anglo-Saxon, Protestant values which they then imagined were universal, cosmopolitan, and fundamentally natural. Americans therefore judged as fundamentally perverse any nation or people who resisted these "universal" values. Since example and persuasion had failed, therefore, the only option left to "nature's nation" was coercion.

Of the various "perverse" nations, the first to feel coercion's sword were the native Americans, and, consistently, whites justified the policy of Indian removal by appeals to the first age and claims of recovery and restoration. In 1830, for example, George Rockingham Gilmer, later to serve as governor of Georgia, put the white Americans' case in the baldest possible terms: "Treaties were expedients by which ignorant, intractable, and savage people were induced without bloodshed to yield up what civilized people had a right to possess by virtue of that command of the Creator delivered to man upon his formation—be fruitful, multiply, and replenish the earth, and subdue it."[55] Proponents of Indian removal regularly and consistently employed this argument from the Genesis account of creation. And why not? After all, this was precisely the argument regarding Indian lands invoked by New England Puritans, fully as engaged in recovering first times as their nineteenth-century descendants. Thus John Winthrop argued, "The whole earth is the Lord's garden & He hath given it to the sons of men, with a general condition, Gen. 1:28. Increase & multiply, replenish the earth & subdue it. . . . That which lies common and hath never been replenished or subdued is free to any that will possess and improve it."[56] The irony inherent in the nineteenth-century use of this argument, however, lay in the fact that "nature's nation" made ownership of land contingent not on a natural use of the land but on subjugation of the land in conformity with "civilization." But nineteenth-century white Americans who employed this line of reasoning altogether failed to see the irony since they had thoroughly particularized "Nature and Nature's God" with a "civilized," Protestant, Anglo-Saxon content which they then assumed was primordial, eternal, and universal.

Appeals to the Genesis account of creation underpinned claims not only to Indian lands but also to Mexico[57] and even to the Oregon Territory. Thus, John Quincy Adams argued that America's title to Oregon was inescapable and unavoidable on the grounds that the Genesis account of creation "is the foundation not only of our title to the territory of Oregon, but the foundation of all human title to all human possession."[58] But the more common claim to Oregon rested on a far more radical form of the recovery motif than this. It rested, instead, on a complete dismissal of history and an appeal to the universal that lay behind all historic particularities. Thus, John L. O'Sullivan rooted America's claim to the Oregon Territory squarely in America's sense of historylessness. He summarily dismissed "all these antiquated materials of old black-leather international law" along with "all these cobweb tissues" of finite, human history, and rested his case with the Author of the Universe, Himself.[59] He might well have added, in the words of the Mormon proclamation issued that same year, that "the kingdom of God has come, . . . even that Kingdom which shall fill the whole earth and stand forever."

While the American kingdom never filled the earth, it at least came in the waning years of the century to the Philippines, and it came in full military regalia. Its objective was to bring universal values, as Americans understood those values, to a people still shackled by the chains of history. The nature of those supposed universal values was spelled out quite clearly by President McKinley as he explained America's motives in that episode: "to educate the Filipinos, and uplift and Christianize them, and by God's grace do the very best we could by them, as our fellow-men for whom Christ also died."[60]

The trenchant paradox involved in this conflict was the American determination to compel the Filipinos to be free. As Senator Orville Platt of Connecticut put it, "God has placed upon this Government the solemn duty of providing for the people of these islands a government based upon the principle of liberty no matter how many difficulties the problem may present."[61] And in defense of his policy of coercion when criticized for what seemed imperialism, McKinley asked, "Did we need their consent to perform a great act for humanity? We had it in every aspiration of their minds, in every hope of their hearts."[62] In reflecting on all of this, Albert Weinberg remarks that it was "a paradoxical fact . . . indeed, that the same humanitarian ideal which had once been used to discredit conquest was now employed with equal confidence in its justification."[63]

There is, however, an explanation to this seeming paradox, and that, it seems, was that America had so thoroughly rooted its historical particularities in the soil of universality, nurtured and fed by its profound sense of historylessness. Thus, Senator Albert Beveridge, in his well-known defense of American involvement in the Philippines, argued in 1899 that God "has made us the lords of civilization that we may administer civilization." Retreat from the Philippines "would be the betrayal of a trust as sacred as humanity" and "a crime against Christian civilization."[64] The particularities inherent in this vision of supposed universality are evident. But the extent to which the Protestant, Anglo-Saxon particularities of the American *experience* had now undermined the very *premises* of that experiment became evident when Beveridge argued that Filipinos simply "are not capable of self government. How could they be? They are not of a self-governing race. They are Orientals, Malays, instructed by Spaniards in the latter's worst state."[65] Thus, the very ideal of freedom, which Jefferson had argued was a fundamentally inalienable right with which "all men" had been endowed, now was the right only of Anglo-Saxons and perhaps a few others who were "capable of self-government." In this way, America was not only a rebuke to time; the nation also became, by the late nineteenth century a rebuke to the universal and cosmopolitan ideals which had established, in the eighteenth century, its very reason for existence.

V

Sidney Mead has cautioned that genuine patriotism "depends upon the ability to distinguish between the legitimation of a form of government as an ideal type (e.g., 'democracy'), and the legitimation of the acts of a current administration (e.g., Republican or Democrat)."[66] Given this important distinction, Mead may rightly "dream with generations of Americans that our commonwealth is the bearer in history of a political cosmopolitanism" which may eventuate in peace "metamorphosed into an ideal, and its practice into a virtue." Likewise, Americans have every reason to share the hopes Martin Luther King expressed to his people: "Even though we face the difficulties of today and tomorrow, I still have a dream. It is a dream deeply rooted in the American dream. I have a dream that one day this nation will rise up and live out the true meaning of its creed: 'We hold these truths to be self-evident that all men are created equal.'"[67] Both these dreams assume the legitimacy of the theme of recovery in American life, namely, that American ideals do, in fact, embody principles that are universal, cosmopolitan, and even primordial. However, both dreams also implicitly disavow the one-on-one identification of any given historic particularity with the ideals themselves. Put another way, for the recovery of an ideal primordium to be viable in American life, it must be held as process, not as realized, accomplished fact, incarnate in some one or another historical manifestation.[68]

Understood in this sense, American history continues the American Revolution as, through the course of human events and the power of rational debate, successive generations of Americans increasingly discern that the "inalienable rights" to "life, liberty, and the pursuit of happiness" belong not only to "all men" but to all human-kind. The alternative to this understanding of recovery as process is the grim vision Mead portrays: "Sectarianism, religious or national, is a greater threat than secularism or outright atheism, because, as the story of religious persecution reminds us, when it comes in the guise of 'the faith once delivered to the saints' it may legitimate terrible tyrannies."[69]

NOTES

1. J. Hector St. John de Crèvecoeur, *Letters from an American Farmer* (1782; New York: Penguin American Library, 1981), p. 70.

2. Charles Pinckney, address to the Constitutional Convention, June 25, 1787, in *Documents Illustrative of the Formation of the Union of the American States,* ed. Charles Tansell (Washington: Government Printing Office, 1927), pp. 804–5.

3. Gulian C. Verplanck, *The Advantages and Dangers of the American Scholar. A discourse delivered . . . at Union College,* July 26, 1836 (New York, 1836), p. 5.

4. "The Great Nation of Futurity," *Democratic Review* 6 (Nov. 1839): 426–27.

5. For a sampling of the extent to which millennialism has been explored, see Leonard I. Sweet, "Millennialism in America: Recent Studies," *Theological Studies* 40 (Sept. 1979): 510–31; and Hillel Schwartz, "The End of the Beginning: Millenarian Studies, 1969–1975," *Religious Studies Review* 2 (July 1976): 1–15.

6. See, e.g., Mircea Eliade, *The Sacred and the Profane* (New York: Harcourt, Brace, 1959), pp. 20–113. See also *The Myth of the Eternal Return* (Princeton: Princeton University Press, 1954), and *The Quest: History and Meaning in Religion* (Chicago: University of Chicago Press, 1969). For an assessment of the pertinence of Eliade's constructs for historical religions and for the American situation, see Richard T. Hughes, "From Civil Dissent to Civil Religion—and Beyond," *Religion in Life* 49 (Autumn 1980): 270–72.

7. Eliade, *Quest,* p. 101.

8. Alexander Campbell, "A Restoration of the Ancient Order of Things. No. I.," *Christian Baptist* 2 (Feb. 7, 1825): 136.

9. Ernest Tuveson, *Redeemer Nation: The Idea of America's Millennial Role* (Chicago: University of Chicago Press, 1968), p. 11.

10. Ibid., p. 97.

11. Fred Somkin, *Unquiet Eagle: Memory and Desire in the Idea of American Freedom, 1815–1860* (Ithaca: Cornell University Press, 1967), p. 57. Subsequent references to this work are cited in the text.

12. Sidney E. Mead, *The Lively Experiment: The Shaping of Christianity in America* (New York: Harper and Row, 1963), pp. 108–13. Mead addressed in considerably more detail the theme of recovery in American life in "The The-

ology of the Republic and the Orthodox Mind," *Journal of the American Academy of Religion* 44 (Mar. 1976): 105–13.

13. Mead, *Lively Experiment*, p. 111.

14. R. W. B. Lewis, *The American Adam: Innocence, Tragedy and Tradition in the Nineteenth Century* (Chicago: University of Chicago Press, 1955); Henry Nash Smith, *Virgin Land: The American West as Symbol and Myth* (Cambridge: Harvard University Press, 1950); Catherine L. Albanese, *Sons of the Fathers: The Civil Religion of the American Revolution* (Philadelphia: Temple University Press, 1976); and Charles L. Sanford, *The Quest for Paradise: Europe and the American Moral Imagination* (Urbana: University of Illinois Press, 1962).

In addition to these works, Professor T. Dwight Bozeman argues in a major work on New England Puritanism that it was the theme of recovery and not the theme of a millennial errand into the wilderness that prompted the Puritans' Great Migration and that informed and nourished their social, religious, and political life throughout their history. (See *"Live Ancient Lives": The Primitivist Dimension of Puritanism* [Williamsburg: Institute of Early American History and Culture, 1988].) More recently, Professor Leonard Allen and I have completed a book-length study on the relation between the recovery motif and freedom in the American experience (*Illusions of Innocence: Protestant Primitivism in America, 1630–1875* [Chicago: University of Chicago Press, 1988]).

In addition, two conferences are important in this regard. A conference at Pepperdine University in 1975 explored the restoration theme in Christian history and included several papers on the recovery motif in American religion and life. Several of those papers were later published in the *Journal of the American Academy of Religion* 44 (Mar. 1976). From that issue of *JAAR*, see esp. Samuel S. Hill, Jr., "A Typology of American Restitutionism: From Frontier Revivalism and Mormonism to the Jesus Movement," pp. 65–76; Edwin S. Gaustad, "Restitution, Revolution, and the American Dream," pp. 77–86; and Sidney Mead, "The Theology of the Republic and the Orthodox Mind," pp. 105–13. Then, at a conference at Abilene Christian University in 1985, a group of scholars explored the theme of recovery specifically in relation to America's religious and intellectual life. There Robert Handy, Albert Outler, Jan Shipps, Dwight Bozeman, and Grant Wacker, to name a few, found the recovery motif to be fundamental to American traditions as diverse as Puritanism, the Enlightenment, Baptists, Mormonism, and Pentecostalism. Papers from that conference are published as a single volume, *The American Quest for the Primitive Church*, edited by Richard T. Hughes (Urbana: University of Illinois Press, 1988).

15. See Abraham Friesen, "The Impulse toward Restitutionist Thought in Christian Humanism," *Journal of the American Academy of Religion* 44 (Mar. 1976): 29–45.

16. Robert Baillie, "A Parallel or Brief Comparison of the Liturgies with the Masse-Book" (1641), cited in Tuveson, *Redeemer Nation*, p. 140.

17. See James C. Spalding, "Restitution as a Normative Factor for Puritan Dissent," *Journal of the American Academy of Religion* 44 (Mar. 1976): 47–63.

18. See Ronald J. Vander Molen, "Anglican against Puritan: Ideological Origins during the Marian Exile," *Church History* 42 (Mar. 1973): 45–57; and John K. Luoma, "The Primitive Church as a Normative Principle in the Theology of the Sixteenth Century: The Anglican-Puritan Debate over Church Polity as Represented by Richard Hooker and Thomas Cartwright" (Ph.D. diss., Hartford Seminary Foundation, 1974). See also Luoma, "Who Owns the Fathers? Hooker and Cartwright on the Authority of the Primitive Church," *Sixteenth Century Journal* 8 (Oct. 1977): 45–59

19. Thomas Cartwright, preface, *A Replye to An answere made of M. Doctor Whitgifte* (1574). A particularly penetrating analysis of the restoration ideal in New England Puritan dissent is Leonard Allen, "'The Restauration of Zion': Roger Williams and the Quest for the Primitive Church" (Ph.D. diss., University of Iowa, 1984).

20. *The Works of John Robinson*, ed. Robert Ashton (Boston, 1851), vol. 2, p. 43.

21. John Cotton, "A Reply to Mr. Williams," cited in Perry Miller, *Orthodoxy in Massachusetts* (New York: Harper and Row, 1970), p. 160.

22. See Nathan O. Hatch, *The Sacred Cause of Liberty: Republican Thought and the Millennium in Revolutionary New England* (New Haven: Yale University Press, 1977), pp. 29–54.

23. *The Writings of Thomas Paine*, ed. Moncure Daniel Conway (New York: G. P. Putnam's Sons, 1894), vol. 2, pp. 428–29.

24. Timothy Dwight, *The Conquest of Canaan* (1783), cited in Tuveson, *Redeemer Nation*, pp. 107–8.

25. Dwight, *Greenfield Hill* (1794), cited in Tuveson, *Redeemer Nation*, p. 111.

26. Tuveson, *Redeemer Nation*, p. 111.

27. Byron Cecil Lambert, *The Rise of the Anti-Mission Baptists: Sources and Leaders, 1800–1840* (New York: Arno Press, 1980), pp. 2–45, 110–11, and passim.

28. Robert Marshall and John Thompson, *A Brief Historical Account of Sundry Things in the Doctrines and State of the Christian, or as it is Commonly Called, The Newlight Church* (Cincinnati: J. Carpenter & Co., 1811), p. 17.

29. *History of Joseph Smith by His Mother, Lucy Mack Smith*, ed. Preston Nibley, (Salt Lake City: Bookcraft, 1954), p. 36.

30. *The Evangelical Restorationist* was a Universalist sheet published in Troy, New York, in 1825; *Priestcraft Exposed and Primitive Christianity Defended* was published in Lockport, New York, during 1828 and 1829; and *The Gospel Restored* was the title of a volume published by Walter Scott, a colleague of Alexander Campbell, in Cincinnati in 1836. These titles are random selections of many publications during this period with pronounced primitivist sentiments.

31. John Nevin, "The Sect System," *Mercersburg Review* 1 (Sept. 1849): 482–507.

32. Archippus, "Calvinism and Arminianism. Review of Elder D's Letter—No. III.," *Christian Examiner* 1 (May 31, 1830): 159. Nathan O. Hatch explores the Christians' attempt to sidestep history, focusing especially on Elias Smith

of New England, in "The Christian Movement and the Demand for a Theology of the People," *Journal of American History* 67 (Dec. 1980): 545–67.

33. Jacob Creath, Jr., "Human Creeds and Confessions of Faith. Essay II.," *Christian Examiner* 1 (Jan. 1830): 53–54.

34. Walter Scott, "From the Minutes of the Mahoning Association. RE-PORT.," *Christian Examiner* 1 (Nov. 1829): 7–8.

35. See Myer Phillips, "A Historical Study of the Attitude of the Churches of Christ toward Other Denominations" (Ph.D. diss., Baylor University, 1983).

36. Joseph Smith, *History of the Church of Jesus Christ of Latter-day Saints*, vol. 1 (Salt Lake City: Deseret Book Co., 1927), p. 6. The text of Smith's first vision is reprinted in *A Documentary History of Religion in America: To the Civil War*, ed. Edwin S. Gaustad (Grand Rapids: Eerdmans, 1982), pp. 350–52.

The fullest assessment of Mormon primitivism is Marvin S. Hill, "The Role of Christian Primitivism in the Origin and Development of the Mormon Kingdom, 1830–1844" (Ph.D. diss., University of Chicago, 1968). See also Robert Flanders, "To Transform History: Early Mormon Culture and the Concept of Time and Space," *Church History* 40 (Mar. 1971): 108–17; Richard Bushman, *Joseph Smith and the Beginnings of Mormonism* (Urbana: University of Illinois Press, 1984), pp. 179–88; Jan Shipps, *Mormonism: The Story of a New Religious Movement* (Urbana: University of Illinois Press, 1985), esp. pp. 67–85; and Richard T. Hughes, "Soaring with the Gods: Early Mormons and the Eclipse of Religious Pluralism" in *The Lively Experiment Continued*, ed. Jerald C. Brauer (Macon, Ga.: Mercer University Press, forthcoming).

37. Marvin Hill clearly recognizes the ecumenical dimensions of early Mormonism ("Role of Christian Primitivism," p. 152) as does Flanders ("To Transform History," pp. 115–16).

38. On this particular theme, see Hughes, "Soaring with the Gods."

39. According to Shipps, "The claim to chosenness became the principle around which they [Mormons] ordered their existence" (*Mormonism*, pp. 118–19).

40. *Proclamation of the Twelve Apostles of the Church of Jesus Christ of Latter-day Saints. To All the Kings of the World, to the President of the United States of America; to the Governors of the Several States, and to the Rulers and People of All Nations* (Liverpool: F. D. Richards, 1845), pp. 1, 6, cited in Hill, "Role of Christian Primitivism," pp. 67–68.

41. Eber D. Howe, *Mormonism Unvailed* (Painesville, Ohio, 1834), p. 14, cited in Hill, "Role of Christian Primitivism," p. 74.

42. Parley P. Pratt, *A Voice of Warning and Instruction to All People* (New York: W. Sandford, 1837), pp. 140–42.

43. Sidney Rigdon, Oration on 4th of July, 1838, Far West, Missouri (Far West, Mo., 1838), in *Among the Mormons: Historic Accounts by Contemporary Observers*, ed. William Mulder and A. Russell Mortensen (New York: Alfred A. Knopf, 1958), p. 95.

44. Reed Peck "manuscript" reproduced in L. B. Cake, *Peepstone Joe and the Peck Manuscript* (New York, 1899), p. 109, cited in Hill, "Role of Christian Primitivism," p. 216.

45. Albert P. Rockwood's letters, October 29, 1838, cited in Hill, "Role of Christian Primitivism," p. 219. For a more thorough and systematic analysis of the coercive dimensions of early Mormonism in a primitivist context, see Hughes, "Soaring with the Gods."

46. *Writings of Thomas Paine*, p. 303.

47. Parley P. Pratt, "Declaration of Independence—Constitution of the United States . . . ," in *Journal of Discourses,* vol. 1 (Liverpool and London, 1854), p. 139.

48. Sidney E. Mead, *The Nation with the Soul of a Church* (New York: Harper and Row, 1975), p. 77.

49. Lyman Beecher, "The Memory of Our Fathers," a sermon delivered on Dec. 22, 1827, in *Nationalism and Religion in America,* ed. Winthrop Hudson (New York: Harper and Row, 1970), pp. 104–5.

50. Beecher, *Republican Elements in the Old Testament: Lectures on Political Atheism and Kindred Subjects* (Boston, 1852), p. 189.

51. Mead, *Lively Experiment,* p. 53.

52. Albanese, *Sons of the Fathers,* p. 114.

53. Mead, *Lively Experiment,* p. 112.

54. Henry Bowden, response to Albert Outler, Robert Handy, and David Holmes, on "The Restoration Ideal in American History" (conference, Abilene Christian University, summer 1985).

55. George Rockingham Gilmer, *Journal of the House of Representatives of the State of Georgia, 1830,* cited in Albert K. Weinberg, *Manifest Destiny: A Study of Nationalist Expansionism in American History* (Chicago: Quadrangle Books, 1963), p. 83.

56. John Winthrop, *Conclusions for the Plantation in New England,* in *Old South Leaflets,* No. 50, pp. 5–7, cited in Weinberg, *Manifest Destiny,* pp. 74–75. In line with this perspective, Winthrop argued that "this savage people ruleth over many lands without title or property; for they enclose no ground, neither have they cattle to maintain it" (Charles M. Segal and David C. Stineback, *Puritans, Indians & Manifest Destiny* [New York: G. P. Putnam's Sons, 1977], p. 50.) John Cotton concurred and argued that a country could be void of inhabitants even where inhabitants reside if those inhabitants had failed to replenish the earth and subdue it. Thus, "in a vacant soil, he that taketh possession of it, and bestoweth culture and husbandry upon it, his right it is. And the ground of this is from the Grand Charter given to *Adam* and his posterity in Paradise, *Gen.* 1:28. *Multiply, and replenish the earth,* and subdue it." (See Segal and Stineback, ibid., p. 53.) The Puritans' conviction that they represented a primordial order and that Indians represented a fallen, decayed order of things may even help explain why Puritans were so reluctant to engage in serious missions to the Indians. For an illuminating discussion of this Puritan failure, see Henry Bowden, *American Indians and Christian Missions* (Chicago: University of Chicago Press, 1981), pp. 111–33.

57. Weinberg, *Manifest Destiny,* pp. 168 and 185. The theme of subduing the earth, however, did not play the role in the campaign against Mexico that it played in Indian removal or even in claims to the Oregon Territory. The

reason seems obvious, namely, that Mexico was a settled region. Thus, a Whig diplomat, Waddy Thompson, argued in South Carolina that Mexico "is not the country of a savage people whose lands are held in common, but a country in which grants have been made for three hundred and twenty-five years" (cited in Frederick Merk, *Manifest Destiny and Mission* [New York: Vintage Books, 1963], p. 165).

58. John Quincy Adams, *Congressional Globe*, 29th Congress, 1st session, p. 340, cited in Weinberg, *Manifest Destiny*, p. 149.

59. John L. O'Sullivan in the *New York Morning News*, Dec. 27, 1845, in *God's New Israel: Religious Interpretations of American Destiny*, ed. Conrad Cherry (Englewood Cliffs: Prentice-Hall, 1971), pp. 128–29.

60. Charles Olcott, *Life of William McKinley*, vol. 2 (Boston, 1916), pp. 110–11.

61. Cited in Weinberg, *Manifest Destiny*, p. 290.

62. Cited in ibid., p. 294.

63. Ibid., p. 284.   .

64. Albert J. Beveridge, "For the Greater Republic, Not for Imperialism," an address given Feb. 15, 1899, cited in *Nationalism and Religion in America,* ed. Winthrop Hudson, pp. 117–19.

65. Cited in Weinberg, *Manifest Destiny*, p. 307. Beveridge's own rejection of the jurisdiction of history over America emerged in his "The March of the Flag" speech in Indianapolis, Sept. 1898: "It is a glorious history our God has bestowed upon His chosen people; . . . a history of prophets who saw the consequences of evils inherited from the past and of martyrs who died to save us from them; a history divinely logical, in the process of whose tremendous reasoning we find ourselves today" (in *An American Harvest: Readings in American History,* ed. J. R. Conlin and C. H. Peterson, vol. 2 [New York: Harcourt Brace Jovanovich, 1986], p. 88).

66. Mead, "Theology of the Republic," pp. 111–12.

67. Martin Luther King, Jr., "I Have a Dream," in *The Negro in Twentieth Century America: A Reader on the Struggle for Civil Rights,* ed. John Hope Franklin and Isidore Starr (New York: Vintage Books, 1967), p. 146.

68. Also basing his insights on the perspectives of Sidney Mead, Franklin I. Gamwell finally concludes that the ultimate purpose of public debate in America is not to arrive at some final answer or set of answers, since all particular answers are finite and bound by time and place to historic particularities. The ultimate purpose of the debate, therefore, is to further the debate, itself ("Religion and the Public Purpose," *Journal of Religion* 62 [July 1982]: 283).

69. Mead, *Nation with the Soul of a Church,* p. 76.

AMANDA PORTERFIELD

Tecumseh, Tenskwatawa, and the Complex Relationship between Religious and Political Power

Tecumseh was a Shawnee war chief whose name has become a symbol of fierce valor and patriotism. In the last decade of the eighteenth century, he stood by the Treaty of Fort Stanwix of 1768, which declared the Ohio River to be the permanent western boundary of American territory.[1] He also promoted the communal ownership of Indian lands by arguing that village chiefs had no right to sell land to the United States. As his political vision expanded, Tecumseh worked to build a confederacy joining disparate tribes from the Great Lakes to the Southeast. On his recruiting trips during the early years of the nineteenth century, Tecumseh encouraged Indians to unite and drive the white man back toward the sea. His confederacy was destroyed at the Battle of Tippecanoe in 1811, and he was killed two years later, fighting Americans in Canada.

Many Americans have admired Tecumseh's valor and identified with his cause. His archrival William Henry Harrison, who rode to the White House in 1840 on the glory he won routing Tecumseh's warriors at Tippecanoe, praised the Shawnee war chief shortly before that battle as

> one of those uncommon geniuses which spring up occasionally to produce revolutions, and overturn the established order of things. If it were not for the vicinity of the United States, he would, perhaps, be the founder of an empire that would rival in glory Mexico or Peru. No difficulties deter him. For four years he has been in constant motion. You see him to-day on the Wabash, and in a short time hear of him on the shores of lake Erie or Michigan, or on the banks of the Mississippi; and wherever he goes he makes an impression favorable to his purposes.[2]

Even though Tecumseh disdained American culture and devoted his life to resistance against the United States, Americans have held him in great esteem, attaching his name to streets and schools across the country. This eulogizing of Tecumseh illustrates the ironic process by which Indian enemies of American culture have become exemplars of American character. Like Pontiac, Chief Joseph, Geronimo, Sitting Bull, Black Elk, and Lame Deer, Tecumseh captured the respect of his colonizers.

Noel W. Shultz, a historian of Shawnee culture, revealed the nature of Tecumseh's hold on American imaginations in an almost casual figure of speech describing Tecumseh's influence among Indians. In picturing him as "the Shawnee Moses . . . uniting Indian tribes against the heathen whites,"[3] Shultz placed Tecumseh in the context of biblical mythology. Tecumseh's heroism in American eyes can be explained by elaborating on this insight. From the perspective of a biblical worldview, Tecumseh represents Mosaic hopes for a righteous society. Like Moses, Tecumseh called for justice and freedom from oppression for his people. Like Moses, Tecumseh led his people toward a promised land. However, Tecumseh's vision failed to be realized, and in its failure, it compares with the fate of biblical visions of America. If Tecumseh represents Moses in America, he represents a Moses whose vision of a homeland was not realized.

Like Tecumseh's, other visions of America have failed. For example, the New England Puritans believed that God had sent them to America to establish a holy way of life that would serve as a model for other peoples. They imagined America as a latter-day Israel and themselves as the people of God chosen to follow his ordinances and represent his righteousness to the world. However, the social reality established by the Puritans never measured up to the vision of goodness, justice, and honesty they hoped to realize. As Roger Williams was only the first to point out, biblical ideals for holy living were as much an indictment as a pattern for social reality in New England. Religious and political leadership in subsequent periods of American history has suffered similar embarrassments. Biblically rooted visions of America as a land of freedom and righteousness have characterized the idealism of America's leaders but not the reality over which they have presided.

Closer analysis of Tecumseh's story will provide a basis for understanding why visionary hopes for America have perpetuated disappointing realities. In the analysis that follows, Tecumseh's story will be taken not only as a heroic episode in American Indian history but also as an example of a tragic process characteristic of the larger history of American culture. This tragic process centers on a complex relationship between religion and politics in which religious visions of America have inspired but also undermined political achievements. Religious visions have generated not only enthusiasm for political justice but also the very images in terms of which political life has been conceived in America. At the same time, they have produced inflated ideas of self and cause that have led both to imperialism and to devastating misjudgments about political reality. This complex relationship between religion and politics characterizes not only Tecumseh's career but the careers of John Winthrop, Abraham Lincoln, Ronald Reagan, and other American leaders as well. For Indians and Euroamericans alike, idealism about America has frequently been rooted in religious myth and vision but limited by religious self-righteousness.

A full grasp of this complex relationship between religion and politics is hampered by not understanding the causes and expressions of religious self-righteousness and by not distinguishing that self-righteousness from mythological patterns that shape perception and behavior. This essay will argue that social and psychological deprivation led Indians associated with Tecumseh's movement to a desperate belief in supernatural power and that supernaturalism was a blinding form of self-glorification which ultimately destroyed Tecumseh's political confederacy. The essay will argue with equal vigor that religious visions inspire political reason. The religious visions associated with Tecumseh's movement drew on mythological imagery as resources for coping with colonization. Through their mythic images of freedom, justice, and Indian strength, these visions helped generate the political power of Tecumseh's movement. By distinguishing the supernatural from the mythological aspects of these visions, we can decipher the complexity of Tecumseh's political situation and understand analogous relationships between religion and politics in other eras of American history. Thus analysis of Tecumseh's story can provide a basis for recovering the essential role that religious myths have played in American political movements. Such analysis may also provide a basis for understanding how Americans might recover from the politically destructive aspects of religious zeal.

• • •

Tecumseh's career as a political leader was tied to the career of his brother Tenskwatawa, known as the Prophet. Tenskwatawa received a vision from the Great Spirit in 1805 and founded a new religion shortly thereafter. This new religion had such widespread appeal among Indians that U.S. government officials considered it a political threat. Government agents were alarmed when, during a "short time" in the summer of 1807, "soldiers at Fort Wayne counted 1500 Indians passing by on the way to pay homage to the Prophet."[4] Tecumseh's support of his brother's religion was at least partly motivated by political necessity. He had little choice but to collaborate: Tenskwatawa's converts were potentially his own warriors, and Tecumseh's hopes for military success depended on his brother's popularity.

In public, Tecumseh and Tenskwatawa identified with one another and represented themselves as working for the same goals. Tenskwatawa incorporated Tecumseh's idea of communal ownership of Indian lands into his religion. And for his part, Tecumseh carried news of his brother's message from the Great Spirit on his diplomatic missions around the Great Lakes and in the Southeast. Tecumseh related his brother's message that the Great Spirit would restore well-being to the Indians if they abandoned the ways of the white man and returned to their own traditions. But beneath the harmonious surface of their partnership, there was a certain tension, which can be partly accounted for by differences in upbringing, behavior, and temperament between the two brothers. These, in turn, begin to explain the tension between religion and politics in the movement they founded.

Tecumseh, the older brother, was born in 1768 in Old Piqua, a Shawnee town in western Ohio, to Methoataske, a Creek woman, and Puckeshinwa, a Shawnee war chief who was fatally wounded in 1775 after fighting for more than a decade to keep Virginians out of the Ohio River valley. While Tecumseh was old enough to remember his heroic father, Tenskwatawa, whose boyhood name was Lalawetheka, was one of two surviving triplets born after his father's death. When Lalawetheka was only four and Tecumseh eleven, their mother fled from Ohio with one of her daughters and settled in Missouri.[5] Tecumseh was almost grown when his mother left; Lalawetheka was a twice-abandoned child.

Tecumseh was a bold and handsome boy whose athletic talent made him the pride of his village. Lalawetheka, who blinded himself in one eye with an arrow as a boy, was uncoordinated, unattractive, and neglected. These several handicaps led to another, namely a "disposition to boast." The habit of proclaiming his own importance was reflected in the name Lalawetheka, which meant the Rattle or Noise-maker, and in later years found outlet in his role as a prophet.[6]

As a young man, the unhappy Lalawetheka relied on Tecumseh for protection and support. Although Tecumseh had fled from his first battle at the age of fourteen, he was a war chief by the time he was twenty-two.[7] As his younger brother stated admiringly in later years, to be recognized as a war chief a Shawnee had to lead "at least four war parties into enemies' country successively, . . . and each time take one or more scalps & . . . return his followers unhurt to their villages."[8] Meeting this criterion not only required a good deal of aggression but also considerable ability to control aggression in oneself and others.

The adopted Shawnee captive Stephen Ruddell recalled that Tecumseh's efforts to control violence began when he was only sixteen or seventeen, when he watched a war party burn a prisoner and then convinced members of the party to agree never to burn another.[9] Tecumseh attempted to enforce this kind of restraint throughout his life. In 1813, in the last year of his life, Indians at the Battle of Fort Meigs were killing American prisoners. According to a British officer's account reported by Benjamin Drake in 1841,

> Whilst this blood-thirsty carnage was raging, a thundering voice was heard in the rear, in the Indian tongue. . . . [T]urning around, [the British officer] saw Tecumseh coming with all the rapidity his horse could carry him, until he drew near to where two Indians had an American, and were in the act of killing him. He sprang from his horse, caught one by the throat and the other by the breast, and threw them to the ground; drawing his tomahawk and scalping knife, he ran in between the Americans and Indians, brandishing them with the fury of a mad man, and daring any one of the hundreds that surrounded him, to attempt to murder another American.[10]

Tecumseh measured both Indians and Americans by his own standards of honor, courage, and self-control. Once when a Kentuckian visiting in Ohio became unduly alarmed about Tecumseh's proximity, the war chief appeared in the house where the Kentuckian was staying, "turned to his host, and pointing to the agitated Kentuckian, exclaimed, 'a big baby! a big baby!' He then stepped up to him, and gently slapping him on the shoulder several times, repeated with a contemptuous manner, the phrase 'a big baby! a big baby!' to the great alarm of the astonished man, and to the amusement of all present."[11]

Like the Kentuckian, Tecumseh's brother Lalawetheka was something of a big baby. During the 1790s, while Tecumseh was establishing a reputation as an intrepid war chief, Lalawetheka was an alcoholic and, despite his brother's lessons, a poor hunter who could not provide for his family. Lalawetheka had none of the self-mastery that lay at the heart of Tecumseh's skill as a political and military leader.

As others have done in similar situations, Lalewatheka sought empowerment through religious means. He was a follower of the Shawnee healer and prophet Penagashea, who was probably a disciple of Pontiac and the Delaware prophet Neolin.[12] In 1804, when Penagashea died, Lalawetheka attempted to assume his mantle but with small success until he received his own great vision. In 1805, after

lighting a pipe at his fire, Lalawetheka fell over on his side; his wife
and neighbors believed he had died. But as plans for his burial were
underway, Lalawetheka revived. He told how his soul had been carried to the spirit world by two emissaries from the Master of Life and
how, once he had arrived there, the Master of Life allowed him a
glimpse of paradise, which was "a rich, fertile country, abounding in
game, fish, pleasant hunting grounds and fine corn fields." As Lalawetheka described it, the souls of people who lived according to
Shawnee traditions as they had been practiced before the coming of
the white man lived on eternally in this natural paradise, hunting,
planting, and playing games as they had in years gone by.

Lalawetheka was not allowed to enter this happy realm but was
taken instead to a great lodge with a huge fire where Indian souls
were punished for their sins. The sins Lalawetheka identified were all
practices Indians had fallen into as a result of their encounters with
white men. Most prominent among them was drunkenness, for which
Indian souls were punished in this spirit world by being forced to
drink molten lead. Once purified by punishment in the fire lodge,
Indian souls were allowed to enter paradise, though not into the full
privileges accorded those who had never taken up white men's vices.
As a result of this vision, Lalawetheka renounced alcohol and encouraged Indians to return to traditional ways of life.[13]

After this vision, Lalawetheka took the name Tenskwatawa, meaning the Open Door, a reference to his status as mediator of divine
truth and supernatural power. Perhaps the Shawnee Prophet borrowed the name Open Door from the saying of Jesus in the tenth
chapter of the Gospel of John: "I am the Door; if any one enters by
me, he will be saved." In any event, Tenskwatawa's relationship with
Christ was a competitive one.[14] Shortly after his great vision, the
Prophet called Shawnee, Wyandot, Ottaway, and Seneca Indians to
his village on the Auglaize River and "unfolded the new character
with which he was clothed." At this meeting Tenskwatawa proclaimed
his power to "cure all diseases, to confound his enemies, and stay the
arm of death, in sickness, or on the battlefield." The Prophet's religion
spread rapidly among many tribes in North America after this dramatic self-proclamation.

Tenskwatawa's preaching made enemies as well as disciples. He
preached that medicine bundles were polluting Indian life and that
people who used them were witches. Most of the people he accused
of witchcraft were influential Indians who resisted his new religion
and who used medicine bundles to carry on their old religion. Tenskwatawa's political animosity to these traditionalists was realized in

the execution of four Delaware Indians—including the "venerable chief" Teteboxti who, refusing to renounce his religion, "calmly assisted in building his own funeral pile" and an old woman named Coltos who was "roasted . . . slowly over a fire for four days" until finally, on the fourth day, she revealed the whereabouts of her medicine bundle.[15] Although Tecumseh opposed these executions, carried out at his brother's will, he had no power to stop them.[16]

The executions alarmed William Henry Harrison, then governor of the Indiana Territory, and eroded Tenskwatawa's influence, especially among the Delaware, as one can well imagine. But the Prophet regained influence through his shrewd response to a letter Harrison wrote to the Delaware denouncing him and urging them to "demand of him some proofs at least, of his being the messenger of the Deity. . . . If he is really a prophet, ask him to cause the sun to stand still—the moon to alter its course—the rivers to cease to flow—or the dead to rise from their graves." After hearing about the letter, Tenskwatawa announced that he would shortly demonstrate his supernatural powers by darkening the sun. When a solar eclipse occurred during the summer of 1806, just a few weeks after Harrison's letter, Tenskwatawa claimed responsibility for it.[17] Apparently he knew about the eclipse beforehand and manipulated the credulity of his followers in order to enlarge his influence and silence his enemies.

As well as providing a means of manipulating others, Tenskwatawa's claims to supernatural power illustrate two theories advanced by students of messianic movements—first, that reliance on supernatural power is a means of defending self and society against destruction and, second, that promises of supernatural intervention are appealing when personal and social crisis seem to admit of no human solution.[18] The abandonment, disgrace, and disease that characterized Tenskwatawa's life before his great vision in 1805 exemplified the social and spiritual crises that beset many Indians devastated by colonization. The plight of being an outcast, which lay at the root of Tenskwatawa's failures, is characteristic of colonized peoples. Tenskwatawa's claim to supernatural power was a means of compensating for being outcast, disgraced, and colonized. His visions offered supernatural solutions to difficulties that he and his followers found otherwise insurmountable.

While Tenskwatawa was attracting many Indians by his claims to supernatural power, Tecumseh was making use of his brother's popularity to build a military confederacy. Tecumseh's animosity toward the U.S. government escalated in 1809 when Harrison signed a secret treaty with Miami, Potawatomi, and Delaware chiefs friendly to the

Americans in which over three million acres were ceded to the U.S. Incensed at Harrison's treachery, Tecumseh accepted free ammunition from the British and increased his efforts to enlarge and establish his confederacy.

In 1811, Tecumseh discussed his confederacy with Harrison and announced his intention to negotiate directly with President Madison. After instructing his brother to guard against any outbreak of aggression against the United States among the Indians at Tippecanoe, Tecumseh left for a final recruiting mission in the Southeast. Making the most of Tecumseh's absence, Harrison and his army surrounded the Indian fort at Tippecanoe and provoked Tenskwatawa to order an attack. The Prophet rose to the bait but not before assuring "his followers, that in the coming contest, the Great Spirit would render the arms of the Americans unavailing; that their bullets would fall harmless at the feet of the Indians; that the latter should have light in abundance, while the former would be involved in thick darkness. Availing himself of the privilege conferred by his peculiar office," as Drake put it, "he prudently took a position on an adjacent eminence; and when the action began, he entered upon the performance of certain mystic rites, at the same time singing a war-song. In the course of the engagement, he was informed that his men were falling: he told them to fight on,—it would soon be as he had predicted; and then, in louder and wilder strains, his inspiring battle-song was heard commingling with the sharp crack of the rifle and the shrill war-whoop of his brave but deluded followers." The Indians at Tippecanoe were roundly defeated. As a result of his failure to evoke supernatural aid, many of Tenskwatawa's surviving followers renounced him as a charlatan. When Tecumseh returned from the south a few days after the battle he "reproached [Tenskwatawa] in bitter terms for having departed from his instructions to preserve peace with the United States at all hazards . . . and seizing him by the hair and shaking him violently, he threatened to take his life." [19] His political confederacy undone, Tecumseh abandoned his plans to visit Madison, joined the British army in Canada during the War of 1812, and was killed at the Battle of the Thames in 1813.

The contrasting behaviors of Tecumseh and Tenskwatawa in the events surrounding the Battle of Tippecanoe illustrate both the difference in their temperaments and the conflict between religion and politics in the movement they founded. Tecumseh pursued a carefully designed strategy that involved years of diplomacy and recruiting. Although his ultimate goal of reversing American expansion was no doubt unrealizable, his diplomatic and military strength might have

altered the pace, direction, and tenor of U.S. expansion if his confederacy had survived. Tecumseh's political efforts were realistic
compared to the preoccupation with supernatural power that overwhelmed Tenskwatawa's understanding of human interaction. Belief
in his own ability to command divine power led Tenskwatawa to ignore his brother's counsel, fall into Harrison's trap, and urge his followers to fight on against insurmountable odds. Although his mystic
rites and war songs may have filled his followers with hope, that hope
sent many of them to an early death. Of course it should be recognized that both the expression and the widespread appeal of Tenskwatawa's claims to supernatural power stemmed from the despera-
tion of the Indians whose lives and cultures were being demolished
by colonization. But the fact remains that Tenskwatawa's supernaturalism destroyed the political confederacy associated with his religious
movement. His impulsive and politically stupid behavior at Tippecanoe was precipitated, sanctioned, and expressed through his belief
in supernatural power.

This situation has certain analogues in American history. For example, a similarly counterproductive relationship between religion
and politics also characterized New England Puritanism. Like Tecumseh, New England Puritans hoped to establish a just society, but they
were prevented from realizing this political vision and led to imperialism by belief in their privileged relationship to God. Like Tenskwatawa's claims to supernatural power, the Puritans' claims to be the chosen people of God grew at least in part out of insecurity, emotional
deprivation, and marginalization with respect to English society. The
supernaturalist hopes of both Tenskwatawa and the Puritans sprung
out of despair.

Claims to supernatural power, divine election, and moral superiority have often had harmful political effects. Perhaps the most devastating instance of religious self-righteousness in American history is
the Civil War. Although that bloodbath did little to remedy the dehumanization of black Americans and may even have retarded the
destruction of racism in America, many Northerners wanted the war
as a crusade against slavery. The war precipitated by their moral self-
righteousness was politically counterproductive.

A structurally analogous situation may exist today among members
of the new political right who base their arguments for nuclear defense in the religious idea that human history is directed by God and
that nuclear war may be a part of God's plan; it may be the Armageddon foretold in scripture. This supernaturalist argument has the effect of making nuclear war seem reasonable and, if one is assuredly

Christian, ultimately nonthreatening. As in the case of Tenskwatawa's supernaturalism, the belief that God may soon bring the world to an end ought to be understood as a means of compensating for and expressing psychological hardship and social insecurity. But if the case of Tenskwatawa invites compassion for the deprivation that breeds such supernaturalism, it is also instructive about supernaturalism's negative effects on political life. Nuclear readings of Armageddon make nuclear war seem inevitable and arms control relatively unimportant. Like Tenskwatawa's belief in supernatural power, belief in nuclear Armageddon is politically nonproductive.

•   •   •

However revealing these cases might be with respect to the destructive political effects of supernaturalism, it is, of course, not the whole story of religion and politics in America. Religion also played a constructive role in shaping the worldview of the Shawnee brothers, as it has in other areas of American history. The political values expressed by the Shawnee brothers, and the political influence they exerted, can be traced to patterns of organizing reality characteristic of Shawnee and Christian mythologies. In the movement they led, as in other realms of American culture, mythological patterns served as foundational elements of political life.

While Tenskwatawa's claims to supernatural power eventually undermined political solidarity, his visions generated it. They defined the spiritual structure of the cosmos, thereby reinvigorating his followers' sense of cosmic order and providing a mythic reconstruction of reality that banded Indians together against Western culture. The mythic reconstruction of reality presented in Tenskwatawa's visions was the basis of Tecumseh's political confederacy.

Tenskwatawa's visions contained symbols borrowed from Western culture. His vision of the spirit world as a realm divided by a forked road, one side leading to a natural paradise and the other to a realm of punishment, reflected Catholic teachings about heaven and purgatory. In preaching this Christianized schema of the spirit world, and in consigning Indian souls who followed the white man's ways to purgatory, the Prophet pitted Christian teachings against Western culture. The brutal and immoral heathens in Tenskwatawa's religion were the whites; the Indians were the chosen people of America who had lost their way among these heathens and were called back to their ancient faith and purity by the Prophet.

In promulgating this religion, the Prophet established a number of rituals designed to align followers with the cosmic structure outlined in his visions. Two of these were adaptations of Catholic rituals—a rite of confession of sins and a practice known as "shaking hands with the Prophet" in which converts were given a strand of beads to manipulate with their fingers. These rituals and the teachings that accompanied them offered Indians from different cultural backgrounds a common religion. In providing a religion that could compete with Christianity and could fortify Indians against further incursions of Western culture, Tenskwatawa was engaged in political defense. His religion enabled Indians beleaguered by colonization to reestablish personal and cultural integrity and thereby better withstand colonization. In providing a religion based on images and ideas borrowed from Christianity, he was engaged in the political subversion of the colonizing culture. The images and rituals Tenskwatawa adopted from Christianity were symbols of Western authority. By relocating those symbols within his own tradition and appealing to them in his denunciations of whites, Tenskwatawa reauthorized his own tradition and demeaned his adversaries.

This strategy of subverting alien power is represented in the Shawnee creation story, which was as much a source of Tenskwatawa's visions and ceremonies as Christian mythology. Though the details of the Shawnee creation story have changed over time, all extant versions include the discovery or regaining of a homeland after crossing an ocean or surviving a flood. In the process of establishing a home place the people in the creation story do battle with a serpent who embodies the terrible chaos of the sea in which he lives. The people take their power from this enemy by making medicine bundles out of his body.

Tenskwatawa made this myth come alive for his followers by retelling it in terms of the crisis of colonization. He identified the serpent rising out of the waters with the white man's coming to America. Although in his retelling of the story, the serpent's body "forms the medicine which the witches use,"[20] Tenskwatawa's own relationship to Christianity suggests an alternative interpretation of the myth of making medicine bundles out of the serpent of chaos. By fortifying Indians against Western culture with the power of Christian symbols, Tenskwatawa adopted the same strategy for subverting hostile power that is depicted in the Shawnee creation myth.

Tecumseh also enacted central themes from the Shawnee creation story.[21] In the creation story, searching for a homeland and fighting off enemies who arise out of the sea are strategies for establishing cosmic and political order. As Tecumseh's movement enacted those strategies, his aggressive activity against America carried forward the old story of doing battle with the serpent of chaos in the quest for a homeland.[22] At the most profound level, Tecumseh was as much a religious leader as a political one. He was an exemplar of the heroism celebrated in the Shawnee's most sacred story.

Religion and politics were inextricably bound together in the movement led by Tecumseh and Tenskwatawa. The political power of their movement was a direct result of their ability to draw patterns of perception and behavior from their mythic backgrounds and make mythical imagery come alive in a time of crisis. By reenacting mythical patterns, Tecumseh and Tenskwatawa made conceptual order out of chaos and gave hope and energy to many Indians. Their political power, which for a time was considerable, was fundamentally religious.

• • •

Mythical patterns have shaped American as well as Shawnee history. The biblical vision of America as a nation of righteousness and holy mission has animated political visionaries from colonial days to the present, and biblical themes of transcendence, covenant, and sacrifice have shaped and continue to shape American perception and behavior in the most fundamental ways. Biblical themes are found not only where biblical language is explicitly used, as in the civil-rights movement or among spokespersons for the Moral Majority, but in secular culture and among atheists as well as believers and churchgoers.[23]

Of special relevance to this essay are the powerful ways in which biblical mythology has shaped Euroamerican perceptions of Indians from the earliest days of colonization. Christopher Columbus perceived the Caribbean Indians he met in terms of the biblical myth of Genesis: first he described them as Edenic innocents and later as brutish exemplars of Adam's fall. The political attitudes toward Indians held by English colonists and later by the United States also reflect biblical mythology. The biblical story of Israel in Canaan found reexpression in the condescending attitude Americans often held toward Indians. Americans who thought of themselves as members of a new Israel perceived Indians as Canaanites to be converted or conquered.[24]

American admiration for Tecumseh as a Moses-like visionary leading his people toward righteousness and freedom from oppression draws on the same biblical theme of Israel in Canaan but in a different way. Tecumseh is an American hero because Americans have perceived him as a better exemplar of biblical ideals than many of the Americans he fought against. While Americans have often expressed the violence and greed biblically associated with heathens, Tecumseh's integrity and purposiveness represent the heroism of Moses.

Just as the biblical story of Moses can be used to interpret Tecumseh's heroism, so Shawnee mythology can interpret certain aspects of American history. While it is important to acknowledge that biblical structures of thought have dominated interpretations of American history in the past, there is no reason to limit interpretations of American history to biblical themes. In particular, there is insight to be gained by reading American history in terms of mythic imagery generated from the other side of its frontier. For example, the relish for dead Indians that characterizes certain elements of American culture can be understood in terms of the Shawnee myth of attaining power from the body of one's enemy. The presidential campaign of 1840 reads as an apt illustration of this Shawnee myth. William Henry Harrison ran for president that year with a nickname, "Old Tippecanoe," that literally identified him with Tecumseh and the battle that destroyed Tecumseh's confederacy. Thus Harrison stepped into the presidency with the power he won defeating the Indian "genius" he so admired. On the opposite ticket, running for vice-president, was Colonel Richard M. Johnson from Kentucky, known as "Old Tecumseh" because of his claim to have killed the Shawnee war chief at the Battle of the Thames in 1813. The colonel relished his identification with Tecumseh and the press described him as bearing a remarkable resemblance to the Shawnee chief.[25] Thus Johnson also took his identity from Tecumseh, the hero he claimed to have slain. Johnson may even have converted Tecumseh's body into a talisman of his own power: Tecumseh's body was never found and there were many speculations that it was *"flayed,* and the skin converted to razor-straps by Kentuckians."[26] It was rumored that Johnson wore a belt made out of Tecumseh's skin.

The Shawnee myth of making medicine out of the enemy can interpret not only the American investment in killing Indians but also some of the biblical myths that have shaped American perception and behavior. Israel's conquest of Canaan can be understood as a means of taking power from Canaan as well as a means of wielding it over her. The golden calf can be understood as a source of Yahweh's power as well as an enemy of it. By extending this Shawnee reading of biblical mythology back into American history, it becomes clear why Indians have played a powerful role in the American imagination. The conquerors of Indians have created some of their own power in the image of Indians.

In sum, both Shawnee and biblical mythologies provide useful bases for interpreting political encounters between Indians and Americans. The religious meaning of those encounters can be recovered by interpreting them in terms of mythical themes. On the other hand, Americans might recover from the politically disastrous aspects of religion by distinguishing belief in supernatural power from awareness that myths inevitably shape human perception and behavior. While belief in supernatural power is ultimately an expression of despair in the face of the inhumanity of reality, awareness of the power myths have to shape political reality is a way of facing the humanity of reality. Facing myths as languages through which to live can aid in discriminating and choosing among them.

NOTES

1. Tecumseh refused to participate in treaty proceedings at Greenville in 1795 at which Black Hoof and other tribal leaders ceded most of the Shawnee land in the Ohio River valley to the United States.

Sources on Tecumseh include James Mooney, *The Ghost Dance Religion and the Sioux Outbreak of 1890,* Fourteenth Annual Report of the Bureau of American Ethnology, 2 vols. (Washington, D.C.: Bureau of American Ethnology, 1896), vol. 2, pp. 670–91; Herbert Charles Walter Goltz, Jr., "Tecumseh, The Prophet and the Rise of the Northwest Indian Confederation" (Ph.D. diss., University of Western Ontario, 1973); and R. David Edmunds, *Tecumseh and the Quest for Indian Leadership* (Boston: Little, Brown and Company, 1984). Glenn Tucker's *Tecumseh: Vision of Glory* (1956; rpt. New York: Russell & Russell, 1973) is criticized by Edmunds and Goltz for its confusion of legend with documentary evidence. The earliest, richest, and most essential work on Tecumseh is Benjamin Drake's *Life of Tecumseh, and of his brother The Prophet; with a Historical Sketch of the Shawanoe Indians* (Cincinnati and Philadelphia: Queen City and Quaker City Publishing Houses, 1856).

2. Quoted in Drake, *Life of Tecumseh,* p. 142.

3. Noel W. Schultz, Jr., "The Study of the Shawnee Myth in an Ethnographic and Ethnohistorical Perspective" (Ph.D. diss., Indiana University, 1975), p. 523.

4. Drake, *Life of Tecumseh,* p. 93. For accounts of Tenskwatawa's life and religious teachings in addition to that provided by Drake see Mooney, *Ghost Dance,* vol. 2, pp. 670–80; Richard McNemar, *The Kentucky revival, or a short history of the extraordinary out-pouring of the Spirit of God in the Western States of America* (Albany: E. and E. Hosford, 1808); R. David Edmunds, *The Shawnee Prophet* (Lincoln: University of Nebraska Press, 1983).

5. Schultz, "Study of the Shawnee Myth," p. 39.

6. Drake, *Life of Tecumseh,* p. 63.

7. Edmunds, *Tecumseh,* p. 29.

8. *Shawnese Traditions: C. C. Trowbridge's Account,* ed. Vernon K. Voegelin and Erminie W. Voegelin, occasional contributions from the Museum of Anthropology of the University of Michigan, No. 9 (Ann Arbor: University of Michigan Press, 1939), pp. 11–12.

9. Drake, *Life of Tecumseh,* pp. 68–69.

10. Ibid., p. 181; also see pp. 226–27.

11. From James Galloway's account, ibid., pp. 85–86.

12. Schultz, "Study of the Shawnee Myth," pp. 525–26; for further information about Neolin see Mooney, *Ghost Dance,* vol. 2, pp. 662–69; John Heckewelder, *History, Manners, and Customs of the Indians Nations* . . . (1819; Philadelphia: Historical Society of Pennsylvania, 1876), pp. 291–93; and Anthony F. C. Wallace, *The Death and Rebirth of the Seneca* (1969; rpt. New York: Vintage Books, 1972), pp. 117–21.

13. Mooney, *Ghost Dance,* vol. 2, pp. 672–73; Edmunds, *Shawnee Prophet,* p. 33.

14. Christian influences may have come through Wyandot Indians who converted to the Prophet's religion after having previously been converted to Catholicism. See J. P. MacLean, "Shaker Mission to the Shawnee Indians," *Ohio Archeological and Historical Publications,* vol. 11 (Columbus: Fred J. Heer, 1903), pp. 215–29, esp. pp. 224–25.

15. Drake, *Life of Tecumseh,* p. 88; Goltz, "Tecumseh," pp. 68ff.

16. Goltz, "Tecumseh," pp. 74–75. Goltz interprets Tecumseh's inability to stop the Delaware executions as evidence of his relative powerlessness compared with Tenskwatawa. Goltz takes the position that while legend has elevated the importance of Tecumseh and diminished the importance of Tenskwatawa, contemporary documents reveal Tenskwatawa to have been far more important than his brother.

17. Drake, *Life of Tecumseh,* pp. 90–91. The Prophet also claimed to be able to make the dead rise from their graves. The mysterious corpse-sized object that played a role in his secret ceremonies suggests that initiation into Tenskwatawa's religion may have involved some ritual based on this claim.

18. See for example, Weston LaBarre, *The Ghost Dance: Origins of Religion* (New York: Dell, 1970).

19. Drake, *Life of Tecumseh,* pp. 152, 156. The remainder of Tenskwatawa's life was uneventful. George Catlin, who interviewed and painted Tenskwatawa in Kansas in 1832, four years before his death, described him as "a shrewd and influential man but circumstances have destroyed him" (George Catlin, *Letters and Notes on the Manners, Customs, and Conditions of the North American Indians,* 2 vols. [1844; New York: Dover Publications, 1973], vol. 2, p. 118).

20. See Schultz, "Study of the Shawnee Myth"; and C. F. Voegelin and E. W. Voegelin, "The Shawnee Female Deity in Historical Perspective," *American Anthropologist* 46 (1944): 370–75; *Trowbridge's Account,* p. 45.

Following Tenskwatawa's version of the creation story, Schultz distinguishes the witchcraft bundles taken from the body of the evil serpent from the sacred bundle given to the Shawnee by the Great Spirit (p. 210). But he cites two pieces of evidence that show that medicine bundles were perceived to be beneficial. In 1648 the Huron wore Algonquian amulets said to have been made from the body of the slain sea monster for good luck (p. 163). More recently, the chief of a war dance "left" by Tecumseh, which was performed for Indians returning from the U.S. Army, wore a bone necklace from Tecumseh's medicine bundle. Some modern-day Shawnee claim that Tecumseh will return to earth, take up his medicine bundle, and "lead America in war against the Communists" (p. 247–48). This evidence leads me to conclude that the legendary sacred bundle and the actual medicine bundles used by Shawnee people are closely and positively identified except in Tenskwatawa's version of Shawnee religion.

21. Tecumseh's confederacy, and the search for cosmic renewal it implied, was part of a history of attempts by the Shawnee to gain a homeland and fend off chaos. In the seventeenth century, Shawnee living in the Ohio and Cumberland river valleys were forced by other Indian groups to migrate south, east, and north. Warfare with Iroquois at the end of the century further rent and scattered the tribe until the end of the French and Indian wars when many Shawnee resettled in the Ohio River valley, where they were stirred by the preachings of Pontiac and the Delaware prophet Neolin. Shawnee bands had been anti-American since the 1740s when Peter Chartier, the son of a Shawnee woman and a Frenchman who deserted LaSalle, attempted to unite Shawnee, Creek, and Cherokee Indians against white settlers on the southern frontier. Thus the history of the Shawnee people represents the myth of fighting the serpent and the waters of chaos in the quest for a homeland (James H. Howard, *Shawnee! The Ceremonialism of a Native Indian Tribe and Its Cultural Background* [Athens: Ohio University Press, 1981], pp. 1–12; Schultz, "Study of the Shawnee Myth," pp. 463–64, 468, 478, 515–52).

22. Tecumseh's strategies for defending his people against colonization also illustrate the myth of making medicine out of the serpent of chaos. Tecumseh hoped to grasp some of the power lodged within the United States by instituting a similar confederacy of Native peoples. Tecumseh's concept of Indianness was also borrowed from Americans. The far-flung and culturally diverse Natives of North America did not think of themselves as one kind of people until Westerners saw them that way and called them Indians. In his emphasis on cultural similarities and common interests among disparate Native peoples, Tecumseh subverted this homogenized view of Native Americans for their own good. Tecumseh took the alien name Indian from the enemy and made it into his own power.

23. See, for example, Thomas J. J. Altizer, *Total Presence: The Language of Jesus and the Language of Today* (New York: Seabury Press, 1980).

24. For discussion along these lines, see Frederick Turner, *Beyond Geography: The Western Spirit against the Wilderness* (New York: Viking Press, 1980).

25. Leland Winfield Meyer, *The Life and Times of Colonel Richard M. Johnson of Kentucky* (New York: Columbia University Press, 1932), pp. 413, 133, 306.

26. Drake, *Life of Tecumseh,* p. 198.

James G. Moseley

Winthrop's *Journal:*
Religion, Politics, and Narrative in
Early America

John Winthrop has often been portrayed as a self-righteous martinet, a Puritan dictator whose love for power was matched only by his unthinking Calvinist orthodoxy. Yet reading his three-volume *Journal* enables us to recover a more credible, if more complicated, image of the foremost founder of the Massachusetts Bay Colony.[1] Several years ago historian Edmund Morgan wisely eschewed the authoritarian caricature and, instead, cast Winthrop as representative of "the Puritan dilemma," that characteristic tension between the transcendent exuberance of an awakened spiritual life and the mundane requirements of living responsibly in a fallen world. Because Morgan pictured Winthrop as quite thoroughly molded by his spiritual experiences as a young man in England, he tended to read Winthrop's *Journal* as a straightforward chronicle of how Puritan religious convictions were translated into political realities in early New England. Yet Winthrop did not simply reach his religious conclusions in England and then embark prepared to govern accordingly in the New World. Reading the *Journal* with an ear for changes in Winthrop's narrative voice reveals that his character, attitudes, and beliefs were not so thoroughly formed by the time of migration as Morgan implied.[2] Indeed, Winthrop's thinking underwent significant transformations in New England, and writing the *Journal* became his way of making sense of these revisions.

Winthrop's *Journal* is thus of more than historiographical interest, for it discloses the development of a prototypically American sensibility. Insofar as it represents a more complex Winthrop than previously known, then, the *Journal* allows us to reclaim one kind of integral response to American experience in religious and political terms which, it can be argued, is presently in danger of being lost to rigid, codified, and inflexible sentiments. Regaining imaginatively the compound of openness and integrity that Winthrop achieved in his *Journal* thus presents a possibility of recovery from the ambivalence that suspends contemporary American life between grandiose delusions and austere self-denial.

The current malaise is described well in the recipe for "the minimal self" outlined in Christopher Lasch's recent book about "psychic survival in troubled times," when "selfhood becomes a kind of luxury." Since "emotional equilibrium [now] demands a minimal self, not the imperial self of yesteryear," this leading cultural critic is definitely expressing "no indignant outcry against contemporary 'hedonism,' self-seeking, egoism, indifference to the general good—traits commonly associated with 'narcissism.'"[3] Lasch naturally wishes his contemporaries could do more than merely "survive." Yet he knows that the kind of selfhood that "implies a personal history, family, friends, a sense of place" requires "the critical awareness of man's divided nature," and, short of reading Freud, he can recommend no workable access to this crucial resource.[4] He would like to revise the values of his readers, but he distrusts new visions and despairs of renewing the old. In this predicament, which Lasch describes with uncomfortable accuracy, how can recovery begin? Is there an alternative to "the minimal self"?

Winthrop's *Journal* shows that the impetus for revision, recovery, and renewal comes not merely in these late bad times but in the beginnings of the national story. It is true that many Europeans came to America seeking a new way of life. But this novelty was not, as it were, *de novo*. The New World was from its discovery a place of revisioning, a place where the problems of life in the Old World could be corrected or avoided. The ideal of the new was thus consciously or unconsciously formulated in reference to the problems of the old. Few Europeans succeeded in stamping the New World indelibly with the impress of the ideal they brought from the Old, as new geographic and social conditions meant that originating designs had to be recast. Nevertheless, without reference to such ideals novelty overwhelmed, experience became mere flux. Revision, then, was not a static pattern but a living process; revisioning thus integrates action and interpretation into the story of America. Without revisioning, the story disintegrates into wanton dynamism, lifeless traditionalism, or gross self-deceit. While much great American literature has examined the difficulty of integrating the driving energy of the new with the wisdom of respect for the past,[5] the hypothesis here is that in at least one exemplary instance—the *Journal* of Puritan Governor John Winthrop—revisioning began early and worked well. Indeed, Winthrop's *Journal* invites revised thinking about the subsequent revisioning of America.

In the early parts of the *Journal* Winthrop records, as one might in a public diary, the facts and sundry impressions of the transatlantic crossing and the struggle to found a colony in Massachusetts Bay. The reader, then and now, knows Winthrop as a reporter and trusts the factuality of his voice. Within a few years, as Winthrop faces the challenge of chronicling events of greater complexity and duration, the entries are less frequently made and tend to lengthen into stories in which the narrator attempts to re-create mixed motives and to trace the processes of conflicts that defined the terms of life in the Bay Colony. As the *Journal* progresses, Winthrop begins to leave blanks in the text, spaces to which he can return to add more facts or to ponder the significance of the events he records. Likewise, he begins to refer to previous and subsequent entries, to employ obvious authorial rhetoric, to cover longer spans of time in some entries, and to group events according to their significance rather than to strict chronology. At one point, when dealing with Anne Hutchinson in the retrospection of his prose, Winthrop first attempts to record the events leading to and surrounding her expulsion from the colony; later, he writes a "Short Story of the Rise, Reign, and Ruin of the Antinomians, and Libertines that Infected the Churches of New England." The shift in narrative approach does not necessarily betray a change of mind on Winthrop's part about "this American Jesabel." But it does indicate an awareness that her story, and his involvement with it, requires a new way of recounting the experience.

Such changes are at least as significant, if not more so, than a more superficial change of ideas, for the alteration of narrative forms reveals Winthrop's nascent apprehension that life in America will require new structures of understanding and will repay novel interpretations. By the beginning of what was in his own text the third and final volume of the *Journal*, Winthrop is more consistently and more fully engaged as the historian of early America, composing a reflective narrative in which it is plain that events are being remembered and reviewed in terms of what the experiences themselves express—instead of simply what they may be construed to mirror in terms of the purposes of a transcendent God. Yet because Winthrop was not a highly self-conscious modern author, it is not surprising to find a mixture of narrative styles in the second and third sections of his *Journal*. With that caveat in mind, one can begin to see what the patterns of its telling suggest about the meaning of Winthrop's story of New England.

I

The Puritans went—or, from a contemporary perspective, came—to America with the explicit purpose of revising the practice of religion in England. Their reforming vision was articulated by John Winthrop in a lay sermon, "A Modell of Christian Charity," delivered on board the *Arbella* in 1630. The basic model was clear: "GOD ALMIGHTIE in his most holy and wise providence hath soe disposed on the Condicion of mankinde, as in all times some must be rich some poore, some highe and eminent in power and dignitie; others meane and in subieccion." No one in England would have argued with that! The "reasons" behind the model suggest the distinctive mission of the Puritans. As "a Company professing our selues fellow members of Christ" they come "to seeke out a place of Cohabitation and Consorteship vnder a due forme of Government both ciuill and ecclesiasticall." This work will require "extraordinary" means; thus unlike "When we liued in England," now "that which the most in theire Churches maineteine as a truth in profession onely, we must bring into familiar and constant practice." Far from being a project designed and performed by men, Winthrop reminds his fellows that "Thus stands the cause betweene God and vs, wee are entered into Covenant with him for this worke." The covenant means that if God hears our prayers and brings us in peace to our desired place, then he has ratified the agreement and "will expect a strickt performance of the Articles contained in it." In order to muster the requisite love, justice, and humility, "wee must be knitt together in this worke as one man," and then "the God of Israell . . . shall make vs a prayse and glory, that men shall say of succeeding plantacions: the lord make it like that of New England: for we must Consider that wee shall be as a Citty vpon a Hill" with "the eies of all people . . . upon us."[6] Faithfulness to this originating vision, therefore, would spur revision of religion and politics in England and throughout the civilized world.

Much has been written about the Puritans and their "errand into the wilderness,"[7] but the purpose here is to look not so much at what "really happened" as into how John Winthrop interpreted the early history of the project he led. It is not that he initially thought the project would require interpretation—far from it. He was so sure of the "modell" and of his own ability to govern that he began a journal simply to keep a record of the way the Puritan plan unfolded. He was ever in the thick of things, usually as governor, always as the recognized leader of the colony. But an interesting thing happened on the way to reforming England and the world. Not only did England have her own revolution and hence need little advice from Massachusetts but also some American Puritans, as the development of Winthrop's *Journal* reveals, were becoming more committed to revisioning as a process than they were to the society and institutions they set out initially to revise. To be sure, not everyone made this transition. Most were caught up too thoroughly in the rude exigencies of daily life, and those who had visions were generally overpowered by them. As his journal-keeping became an increasingly self-conscious literary project, Winthrop mapped out a "middle landscape," poised precariously between the rampant spirituality and the land-hungry expansionism of his companions. His literary enterprise afforded Winthrop a crucial angle of revision, which if not wholly yet still significantly enabled him to succeed where so many of his contemporaries failed.[8] For Winthrop's writing began to give him a double or combined consciousness of himself both as an active participant in and as an interpretive observer of Puritan life. In the process Winthrop's narrative becomes considerably more than a quotidian chronicle, and the religious and political developments at the heart of his story need to be understood in relation to the changing nature of the narrative itself.

II

In the first and perhaps most obvious place, in the course of the years covered in his *Journal* Winthrop moved from a commitment to reform and renew the Church of England toward an affirmation of a new, more characteristically American religiousness. Tension between the old and the new is evident very early on. Thus on 27 July 1630, about a month after landing in Massachusetts, Winthrop observes: "We of the congregation kept a fast, and chose Mr. Wilson our teacher, and Mr. Nowell an elder, and Mr. Gager and Mr. Aspinwall, deacons. We used imposition of hands, but with this protestation by all, that it was only as a sign of election and confirmation, not of any intent that Mr. Wilson should renounce his ministry he received in England." Despite their protestations, such balancing became increasingly difficult.

The original idea was that, while the corrupt Anglicans required purifying, the separatists, such as those at nearby Plymouth, had severed their bonds with the communion of the saints. The Bay Colony was to chart a middle course, and Winthrop and the others were prepared to be welcomed back by a mother country awakened by New England's shining example. But William Bradford visited Boston in 1631, and on 25 October 1632 Winthrop records that when he and John Wilson and two Puritan captains visited the Pilgrims:

> The governour of Plimouth, Mr. William Bradford, (a very discreet and grave man,) with Mr. Brewster, the elder, and some others, came forth and met them without the town, and conducted them to the governour's house, where they were very kindly entertained, and feasted every day at several houses. On the Lord's day there was a sacrament, which they

did partake in; and, in the afternoon, Mr. Roger Williams (according to
their custom) propounded a question, to which the pastor, Mr. Smith,
spake briefly; then Mr. Williams prophesied; and after the governour
of Plimouth spake to the question; after him the elder; then some two
or three more of the congregation. Then the elder desired the governour of Massachusetts and Mr. Wilson to speak to it, which they did.
When this ended, the deacon, Mr. Fuller, put the congregation in mind
of their duty of contribution; whereupon the governour and all the rest
went down to the deacon's seat, and put into the box, and then
returned.

Winthrop soon saw the Pilgrims as allies and even spiritual brothers,
and he did not return "home" when the Puritans came to power in
England. New World associations had replaced ties from the Old.

Then, too, it was useful to convene elders from the various
churches for specific causes and occasions, and in such meetings new
steps were taken. In November of 1633, for example, Winthrop
notes:

The ministers in the bay and Sagus did meet, once a fortnight, at one
of their houses by course, where some question of moment was debated.
Mr. Skelton, the pastor of Salem, and Mr. Williams, who was removed
from Plimouth thither, (but not in any office, though he exercised by
way of prophecy,) took some exception against it, as fearing it might
grow in time to a presbytery or superintendency, to the prejudice of the
churches' liberties. But this fear was without cause; for they were all
clear in that point, that no church or person can have power over another church; neither did they in their meetings excercise any such
jurisdiction.

By denying so fervently the dangerous extreme of Presbyterianism,
they abandoned the middle ground and forthrightly espoused radical
congregationalism. There were indeed no bishops in New England!

The planting of new churches in new settlements seemed natural;
nevertheless, in practice, such new developments required monitor-
ing. As Winthrop explains on 1 April 1636, there were good reasons
for keeping a close eye even on people led by a man of "bright learning and high piety" such as Richard Mather:

Mr. Mather and others, of Dorchester, intending to begin a new church
there, (a great part of the old one being gone to Connecticut,) desired
the approbation of the other churches and of the magistrates; and, accordingly, they assembled this day, and, after some of them had given
proof of their gifts, they made confession of their faith, which was approved of; but proceeding to manifest the work of God's grace in themselves, the churches, by their elders, and the magistrates, &c. thought

them not meet, at present, to be the foundation of a church; and there-upon they were content to forbear to join till further consideration. The reason was, for that most of them (Mr. Mather and one more excepted) had builded their comfort of salvation upon unsound grounds, viz. some upon dreams and ravishes of spirit by fits; others upon the reformation of their lives; other upon duties and performances, &c; wherein they discovered three special errours: 1. That they had not come to hate sin, because it was filthy, but only left it, because it was hurtful. 2. That, by reason of this, they had never truly closed with Christ, (or rather Christ with them,) but had made use of him only to help the imperfection of their sanctification and duties, and not made him their sanctification, wisdom, &c. 3. They expected to believe by some power of their own, and not only and wholly from Christ.

Evidently such guidance was effective, for four months later "a new church was gathered at Dorchester, with approprobation of the magistrates and elders." Thus some new form of church order appeared to be in line with God's purposes in New England. Although the full flowering was many years away, some of the seeds of denominationalism—America's distinctive contribution to ecclesiastical organization—found native soil in the early towns of New England.[9]

In religious matters Winthrop entered arguments and made his own beliefs clear but finally moved against only those whose beliefs appeared to threaten the public order. No doubt he was heavy-handed and crude in the ways he orchestrated the removal of Anne Hutchinson and her followers from Massachusetts, but there is also no doubt that he acted in response to what he perceived as the clear and present danger her antinomian teachings involved. She was "a woman of a ready wit and bold spirit," he observed on 21 October 1636, who "brought over with her two dangerous errours: 1. That the person of the Holy Ghost dwells in a justified person. 2. That no sanctification can help us to evidence our justification." Winthrop knew instinctively that "From these two grew many branches," which would sprout beyond the bounds of decent communal order.

If they could not be pruned by the elders, the antinomians would have to be removed "root and branch" by the magistrates. As Winthrop saw it, Mrs. Hutchinson did more than sow dissent; she encouraged people to believe that since they were actually one with the Holy Spirit, they could live entirely as they pleased, without need for religious instruction and moral constraint. By December, John Wilson laid the blame for the growing and "inevitable danger of separation" squarely "upon these new opinions risen up amongst us, which all the magistrates, except the governour and two others, did confirm, and all the ministers but two." Winthrop defended Wilson in the church and in writing to the fence-sitting John Cotton, but to no avail. Given the spreading disturbances, it is not surprising that Winthrop's party applied increasingly unseemly pressure until Mrs. Hutchinson finally broke down in court, rapturously affirmed her erroneous beliefs, and was banished. Recalling the tenacity of the mainline's counterattack, one has to remember the overwhelming importance of spiritual affairs in Puritan life in order to understand—not to say excuse—Winthrop's treatment of these "familists."

In the heat of the controversy, when the future of the Bay Colony as a coherent religious community seemed most in doubt, one of Winthrop's observations on 17 May 1637 reveals the more constant side of his character: "The intent of the court in deferring the sentence was, that, being thus provoked by their tumultuous course, and divers insolent speeches, which some of that party had uttered in the court, and having now power enough to have crushed them, their moderation and desire of reconciliation might appear to all." Such ambivalent sentiments were not simply for the sake of noble public appearance. In fact, Winthrop's characteristic tendency was toward leniency, as can be seen in his relations with Roger Williams and in Thomas Morton's personification of Winthrop as "Joshua Temperwell." In the entry for 29 October 1645 he points out that "sure the rule of hospitality to strangers, and of seeking to pluck out of the fire such as there may be hope of to be reduced out of error and the snare of the devil, do seem to require more moderation and indulgence of human infirmity where there appears not obstinancy against the clear truth." Thus he was at odds with spiritually adolescent hotheads such as Henry Vane and pedestrian precisionists such as Thomas Dudley. In the heat of the moment, the passionate found Winthrop's temperance objectionable; over the course of his life, though, the people often preferred Winthrop's spiritual moderation to Hutchinson's abandon or Dudley's authoritarianism.

While he could not abide Anne Hutchinson's bold antinomianism, Winthrop was no certain enemy of Roger Williams, who came to consider the governor a wise and trusted adviser. The "inner light," in Winthrop's eyes, needed the focus of orthodox doctrine to produce useful insight, and spiritual heat required the regulation of social sanction to fuel "a Citty vpon a Hill." Thus in late August of 1637 "the synod, called the assembly, of all the teaching elders" met to consider "about eighty opinions, some blasphemous, others erroneous, all unsafe, condemned by the whole assembly; whereto near all the elders, and others sent by the churches, subscribed their names; but some few liked not the subscription, though they consented to the condemning of them."

If theological opinions without critical consideration by the elders might have consequences that were unsafe for the community, outright immorality without clear punishment was at least equally pernicious. On 12 November 1641 Winthrop enables his readers to witness the fate of one Hackett, a young servant in Salem who "was found in buggery with a cow, upon the Lord's day." Even upon the ladder prepared to be hanged, full repentance had not come; "but the cow (with which he had committed that abomination) being brought forth and slain before him, he brake out into a loud and doleful complaint against himself" and was led in prayer by John Wilson and the other attendant elders. Winthrop's observation upon the lad's execution is noteworthy: "There is no doubt to be made but the Lord hath received his soul to his mercy; and he was pleased to lift up the light of his countenance so far towards him, as to keep him from despair, and to hold him close to his grace in a seeking condition; but he was not pleased to afford him that measure of peace and comfort as he might be able to hold out to others, lest sinful men, in the love of their lusts, should set mercy and repentance at too low a rate, and so miss of it when they vainly expect it." With such precise moral calibration, the Bay Colony would be no "burned-over district."

True piety required the guidance of a learned clergy. The weird misbeliefs and violence fostered by Samuel Gorton and his cohorts sprang from the fact, as Winthrop notes on 13 October 1643, that "they were all illiterate men, the ablest of them could not write true English, no not common words, yet they would take upon them the interpretation of the most difficult places of scripture, and wrest them any way to serve their own turns." Nevertheless, Winthrop's goal was not to douse the flame of religious enthusiasm but to sustain it within a steady range. Charismatic spirituality might lead either to disregard for moral regulations or to compulsive moralism. Winthrop wanted to keep true religion alive by avoiding both extremes, and he often found himself needing to protect the unwary from their neighbors' ire. While it certainly had its limits, Winthrop's lenity in such matters did more than get him in trouble with the inflexible among the saints. It also nurtured resources that could be tapped a century later by Jonathan Edwards in the Great Awakening. And the development of these spiritual resources can best be seen in the increasing creativity of the narrative voice in Winthrop's *Journal*. Looking at Puritan religious life through the changes in the *Journal*, then, suggests crucial relations between institutional and imaginative expressions of American spirituality.

III

Because of its overriding religious purposes, the Bay Colony's political life was supposed to be different from what its people had known in the old country. Unlike the factionalism that "hath been usual in the council of England and other states, who walk by politic principles only," asserted Winthrop on 30 October 1644, in Massachusetts:

> these gentlemen were such as feared God, and endeavored to walk to the rules of his word in all their proceedings, so as it might be conceived in charity, that they walked according to their judgments and conscience, and where they went aside, it was merely for want of light, or their eyes were held through some temptation for a time, that they could not make use of the light they had, for in all these differences and agitations about them, they continued in brotherly love, and in the exercise of all friendly offices each to other, as occasion required.

But, try as he might to see Puritan politics in terms of religion, Winthrop, as his friends in the ministry had on occasion to remind him, was no theologian; he was a leader of men and manager of worldly affairs, and so it is, in the second place, in the realm of politics itself that one looks for an understanding of the man. Indeed, much of the *Journal* is taken up with observing the hero's political reasoning and tact in the face of his opponents' passion and contrariness. Just as his style of religion changes, so too in politics the *Journal* reveals Winthrop's transformation (incomplete but undeniable) from being governor as ruler to being governor as first citizen. The architect of "A Modell of Christian Charity," who sees power rightly held by the governor and dispensed through his wisdom on behalf of the governed, becomes in the press of founding, sustaining, and directing a successful colony the engineer of an increasingly political structure, who writes "A Discourse on Arbitrary Gouerment." [10]

While remaining the elected governor more often than not throughout his life in the New World, Winthrop is continually in the process of giving away political power. In 1631 the people of Watertown agreed to pay their assessment for new fortifications after admitting their misunderstanding of the nature of the Bay Colony's government. "The ground of their errour," Winthrop notes on 17 February, was that

they took this government to be no other but as of a major and alder-
men, who have not power to make laws or raise taxations without the
people; but understanding that this government was rather in the nature of a parliament, and that no assistant could be chosen but by the
freemen, who had power likewise to remove the assistants and put in
others, and therefore at every general court (which was to be held once
every year) they had free liberty to consider and propound any thing
concerning the same, and to declare their grievances, without being
subject to question, or, &c. they were fully satisfied; and so their sub-
mission was accepted, and their offence pardoned.

This right of the freemen to elect their leaders was important—to
Winthrop, to the freemen, and to others within the colony. Virtually
from the outset, and then steadily, Winthrop oversaw the expansion
of the franchise. During a private meeting of the assistants on 1 May
1632, "after dinner, the governour told them, that he had heard, that
the people intended, at the next general court, to desire, that the assistants might be chosen anew every year and that the governour
might be chosen by the whole court, and not by the assistants only."
The news distressed at least one of the others, but his objections were
"answered and cleared in the judgment of the rest," and Winthrop's
information proved accurate. A week later, when the general court
met in Boston, the change was made: "Whereas it was (at our first
coming) agreed, that the freemen should choose the assistants, and
they the governour, the whole court agreed now, that the governour
and assistants should all be new chosen every year by the general
court, (the governour to be always chosen out of the assistants;) and
accordingly the old governour, John Winthrop, was chosen; accordingly all the rest as before, and Mr. Humfrey and Mr. Coddington
also, because they were daily expected." For the moment, a more general electoral process was simply a better way of choosing the same
leaders. Within a few years, however, religious unrest fueled political
passions; new men were elected, and offices rotated among the old
guard. By 1644 there was a move to grant the freemen's privileges to
non-churchmen, and in May of 1646 the rights of freemen were given
to non-freemen as well. Until his death in 1649, Winthrop remained
the one most often elected. The people usually trusted his leadership,
always respected his judgment, and approved of his judicious broad-
ening of the franchise.

Likewise, Winthrop worked steadily to balance the power of the
generally elected "assistants" and the locally representative "deputies," never yielding enough to satisfy the more "democratical" deputies, nevertheless leading toward a form of legislative power that was

fully bicameral by 1644. Then, too, while seeking to retain an arena
for judicial discretion, he oversaw the formulation of a general body
of laws for adjudication within the colony—never minutely specific
enough to satisfy the precisionists but nevertheless far from the arbi-
trariness of autocracy.

In politics as in religion, Winthrop was characteristically ambivalent. On the one hand, as a good Calvinist, he agreed with the elders
who affirmed on 18 October 1642 that "in a commonwealth, rightly
and religiously constituted, there is no power, office, administration,
or authority, but such as are commanded and ordained by God" and
that the political institutions of such a commonwealth "ought not to
be by them either changed or altered, but upon such grounds, for
such ends, in that manner, and only so far as the mind of God may be
manifested therein." Yet on the other hand, compassion for others led
him on 18 January 1635 to profess "that it was his judgment, that, in
the infancy of plantations, justice should be administered with more
lenity than in a settled state, because people were then more apt to
transgress, partly of ignorance of new laws and orders, partly through
oppression of business and other straits." Given the ongoing tug-of-
war between antinomians and precisionists, Winthrop's ambivalence
embroiled him in—and saw the colony through—many controversies.
In all he sought balance: in "a little speech" in 1645 Winthrop reminded the people, as he notes on 14 May, "so shall your liberties be
preserved, in upholding the honor and power of authority amongst
you." And he welcomed the development in 1643 of an intercolonial
government called the United Colonies, with its own commissioners—
elected by all freemen by May of 1645—to resolve disputes between
the several colonies of New England and to coordinate their common
defense. On the one hand, yielding power seemed to increase Winthrop's authority; on the other, in all these ways he was preparing the
colony for orderly continuity following the passage of his personal
charisma.

Caught in a tug-of-war between enemies in England who wanted
to install a "general governor" over all the colonies of New England
and the deputies from the several towns who wanted more democratic
decision-making, Winthrop moved from advocating aristocracy to
supporting a mixed government, or "buffered democracy," at its heart
much like the concept developed a century and a half later by the
more conservative among the founders of the American republic. On
the one hand, Winthrop suggested the expansion of the franchise, the
development of a bicameral legislature, the formulation of a general
body of laws, and the constitution of an intercolonial government. Yet

he did not go as far in any of these matters as their proponents wished. For, on the other hand, he believed that an excess of democracy would lead to instability. He agreed with those who spoke for the rights of the minority in a church dispute in September of 1646 "that it was not to be expected, that the major party should complain of their own act, and if the minor party, or the party grieved, should not be heard, then God should have left no means of redress in such a case, which could not be." This particular case had a Winthropian happy ending, for "some failing was found in both parties, the woman had not given so full satisfaction as she ought to have done, and the major party of the church had proceeded too hastily against a considerable party of the dissenting brethren, whereupon the woman who had offended was convinced of her failing, and bewailed it with many tears, the major party also acknowledged their errour, and gave the elders thanks for their care and pains." Thus it seems possible that Winthrop's changing attitudes toward governance may provide a clue for interpreting relations between the federal theology of the Puritans and the federalism of such "revolutionaries" as John Adams and Alexander Hamilton. In the later stages of his *Journal* Winthrop moves from reporting events to telling stories that let the experiences of various characters speak increasingly for themselves. This move reflects his growing willingness to give the people and their deputies a voice in government, and so it is through the *Journal* that one begins to observe connections between the political, religious, and imaginative forms of the American story.

IV

Winthrop's sense of vocation evolves in several stages. While still in England, when the altogether prepared but somewhat skeptical and unwilling Winthrop is recruited, he joins the Puritan project with a plan for action. As the chief actor, formed for heroic leadership, he has a design, or "modell," with which he informs and charges the group's sense of common purpose. Then, in the New World, he guides his model into action, usually playing the hero but sometimes forced into a supporting role—a new stance which, by making him from time to time an observer, heightens his powers of perception and gives him a crucial angle of interpretation through which to view the development of his design. Thus in December of 1636, in the midst of the antinomian turmoil, while Winthrop is out of office he has time to write a long entry describing Henry Vane's petulant attempt to resign as governor and relating his own and John Wilson's wise probity during the turbulence surrounding Anne Hutchinson.

As Winthrop begins to see himself as both interpreter and actor, he examines the people whose actions he records with increasing attention to their unique circumstances and personal complexities. Winthrop's entry for 9 November 1641 begins with "Query, whether the following be fit to be published," indicating an increasingly discriminating awareness of his role as a writer, and then proceeds to recount how Governor Bellingham stole the affections of a young woman residing in his own house and induced her to marry him instead of the man to whom she was betrothed. The relation of this compromising incident, which led perhaps to Winthrop's becoming governor again at the next election, is followed three days later by another tale of infidelity:

> Mr. Stephen Batchellor, the pastor of the church at Hampton, who had suffered much at the hands of the bishops of England, being about 80 years of age, and having a lusty comely woman to his wife, did solicit the chastity of his neighbour's wife, who acquainted her husband therewith; whereupon he was dealt with, but denied it, as he had told the woman he would do, and complained to the magistrates against the woman and her husband for slandering him. The church likewise dealing with him, he stiffly denied it, but soon after, when the Lord's supper was to be administered, he did voluntarily confess the attempt, and that he did intend to have defiled her, if she would have consented. The church, being moved with his free confession and tears, silently forgave him, and communicated with him: but after, finding how scandalous it was, they took advice of other elders, and after long debate and much pleading and standing upon the church's forgiving and being reconciled to him in communicating with him after he had confessed it, they proceeded to cast him out.

Winthrop notes that "after this he went on in a variable course" and finally nearly two years later "he was released of his excommunication, but not received to his pastor's office." In this narrative, told primarily for the sake of its own interest, though perhaps in some measure also to document the scandals occurring during Bellingham's administration, Winthrop uses adjectives deftly to delineate a memorable character, and he compresses events of two years' duration into a coherent short story.

This little story within a story is followed by a four-page tale of "a very foul sin, committed by three persons" involving the debauchery of a young girl who was abused "many times, so as she was grown capable of man's fellowship, and took pleasure in it." Then, following an authorial observation that "as people increased, so sin abounded, and especially the sin of uncleanness, and still the providence of God found them out," Winthrop tells the story of poor Hackett and the cow, and various other tales of disorder before this long entry is completed. By this time Winthrop is more than governor; he is working consciously as the author of early New England. By 1642 the form of his work is no longer that of journal entries; Winthrop begins simply to intersperse dates in the text of a flowing narrative. In 1643 a single entry covers two months, looking back in time in order to show present events in their proper light. And the entries themselves lengthen, with those of May 1645 and November 1646 surpassing twenty pages each. Thus in terms of particular literary devices, such as characterization, retrospective narration, and the avoidance of authorial intrusion, as well as in terms of the increasing flow and continuity of the narrative as a whole, Winthrop's text ceases to be a matter of record-keeping and becomes a matter of history as literature.

More nuanced characterization of others and more awareness of their roles in the drama of the Bay Colony as a whole provide Winthrop an increasingly distanced perspective on his own motives and actions as a character in the story he tells. The decency and sympathy with which he treats the characters in his *Journal* is perhaps related to his characteristic leniency toward those in trouble and his urge to understand their motivations—tendencies which sometimes cost him his office when public passions ran high but which also made him a better writer. While in roughly equal measure hero and narrator, Winthrop develops a literary form that can embrace confrontations and hence a narrative vision that sustains and includes challenges in ways beyond his capacities as one of the actors in the drama of the Bay Colony. On 12 June 1643 Winthrop records his apology for the style of one of his writings in which he had made "appeal to the judgment of religion and reason, but, as I there carried it, I did arrogate too much to myself and ascribe too little to others." A few months later, on 14 July, he notes in his *Journal* one of his failings as governor: "this fault hath been many times found in the governour to be over-sudden in his resolutions, for although the course were both warrantable and safe, yet it had beseemed men of wisdom and gravity to have proceeded with more deliberation and further advice." Thus sometimes directly in power and sometimes not, Winthrop emerges more as narrator than as actor, freer to tell the history of early America in its own terms, still bearing witness to the motivating power of his original model but more intrigued now with discovering what the model has engendered than with forcing the New World's light through the prism of his initial design. As he observes on 12 November 1641, "God hath not confined all wisdom etc. to any one generation, that they should set rules for others to walk by."

Winthrop's opponents seem to have been people of single visions. As a man of action and of observation, however, Winthrop learned that the spiritual power of a vision lives only in the ongoing revisioning it engenders. When visions are codified and institutionalized, they begin to die as authority degenerates into control. Models imposed on experience stifle vitality and become relics, whether venerated or despised. In some crucial ways a moderate from the outset, Winthrop discovered in writing his *Journal* that interpretation, through reference to a past ideal of the future, yields a kind of authority that need not violate the experience of the present. The ideal is reshaped as experience is represented. As a writer, Winthrop was able to respect the integrity of the present without losing sight of the ideal and without using the ideal to disfigure the vitality of the present. Like his movements in religion and politics, in his *Journal* Winthrop moves toward freedom even while he gains authority. It is in the product of his double vision, the text itself, that all the people of single vision continue to live for us. Their descendants made the jeremiad the literary form most characteristic of second- and third-generation Puritans. For them, as Sacvan Bercovitch says, "every crisis called forth a reassertion of the design."[11] In contrast, Winthrop kept the design alive by remaining open to the unexpected. Vision endures in revision; as he said on 12 November 1641, "for history must tell the whole truth."

The whole truth can be neither wholly expressed in action nor fully relished in observation. As a certain kind of conscious and unconscious experience, Winthrop's changing engagement in and interpretation of life in the New World generated a new literary form. Hence we might see the *Journal* as the first example of what Sacvan Bercovitch calls "auto-American-biography," the telling of one's own and America's story in the same imaginative act.[12] Or we might consider Winthrop's *Journal* to be something like the first American "novel," especially insofar as the meaning Winthrop articulates as narrator is generated from the alteration of his original governing design and therein initiates what David Minter calls "the interpreted design as a structural principle in American prose."[13] In any case, in Winthrop's *Journal* this is all rudimentary rather than full-blown. On the one hand, when we see Winthrop as an actor who begins with a design upon the world and ends as a narrator or historian, we are not yet dealing with the developed literary genius of Hawthorne, James, Fitzgerald, or Faulkner that Minter explicates. Yet on the other hand, there is in Winthrop's *Journal* something akin to the impulse that led Norman Mailer to call the major sections of *The Armies of the Night* "history as a novel" and "the novel as history." [14] There are certainly few other than inverse personal comparisons to be drawn between Mailer and Winthrop, but Mailer's intuitions about America hark back to an ancestry that might surprise him. Mailer and other recent keepers of the American dream have, like Winthrop, discovered that politics, religion, and narrative are modes of power, ways not only of responding to experience but also ways of controlling life by shaping its manifold energies into tractable, intelligible, forms. Revisioning America involves charting their ebbs and flows.

V

Recovering a sense of Winthrop's compound of integrity and openness yields resources for recovery from the ambivalent malaise of contemporary American life. Because he charted a course between the whirlpools of spiritual exuberance and the stagnation of moral precisionism, Winthrop's project suggests a strategy for coping with the expansive religious and political visions of Anne Hutchinson's cultural descendants and with the self-centered programs of latter-day Thomas Dudleys. Neither the grandiose delusions of religious and political imperialism nor the cunning austerity of an individual and cultural style that is "taut, toned, and coming on strong" will suffice to sustain a sense of purpose commensurate with American promise. Christopher Lasch's recipe for "minimal selfhood," for example, is more puritanical than authentically Puritan; Lasch's work, like much neoconservative cultural criticism, follows the form of the jeremiad while lacking its theological substance. Winthrop's revisioning defines an alternative to Lasch's studied pessimism as well as to the wistfully Emersonian optimism in many dreams of a larger and better life. Winthrop knew the answer to Emerson's Transcendentalist query, "Why should not we also enjoy an original relation to the universe?" [15] Such dreams for a larger and better life are inevitably fashioned from fallible, if not meretricious, materials. An original relation to the universe, like the Puritans' "Modell of Christian Charity," is already unreachably in the past. Although it is a lesson remembered usually in— or just after—times of crisis, revisioning is the only real way of having America at all.

Pointing to "some strange resistance in itself," Robert Frost says, "It is this backward motion toward the source, / Against the stream, that most we see ourselves in, / The tribute of the current to the source." [16] Readers who recall the elegiac ending of *The Great Gatsby*—Nick Carraway's remembrance of "a fresh green breast of the new world" that "had once pandered in whispers to the last and greatest of all human dreams; for a transitory enchanted moment man must have held his breath in the presence of this continent, compelled into an aesthetic contemplation he neither understood nor desired, face to face for the last time in history with something commensurate to his capacity for wonder" [17]—such readers will confront Winthrop's journal entry for Tuesday 8 June 1630 with a start of recognition:

> The wind still W. and by S. fair weather, but close and cold. We stood N.N.W. with a stiff gale, and, about three in the afternoon, we had sight of land to the N.W. about ten leagues, which we supposed was the Isles of Monhegan, but it proved Mount Mansell. Then we tacked and stood W.S.W. We now had fair sun-shine weather, and so pleasant a sweet air as did much refresh us, and there came a smell off the shore like the smell of a garden.
> There came a wild pigeon into our ship, and another small land bird.

The Puritan imagination was saturated with Old Testament images: the birds present an antitype of the end of the Flood, and days of rain and fog end when sight of land is coupled with new sunshine and the smell of a garden!

Winthrop began with a vision and discovered the value of revisioning. Revisioning is where Americans begin. While "we can believe only by interpreting," Paul Ricouer points out that "it is by *interpreting* that we can *hear* again." [18] Or as Nick Carraway concludes, "So we beat on, boats against the current, borne back ceaselessly into the past." [19] Thus recovering Winthrop involves more than pointing to the Puritan foundation of the American cultural edifice. Winthrop's achievement, the commitment to revisioning that informs his *Journal,* is more model than monument. He kept in play certain contradictory attitudes—individualism and communalism, innocent optimism and studied pessimism, interpretation and action—that work as antinomies throughout subsequent American cultural history. Neither in politics nor in literature was his work complete: governance of the Bay Colony often lacked Winthrop's guiding moderation, and his *Journal* is unabashedly an unfinished text. What can be recovered by looking backward at this curious blend of authoritarianism and moderation, of involvement and detachment, is the knowledge that the return of possibilities comes in the process of revisioning.

However much Americans now may wish for a reappearance of

leadership with Winthrop's balanced sense of purpose, such renaissances depend on complicated historical and psychological processes that scholarship can investigate but not generate. Historical scholars contribute best to cultural recovery by rethinking the kind of history they write. The world of recent historical inquiry has been divided, if not between spiritual visionaries and moral precisionists, then between "humanists" who love theory and interpretation and "social scientists" who thrive on statistics and facts. Clifford Geertz is right to celebrate the blurring of these genres,[20] and one goal of the present essay is to suggest that to undertake such interdisciplinary analysis— blending together in this case thinking about religion, politics, and narrative—is simply to render scholarship apposite to the variegated stuff of historical experience. The inability ever completely to fulfill such complex hermeneutical goals is the unavoidable price of wanting to see whole; to attempt, and thereby to achieve, less is the greater failure.

Study of the past may be hampered by artificial boundaries between various areas of life, and attempts to see the past whole may disclose distinctions more important than those made between academic disciplines. There is an irony, for example, in seeking faultless political candidates and then castigating them when their deficiencies inevitably appear. As Lewis Lapham asks, "who could bear the thought of being governed by human beings, by people as confused and imperfect as oneself? If a politician confessed to an honest doubt or emotion, how would it be possible to grant him the authority of a god?"[21] In contrast, after being acquitted in an invidious political trial, on 14 May 1645 Winthrop reminds his fellow citizens that "it is you yourselves who have called us to this office, and being called by you, we have our authority from God" and then entreated them "to consider, that when you choose magistrates, you take them from among yourselves, men subject to like passions as you are. Therefore when you see infirmities in us, you should reflect upon your own, and that would make you bear the more with us, and not be severe censurers of the failings of your magistrates, when you have continual experience of like infirmaties in yourselves and others." Winthrop does not distinguish between the people and their leaders in terms of moral quality. He draws the line elsewhere:

> The covenant between you and us is the oath you have taken of us, which is to this purpose, that we shall govern you and judge your causes by the rules of God's laws and our own, according to our best skill. When you agree with a workman to build you a ship or house &c. he undertakes as well for his skill as for his faithfulness, for it is his profes-

sion, and you pay him for both. But when you call one to be a magistrate, he doth not profess nor undertake to have sufficient skill for that office, nor can you furnish him with gifts &c. therefore you must run the hazard of his skill and ability. But if he fail in faithfulness, which by his oath he is bound unto, that he must answer for. If it fall out that the case be clear to common apprehension, and the rule clear also, if he transgress here, the errour is not in the skill, but in the evil of the will: it must be required of him. But if the cause be doubtful, or the rule doubtful, to men of such understanding and parts as your magistrates are, if your magistrates should err here, yourselves must bear it.

Assessing leaders in Winthrop's way would require continual self-assessment, which is always difficult, and might improve the quality and realism of American political discourse.

If self-scrutiny is the price of revisioning America, some things have not changed. For, as Winthrop went on to say, "concerning liberty, I observe a great mistake in the country." American life is still bedeviled by this mistake, although most people may no longer—perhaps for good reasons—be able to acknowledge it. As a true son of the Reformation, Winthrop distinguished between two kinds of liberty. On the one hand, there is everyone's "natural" liberty "to do what he lists." Such freedom to "do your own thing" is one of the few values Americans today now hold in common, even while recognizing that this "is a liberty to evil as well as to good" and that "this liberty is incompatible and inconsistent with authority." Unlike Winthrop, however, Americans now reject authority that curtails freedom. Certainly no one wants to reinhabit the cramped moral space of early New England. Yet in taking a stand for freedom, Americans may have forgotten what Winthrop envisioned, on the other hand, as the true form of liberty:

> The other kind of liberty I call civil or federal, it may also be termed moral, in reference to the covenant between God and man, in the moral law, and the politic covenants and constitutions, amongst men themselves. This liberty is the proper end and object of authority, and cannot subsist without it; and it is a liberty to that only which is good, just and honest. This liberty you are to stand for, with the hazard (not only of your good, but) of your lives, if need be. Whatsoever crosseth this, is not authority, but a distemper thereof. This liberty is maintained and exercised in a way of subjection to authority; it is of the same kind of liberty wherewith Christ hath made us free.

Without something like "civil" or "federal" or "moral" liberty, as Winthrop wrote on 22 September 1642, the Puritan community could not endure:

Others who went to other places, upon like grounds, succeeded no better. They fled for fear of want, and many of them fell into it, even to extremity, as if they had hastened into the misery which they feared and fled from, besides the depriving themselves of the ordinances and church fellowship, and those civil liberties which they enjoyed here; whereas, such as staid in their places, kept their peace and ease, and enjoyed still the blessing of the ordinances, and never tasted of those troubles and miseries, which they heard to have befallen those who departed. Much disputation there was about liberty of removing for outward advantages, and all ways were sought for an open door to get out at; but it is to be feared many crept out at a broken wall. For such as come together into a wilderness, where are nothing but wild beasts and beastlike men, and there confederate together in civil and church estate, whereby they do, implicitly at least, bind themselves to support each other, and all of them that society, whether civil or sacred, whereof they are members, how they can break from this without free consent, is hard to find, so as may satisfy a tender or good conscience in time of trial. Ask thy conscience, if thou wouldst have plucked up thy stakes, and brought thy family 3000 miles, if thou hadst expected that all, or most, would have forsaken thee there. Ask again, what liberty thou hast towards others, which thou likest not to allow others towards theyself; for if one may go, another may, and so the greater part, and so church and commonwealth may be left destitute in a wilderness, exposed to misery and reproach, and all for thy ease and pleasure, whereas these all, being now thy brethren, as near to thee as the Israelites were to Moses, it were much safer for thee, after his example, to choose rather to suffer affliction with thy brethren, than to enlarge thy ease and pleasure by furthering the occasion of their ruin.

The notion that freedom means staying rather than moving on, accepting hardship and confinement rather than seeking openness and a better life, is an idea that Americans learned to admire but not to emulate, a sentiment that makes the seventeenth-century mind remote from modern sensibility. Winthrop's commitment to such ideas is what makes it inappropriate, finally, to read him as a proto-Romantic who found change exhilarating. However much he made way for novelty, Winthrop's steadfast Puritanism cannot be overlooked. In fact, to interpret him as more modern than he was would be to miss the ways his life and work calls ours into question.

It is only by honoring his irreducible otherness that we can appreciate his way of revisioning America. Without his originating beliefs, his revisions in religion, politics, and narrative make the wrong kind of sense. Revision for its own sake keeps little but criticism alive; in this sense it is still true that where there is no vision, the people perish. Hence if we lack a coherent sense of purpose as a people, we could do worse than hypothetically to adopt Winthrop's model of civil liberty. It is so different from our conventional ideas that it might force us to begin the process of revision. Winthrop's Puritan vision will not provide the answers we need, but by framing the right questions it might inaugurate our own revisioning. The will for that task, and a steady commitment to it, is what Winthrop's *Journal* has to offer. In undertaking it, we keep something alive that is more important, finally, than any particular origin.

In life as in scholarship, possibilities come into focus only when limitations are recognized; one never grasps them whole, yet one doesn't simply have to get by without them. If historian John P. Diggins is right about "the lost soul of American politics,"[22] Winthropian revisioning presents a real alternative to the apparent contemporary options of nostalgic communalism and narcissistic individualism. Our world is different from but not more difficult than that of the Puritans. Winthrop sold all that he had to come to America and lost most of what he acquired here. Our sacrifices are more subtle but no less uncomfortable. Revising America will cost more than we imagine and require resources beyond ourselves. There is no other way to keep the dream alive. History that tells the whole truth is a rock against the current as it runs away. Resistance is all. Revisioning is most us.

NOTES

1. John Winthrop's *Journal* is a crucial document for understanding the relationship between religion and politics in America. It is our best guide to the foundation and early years of the Massachusetts Bay Colony, a settlement unmatched for its influence on later American life and thought. Yet the nature—even the title—of Winthrop's work is anything but clear. The text has been published several times—once as a "journal," once as a "history," once as a hybrid *Winthrop's Journal "History of New England," 1630–1649*. The editors of a new edition, Richard S. Dunn and Laetitia Yeandle, have opted for *The Journal of John Winthrop, 1630–1649* (Boston: Harvard University Press, for the Massachusetts Historical Society, forthcoming). In the essay that will serve as the introduction to this new edition, Dunn points out the anomalies in the text's titles over the years and suggests some changes of style within the text itself. The restricted scope of Dunn's essay and its orientation toward matters of textual history prohibit him from developing any sustained correlations between the experiences and ideas at the heart of Winthrop's writing and the nature of the text he produced. Yet several of these correlations are quite important, and they define the basic ideas, problems, or questions my essay examines. See Dunn's "John Winthrop Writes His Journal," *William and Mary Quarterly*, 3d series, 41 (Apr. 1984): 185–212. References in my essay are to

James Savage's two-volume edition of 1825 and 1826, as reprinted by Arno Press in 1972; given the several editions extant, I cite quotations by date rather than page.

2. The separation *and* interworking of religion and politics was Winthrop's life's work, and investigating that complex relationship is the remarkable achievement of Edmund S. Morgan's *The Puritan Dilemma: The Story of John Winthrop* (Boston: Little, Brown and Company, 1958). Despite the insights of his fine book, however, Morgan tends to see Winthrop's character, attitudes, and beliefs as so thoroughly formed by the time of migration that the significant changes Winthrop experiences in America are insufficiently articulated in Morgan's biography. Morgan's oversight is, I think, a consequence of failing to read his hero's *Journal* as a literary creation every bit as complex and demanding as Winthrop's accomplishments in religion and politics.

3. Christopher Lasch, *The Minimal Self: Psychic Survival in Troubled Times* (New York: W. W. Norton and Company, 1984), p. 15.

4. Ibid., pp. 15, 258.

5. See R. W. B. Lewis, *The American Adam: Innocence, Tragedy, and Tradition in the Nineteenth Century* (Chicago: University of Chicago Press, 1955) for a discussion of the interplay of these contraries two centuries after Winthrop. I agree with Lewis's argument that our greatest works are those which do not simply contribute to but contain or express this cultural dialectic in some novel way.

6. John Winthrop, "A Modell of Christian Charity," in *Winthrop Papers*, vol. 2, ed. Stewart Mitchell, (Boston: Massachusetts Historical Society, 1931), pp. 282–95.

7. See Perry Miller, *Errand into the Wilderness* (Cambridge: Belknap Press of Harvard University Press, 1956); and my *Cultural History of Religion in America* (Westport, Conn.: Greenwood Press, 1981), pp. 3–15, 168–69. For annotated bibliographic references, see Michael McGiffert, "American Puritan Studies in the 1960's," *William and Mary Quarterly*, 3d series, 27 (1970): 36–67; and David R. Williams, "New Directions in Puritan Studies," *American Quarterly* 37 (1985): 156–61.

8. Thus my reading of Winthrop differs radically from that of John Seelye in *Prophetic Waters: The River in Early American Life and Literature* (New York: Oxford University Press, 1977), pp. 131–58.

9. For a helpful summary of the basic elements of denominationalism, see Sidney E. Mead, *The Lively Experiment: The Shaping of Christianity in America* (New York: Harper and Row, 1963), pp. 103–33.

10. John Winthrop, "A Discourse on Arbitrary Gouerment," in *Winthrop Papers*, vol. 4, ed. Allyn Bailey Forbes, (Boston: Massachusetts Historical Society, 1944), pp. 468–88.

11. Sacvan Bercovitch, *The Puritan Origins of the American Self* (New Haven: Yale University Press, 1975), p. 88. On the jeremiad, see Bercovitch, *The American Jeremiad* (Madison: University of Wisconsin Press, 1978).

12. Bercovitch's *Puritan Origins* is a fecund rumination on Cotton Mather's *Nehemias Americanus: The Life of John Winthrop, Esq., Governor of the Massachusetts*

Colony. My suggestion is that Winthrop's own *Journal* may be as fruitfully analyzed in terms of what Bercovitch calls "auto-American-biography" as is Mather's hagiographic biography.

13. Minter does not discuss Winthrop's *Journal* in relation to his basic case about the structure of American prose; I am thus suggesting that the structural principle Minter analyzes is adumbrated rather more fully and earlier than he claims. See David L. Minter, *The Interpreted Design as a Structural Principle in American Prose* (New Haven: Yale University Press, 1969).

14. Norman Mailer, *The Armies of the Night: History as a Novel; The Novel as History* (New York: New American Library, Inc., 1968).

15. Ralph Waldo Emerson, "Nature," in *The Selected Writings of Ralph Waldo Emerson,* ed. Brooks Atkinson (New York: Modern Library, 1940), p. 3.

16. Robert Frost, "West-Running Brook," in *The Complete Poems of Robert Frost* (New York: Holt, Rinehart and Winston, 1956), p. 329.

17. F. Scott Fitzgerald, *The Great Gatsby* (New York: Charles Scribner's Sons, 1925), p. 159.

18. Paul Ricoeur, *The Symbolism of Evil* (Boston: Beacon Press, 1967), pp. 352, 351.

19. Fitzgerald, *Gatsby,* p. 159.

20. Clifford Geertz, "Blurred Genres: The Refiguration of Social Thought," *American Scholar* 49 (1980): 165–79.

21. Lewis H. Lapham, "Notebook: Powdered Roses," *Harper's,* Dec. 1985, p. 10.

22. John P. Diggins, *The Lost Soul of American Politics: Virtue, Self-Interest, and the Foundations of Liberalism* (New York: Basic Books, 1984).

Notes on Contributors

JOEL CARPENTER directs the religion division of the Pew Memorial Trust after several years as administrator of the Institute for the Study of American Evangelicals. He is the author of several articles and chapters on the history of fundamentalism and is working now on fundamentalism during the 1930s and 1940s. While serving as codirector of a research project on American evangelicals and mass communications, he is also the editor of a forty-volume reprint series, *Fundamentalism in America*.

ROLAND A. DELATTRE is Professor of American Studies and Religious Studies at the University of Minnesota, where he served formerly as Chair of the Program in American Studies. A founding editor of the *Journal of Religious Ethics,* he is the author of *Beauty and Sensibility in the Thought of Jonathan Edwards,* several essays on ritual in American culture, and an article on "Desire" in the *Encyclopedia of Religion*. He is presently at work on a book titled *Religious Ethics in America: A Cultural Interpretation*.

RICHARD T. HUGHES teaches on the faculty of Pepperdine University. He is the author of articles on various aspects of civil religion in *Religion in Life* and in the *Journal of Church and State,* a chapter on early Mormonism in *The Lively Experiment Continued,* ed. Jerald Brauer, and a book on the Churches of Christ. Currently editing a collection of essays, *The Restoration Ideal in American History,* he is also co-author of a study on this topic with Leonard Allen.

L. SHANNON JUNG is Associate Professor of Rural Ministry and Christian Ethics at the University of Dubuque Theological Seminary. His publications in the *Journal of the American Academy of Religion* and the *Journal of Religious Ethics* focus on the implications of human spatiality for ethics. His book, *Identity and Community,* is a study of American values, an interest which continues in his current work on the ethics of American agricultural policy.

EDWARD TABOR LINENTHAL is Professor of Religion at the University of Wisconsin at Oshkosh. The author of *Changing Images of the Warrior in America, Symbolic Defense,* and a number of essays on ceremonial performances at historic American battlefields and the symbolism of warfare, he is currently at work on studies of religion in the nuclear age. During the 1986–87 academic year, he was a Sloan Research Fellow in the Defense and Arms Control Studies Program at the Massachusetts Institute of Technology

JAMES G. MOSELEY is Professor of Religion at Chapman College. Director of two summer seminars on early American politics and religion for the National Endowment for the Humanities and a frequent author and reviewer for the scholarly journals, he is also the author of a study of Henry James, Sr., entitled *A Complex Inheritance* and of *A Cultural History of Religion in America.*

AMANDA PORTERFIELD is Associate Professor of Religion and Director of American Studies at Syracuse University. She is the author of *Feminine Spirituality in America* and essays on feminist theology in *Sociological Analysis,* on shamanism in the *Journal of the American Academy of Religion,* and on early American religion in *Horizons.* She is presently at work on a study which compares forms of personhood in Native American and Christian cultures in North America.

ALBERT J. RABOTEAU is Putnam Professor and Chair of Religion at Princeton University. His book *Slave Religion: The Invisible Institution in the Antebellum South* won both the African Roots Award of the International African Institute and the National Religious Book Award. Also the author of essays on Afro-American religious history, he is currently at work on a general history of religious life among black Americans. In 1986, he gave the Stone Lectures at Princeton and delivered the Cole Lectures at Vanderbilt.

JOHN K. ROTH is the Russell K. Pitzer Professor of Philosophy at Claremont McKenna College and the 1988 recipient of the CASE Professor of the Year Award. He has been a Fulbright Lecturer in American Studies (Austria) and has held visiting professorships at the University of Haifa in Israel and at Doshisha University in Japan. Author of numerous essays, he has also co-authored *The American Religious Experience* (with Frederick Sontag), *The American Dream* (with Robert H. Fossum), and *Ideology and American Experience* (with Robert C. Whittemore).

JONATHAN D. SARNA teaches at Brandeis University after serving on the faculty at Hebrew Union College Jewish Institute of Religion (Cincinnati) and serving as Academic Director of its Center for the Study of the American Jewish Experience. He is the co-author of *Jews and the Founding of the Republic* (a curricular package of the Center) and author of *Jacksonian Jew: The Two Worlds of Mordecai Noah* as well as many articles and reviews. He is now at work on a documentary history of American Judaism, a history of the Jewish Publication Society, and a study of Jewish-Christian relations in the United States.

ROWLAND A. SHERRILL is Professor and Chair of Religious Studies and Adjunct Professor of American Studies at Indiana University, Indianapolis. He is the author of *The Prophetic Melville* and a number of chapters, articles, and reviews, including "The Bible and Twentieth Century American Fiction" in *The Bible and American Arts and Letters,* ed. Giles Gunn, and "Melville and Religion" in *A Companion to Melville Studies,* ed. John Bryant.

CHARLES REAGAN WILSON is Associate Professor of History and Southern Studies and co-editor of the *Encyclopedia of Southern Culture* at the University of Mississippi. He is the author of *Baptized in Blood: The Religion of the Lost*

Cause, editor of *Religion in the South,* and co-editor of the annual *Perspectives on the American South,* as well as authoring a number of journal articles. He is currently working on a study of southern attitudes and customs regarding death.

Index